Arsenal 100 GREATEST GAMES

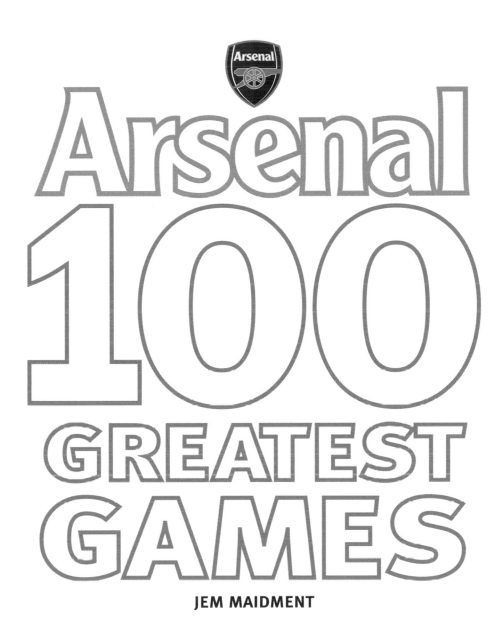

Arsenal 100 GREATEST GAMES

JEM MAIDMENT

hamlyn

Acknowledgements
The author would like to thank the following: Andy Exley, Josh James, Svein Clouston, Julia Wall-Clarke, Thomas Ballegaard, Trevor Davies, Julian Flanders, Rick Glanvill, Giselle Osborne, Andy Beill, Rachel Branson, Dave Smith and, of course, Clare Willis. The publisher would like to thank Joe Cohen and Stuart MacFarlane at Arsenal, Julian Flanders and Kathie Wilson at Butler and Tanner, Andy Cowie at Colorsport, Fred Ollier for his wisdom and Lisa Hughes for her attention to detail.

Words Jem Maidment

Produced for Hamlyn by Butler and Tanner Ltd

First published in 2005 by
Hamlyn, a division of Octopus Publishing Group Ltd, 2–4 Heron Quays, London E14 4JP

ISBN-13: 978-0-600-61376-3
ISBN-10: 0-600-61376-3

A CIP catalogue record for this book is available from the British Library

Printed and bound in the UK by Butler and Tanner Ltd

10 9 8 7 6 5 4 3 2 1

Executive Editor Trevor Davies
Project Editor Julian Flanders at Butler and Tanner
Design Kathie Wilson at Butler and Tanner
Production Martin Croshaw
Index by Indexing Specialists (UK) Ltd

Memorabilia provided by Arsenal, all photographs © Arsenal Football Club Plc/Stuart MacFarlane/David Price except the following: Colorsport 11, 16, 19 (top), 21 (bottom), 24, 27, 41 (both), 45 (bottom), 48, 49 (top), 88, 89 (bottom), 90, 103 (both), 107, 110, 112, 115, 116, 25, 126, 129 (both), 130, 133, 134, 135 and 136; Empics 10, 17 (top), 18, 19 (bottom), 20, 21 (top), 22, 23 (both), 26, 29 (both), 33 (top), 34, 35 (both), 40, 44, 45 (top), 49 (bottom), 50, 54, 58, 67 (both), 73 (top), 75 (bottom), 77 (top), 81, 82, 83, 84, 89 (top), 93, 94, 97, 99, 101, 105, 106, 108, 111, 118, 119, 120, 124, 127 (both), 128, 132 and 137; Hulton-Getty 32, 61, 66 and 72; Popperfoto 64 and 100.

Contents

Introduction

When handed the task of compiling the 100 greatest games in Arsenal's magnificent history, it became apparent very early on that the problem would not be 'padding out' the list, but rather having to make some tough decisions on which classic encounters to omit. You see ours is a football club in an elite category.

Very few football clubs, or indeed any sporting organisations, have quite the history, tradition and class associated with the Arsenal. It is an indisputable fact that Arsenal have been London's premier club since turning professional in 1893 – the first club south of Birmingham to do so. In that time Arsenal have won 13 league titles, more than three times as many as the rest of the capital's club sides put together. This is reflected in the following pages.

From those fledgling days back in Victorian Britain, to the controversial move from south to north London; the magical 1930s courtesy of Herbert Chapman's foresight and genius; more titles under Tom Whittaker in those austere post-war years; the fortitude and spirit of Bertie Mee's 'double' winners; George Graham's Young Guns stunning Anfield in 1989; the emotion of Wonderful, Wonderful Copenhagen and Arsène Wenger's superlative footballing academy, Arsenal have always been a class apart.

Indeed, since Wenger's arrival in September 1996, it could be argued there's a book to be written on the 100 greatest games solely under his stewardship.

First there were 140, then 125 – reluctantly leaving out some quite wonderful games, such as that superb Kanu-inspired 6–1 win at Middlesbrough a few years back – then 110, and finally, after much deliberation throughout the Club, it was down to the magical 100, only for Arsenal to 'spoil' the list by crushing Everton 7–0 in a remarkable Highbury display and then to win the FA Cup against Manchester United for a tenth time a few days later!

Such are the trials and tribulations of supporting the mighty Gunners.

Arsenal fans had, via the Club's official website, matchday programme and official magazine, the opportunity to select a top 20 favourite matches, the other 80 remaining in chronological order. We have retained this format for the following pages.

So what were the criteria for selecting Arsenal's 100 greatest games?

Matches of huge historical significance are obvious inclusions, such as Woolwich Arsenal's first ever professional league game at home to Newcastle United in September 1893, or our Highbury bow 20 years later – a game with even more resonance in this, our final season at the old ground, when Leicester Fosse were dispatched 2–1 in a stadium more akin to a building site than a football ground.

Every cup final victory is featured – and that, of course, includes the sheer drama of our last encounter with Manchester United in Cardiff when inspirational skipper Patrick Vieira's final act for the Club was to fire us to glory in a penalty shootout.

Also featured are those backs-against-the-wall games when nobody gave us a chance; the 1988/89 league title decider away to Liverpool, the defeat of Parma in the Parken Stadium in May 1994, Paul Vaessen's 15 minutes of fame for a famous win at Juventus in 1980 … there's just too many to mention.

The heart-stopping drama of Alan Sunderland's famous FA Cup Final winner warrants a book on its own, while the raw emotion of beating Anderlecht to end a 17-year trophy drought will never leave the memory of any Gunners fan fortunate enough to be at Highbury on that glorious Spring evening in 1970.

Countless victories over the old enemy Spurs obviously made the cut: Alf Kirchen's two-goal debut in a record 6-0 win at the Lane in 1935; the Brady and Sunderland show in 1978; those momentous Littlewoods Cup ties nine years later; FA Cup semi-final wins in 1993 and 2001; Thierry Henry's dazzling 70-yard run and goal in 2002 and that breathless nine-goal thriller not so long ago. Did I mention clinching the title in 1971 or 2004 at the other end of the Seven Sisters Road?

For pure aesthetics Wenger's sides feature heavily, as do near perfect performances under the tutelage of Herbert Chapman and George Allison in the 1930s. And some memorable performances across the Channel feature the 5-1 dismantling of Inter Milan was simply stunning, as was a mammoth 7-0 victory at Standard Liège in Belgium under 'boring' George Graham, still a Club record win in Europe.

And there is even – controversially – a defeat, 4-5 at home to Manchester United, the last occasion Matt Busby's 'babes' would grace an English football stadium before the tragedy of the Munich disaster.

There was even an argument to include England's 3-2 win over world champions Italy in November 1934, the so-called 'Battle of Highbury'. Why? Because seven Arsenal players made the starting line-up, including captain Eddie Hapgood, Tom Whittaker was the England trainer and, of course, the game was staged at Highbury.

At the beginning of the 2006/07 season Arsenal are set to embark on a new era at Emirates Stadium and that will, in time, play host to yet more drama, theatre, success and, no doubt, footballing excellence under Mr Wenger.

If our new home does half as well as the splendour and history of Highbury, there will be few complaints …

Jem Maidment, London, August 2005.

Arsenal's 100 Greatest Games

The Top 20

1   **Liverpool 0 Arsenal 2** – 26 May 1989 (League Division One)

2   **Inter Milan 1 Arsenal 5** – 25 November 2003 (UEFA Champions League, Group Stage)

3   **Manchester United 0 Arsenal 1** – 8 May 2002 (FA Premier League)

4   **Arsenal 3 Manchester United 2** – 12 May 1979 (FA Cup, Final)

5   **Arsenal 4 Everton 0** – 3 May 1998 (FA Premier League)

6   **Tottenham Hotspur 0 Arsenal 1** – 3 May 1971 (League Division One)

7   **Arsenal 3 Anderlecht 0** – 28 April 1970 (European Fairs Cup, Final, 2nd Leg)

8   **Arsenal 2 Liverpool 1** – 8 May 1971 (FA Cup, Final)

9   **Chelsea 2 Arsenal 3** – 23 October 1999 (FA Premier League)

10   **Arsenal 1 Parma 0** – 4 May 1994 (European Cup-Winners' Cup, Final)

11   **Tottenham Hotspur 2 Arsenal 2** – 25 April 2004 (FA Premier League)

12   **Tottenham Hotspur 0 Arsenal 5** – 23 December 1978 (League Division One)

13   **Arsenal 2 Newcastle United 0** – 16 May 1998 (FA Cup, Final)

14   **Arsenal 2 Leicester City 1** – 15 May 2004 (FA Premier League)

15   **Tottenham Hotspur 4 Arsenal 5** – 13 November 2004 (FA Premier League)

16   **Leicester City 3 Arsenal 3** – 27 August 1997 (FA Premier League)

17   **Roma 1 Arsenal 3** – 27 November 2002 (UEFA Champions League, Second Group Stage)

18   **Manchester United 0 Arsenal 1** – 14 March 1998 (FA Premier League)

19   **Arsenal 3 Aston Villa 1** – 16 October 2004 (FA Premier League)

20   **Sampdoria 3 Arsenal 2** – 20 April 1995 (European Cup-Winners' Cup, Semi-Final, 2nd Leg – Arsenal won 3–2 on pens)

Woolwich Arsenal 2 Newcastle United 2
– 2 September 1893 (League Division Two)

Woolwich Arsenal 2 Leicester Fosse 1
– 6 September 1913 (League Division Two)

Hull City 2 Arsenal 2 – 22 March 1930 (FA Cup, Semi-Final)

Leicester City 6 Arsenal 6
– 21 April 1930 (League Division One)

Arsenal 2 Huddersfield Town 0 – 26 April 1930 (FA Cup, Final)

Racing Club de Paris 2 Arsenal 7
– 11 November 1930 (Armistice Day Friendly)

Arsenal 9 Grimsby Town 1
– 28 January 1931 (League Division One)

Arsenal 3 Liverpool 1 – 18 April 1931 (League Division One)

Arsenal 4 Chelsea 1 – 10 December 1932 (League Division One)

Arsenal 8 Liverpool 1 – 1 September 1934 (League Division One)

Tottenham Hotspur 0 Arsenal 6
– 6 March 1935 (League Division One)

Everton 0 Arsenal 2 – 16 March 1935 (League Division One)

Arsenal 8 Middlesbrough 0
– 19 April 1935 (League Division One)

Aston Villa 1 Arsenal 7 – 14 December 1935 (League Division One)

Arsenal 1 Sheffield United 0 – 25 April 1936 (FA Cup, Final)

Arsenal 5 Bolton Wanderers 0
– 7 May 1938 (League Division One)

Charlton Athletic 1 Arsenal 7
– 1 May 1943 (League South Cup, Final)

Manchester United 1 Arsenal 1 (Maine Road)
– 17 January 1948 (League Division One)

Chelsea 2 Arsenal 2 – 18 March 1950 (FA Cup, Semi-Final)

Arsenal 2 Liverpool 0 – 29 April 1950 (FA Cup, Final)

Arsenal 6 Hapoel Tel Aviv 1
– 19 September 1951 (Floodlit Friendly)

Liverpool 1 Arsenal 5 – 15 November 1952 (League Division One)

Bolton Wanderers 4 Arsenal 6
– 25 December 1952 (League Division One)

Arsenal 3 Burnley 2 – 1 May 1953 (League Division One)

Arsenal 4 Manchester United 5
– 1 February 1958 (League Division One)

Everton 1 Arsenal 6 – 6 September 1958 (League Division One)

Blackburn Rovers 5 Arsenal 5
– 3 November 1962 – (League Division One)

Staevnet København 1 Arsenal 7 – 25 September 1963
(Inter-Cities' Fairs Cup, First Round, 1st Leg)

Arsenal 3 Ajax 0 – 8 April 1970
(European Fairs Cup, Semi-Final, 1st Leg)

Stoke City 2 Arsenal 2 – 27 March 1971 (FA Cup, Semi-Final)

Arsenal 5 Newcastle United 3
– 4 December 1976 (League Division One)

Juventus 0 Arsenal 1 – 23 April 1980
(European Cup-Winners' Cup, Semi-Final, 2nd Leg)

Liverpool 0 Arsenal 1 – 1 May 1980
(FA Cup, Semi-Final, 3rd Replay)

Aston Villa 2 Arsenal 6 – 29 October 1983 (League Division One)

Tottenham Hotspur 2 Arsenal 4
– 26 December 1983 (League Division One)

Arsenal 3 Liverpool 1 – 8 September 1984 (League Division One)

Manchester United 0 Arsenal 1
– 21 December 1985 (League Division One)

Arsenal 1 Manchester United 0
– 23 August 1986 (League Division One)

Tottenham Hotspur 1 Arsenal 2 – 1 March 1987
(Littlewoods Challenge Cup, Semi-Final, 2nd Leg)

Tottenham Hotspur 1 Arsenal 2
– 4 March 1987 (Littlewoods Challenge Cup, Semi-Final, Replay)

Arsenal 2 Liverpool 1
– 5 April 1987 (Littlewoods Challenge Cup, Final)

Norwich City 2 Arsenal 4
– 14 November 1987 (League Division One)

Arsenal 2 Manchester United 1
– 20 February 1988 (FA Cup, Fifth Round)

Arsenal 3 Everton 1 – 24 February 1988
(Littlewoods Challenge Cup, Semi-Final, 2nd Leg)

Arsenal 5 Norwich 0 – 1 May 1989 (League Division One)

Arsenal 4 Norwich City 3
– 4 November 1989 (League Division One)

Manchester United 0 Arsenal 1
– 20 October 1990 (League Division One)

Arsenal 3 Liverpool 0
– 2 December 1990 (League Division One)

Liverpool 0 Arsenal 1 – 3 March 1991 (League Division One)

Arsenal 3 Manchester United 1
– 6 May 1991 (League Division One)

Arsenal 6 Coventry City 1 – 11 May 1991 (League Division One)

Arsenal 6 Austria Memphis 1
– 18 September 1991 (European Cup, First Round, 1st Leg)

Southampton 0 Arsenal 4
– 28 September 1991 (League Division One)

Arsenal 4 Everton 2 – 21 December 1991 (League Division One)

Arsenal 7 Sheffield Wednesday 1
– 15 February 1992 (League Division One)

Arsenal 4 Liverpool 0 – 20 April 1992 (League Division One)

Arsenal 5 Southampton 1 – 2 May 1992 (League Division One)

Leeds United 2 Arsenal 3
– 3 February 1993 (FA Cup, Fourth Round, Replay)

Arsenal 1 Tottenham Hotspur 0
– 4 April 1993 (FA Cup, Semi-Final)

Arsenal 2 Sheffield Wednesday 1
– 18 April 1993 (Coca-Cola Cup, Final)

Arsenal 2 Sheffield Wednesday 1
– 20 May 1993 (FA Cup, Final, Replay)

Standard Liège 0 Arsenal 7 – 3 November 1993
(European Cup-Winners' Cup, Second Round, 2nd Leg)

Arsenal 4 Southampton 2
– 23 September 1995 (FA Premier League)

Arsenal 2 Bolton Wanderers 1
– 5 May 1996 (FA Premier League)

Arsenal 4 Bolton Wanderers 1
– 13 September 1997 (FA Premier League)

Arsenal 5 Deportivo La Coruña 1
– 2 March 2000 (UEFA Cup, Fourth Round, 1st Leg)

Werder Bremen 2 Arsenal 4
– 23 March 2000 (UEFA Cup, Quarter-Final, 2nd Leg)

Arsenal 2 Tottenham Hotspur 1
– 8 April 2001 (FA Cup, Semi-Final)

Arsenal 3 Juventus 1 – 4 December 2001
(UEFA Champions League, Second Group Stage)

Newcastle United 0 Arsenal 2
– 2 March 2002 (FA Premier League)

Arsenal 2 Chelsea 0 – 4 May 2002 (FA Cup, Final)

PSV 0 Arsenal 4 – 25 September 2002
(UEFA Champions League, First Group Stage)

Leeds United 1 Arsenal 4
– 28 September 2002 (FA Premier League)

Arsenal 3 Tottenham Hotspur 0
– 16 November 2002 (FA Premier League)

Arsenal 1 Southampton 0 – 17 May 2003 (FA Cup, Final)

Portsmouth 1 Arsenal 5 – 6 March 2004 (FA Cup, Quarter-Final)

Arsenal 4 Liverpool 2 – 9 April 2004 (FA Premier League)

Arsenal 5 Leeds United 0 – 16 April 2004 (FA Premier League)

Arsenal 7 Everton 0 – 11 May 2005 (FA Premier League)

Arsenal 0 Manchester United 0
– 21 May 2005 (FA Cup, Final)

Liverpool 0
Arsenal 2 Smith, Thomas

26 May 1989

Liverpool	Arsenal	
Grobbelaar, Ablett, Staunton,	Lukic, Dixon, Winterburn,	Attendance: **41,728**
Nicol, Whelan, Hansen,	Thomas, Adams, O'Leary,	
Houghton, Aldridge,	Rocastle, Richardson,	
Rush (Beardsley), Barnes,	Smith, Merson (Hayes),	
McMahon	Bould (Groves)	

To many Arsenal fans, this will always remain the greatest victory in the Gunners' history, but it is difficult to describe to younger fans what it was like on that balmy Friday evening on Merseyside. Liverpool had not lost a league game at home by two goals for three years, and had been the dominant force in domestic and European football for the bulk of the previous decade.

So when Arsenal had to travel up the M6 and attempt to win – by two clear goals – to surpass the Reds' goal difference and lift the league championship, it was, according to the press, mission impossible. 'You haven't got a prayer!' screamed one headline on the morning of the game… And they were surely right.

The previous weeks had seen Arsenal's fine season self-destruct spectacularly, culminating in a home defeat to Derby County and, four days later, an equally devastating 2–2 draw at home to perennial party-poopers Wimbledon, which seemed to finally extinguish the Gunners' title bid. Liverpool, however, had to deal with the traumatic events at Hillsborough the previous month.

But, and credit to Kenny Dalglish's 'double'-chasers, their focus on the field remained total and their league form was mighty impressive. The previous week West

Michael Thomas fires his way into Arsenal folklore. He later went on to play for Liverpool.

Arsenal's players celebrate the greatest ever finish to a league season. Goal hero Thomas is on the far right.

Ham had been relegated after a 5–1 mauling at Anfield and the 'Red Machine', confident as ever, was relishing the visit of Arsenal.

Gunners' players handed out bouquets to the Anfield crowd before the game as a mark of respect for those who had perished at Hillsborough six weeks before, but they were to be the only presents offered on the night. From then on it was all about focusing on the job in hand as Arsenal – playing an unusual 5–3–2 formation – produced a performance of courage, charisma and cool heads. Controlling the game from the off, Arsenal, playing in yellow, got among the hosts with gusto. Steve Bould saw his early header deflected just wide with Bruce Grobbelaar beaten, while Ian Rush, shortly to depart through injury, stung John Lukic's hands with a 30-yard snapshot.

Arsenal knew they needed to apply more pressure and shocked the Anfield crowd when Alan Smith got the faintest of touches to Paul Merson's cute free-kick six minutes after the interval and sent the ball past a wrong-footed Grobbelaar. The Liverpool players complained that Smith had not touched the ball and there was an agonising wait for Arsenal fans as the referee consulted the linesman. The goal was given.

For Liverpool, however, the occasion seemed to be too much for some of their players, as they prepared to sit back and defend a 1–0 home defeat – still enough to earn them another championship. Michael Thomas had given them cause for concern with a quarter of an hour to go when he turned and shot straight at Grobbelaar, though it looked like Arsenal were to win the battle – but lose the war.

George Graham flung on Perry Groves and Martin Hayes in one desperate last throw of the dice, but Liverpool appeared to have done enough, John Barnes and Steve McMahon shaking hands, congratulating each other as the seconds ticked down. But, deep into added time and with the Kop demanding the final whistle, John Lukic threw the ball to Lee Dixon, who cleared to Alan Smith and he in turn nudged the ball into the path of Thomas. The young midfielder, aided by a fortunate deflection, then, miraculously, found himself through on goal. Time stood still as Steve Nicol and Ray Houghton desperately tried to get back. Grobbelaar narrowed the angle, but Thomas' momentum took it on and one flick of his right boot later the ball had snuggled into the corner of the net.

For Liverpool it was a hammer blow, but for the travelling contingent of Arsenal fans, wedged into a small corner of the ground, it was sheer ecstasy. Few games, if any, have ever ended in such drama. Arsenal had defied the odds to become champions.

Inter Milan 1 Vieri

25 November 2003 # Arsenal 5 Henry (2), Ljungberg, Edu, Pires

Inter Milan
Toldo, Cordoba, Materazzi,
Cannavaro, J Zanetti, C Zanetti,
Lamouchi (Almeyda), Brechet,
van der Meyde (Cruz),
Vieri, Martins

Arsenal
Lehmann, Toure, Cygan,
Campbell, Cole, Ljungberg,
Parlour, Edu, Pires,
Henry (Aliadiere),
Kanu (Gilberto)

Attendance: **44,884**

There are performances that come out of nowhere and astonish everyone. But even when they do, few have the power to really, as the tabloid clichés go, 'send shockwaves around Europe'. However, Thierry Henry's captivating, brilliant dismantling of Internazionale in their own backyard in Milan did just that.

On a quite miserable Milanese evening in the spaceship-like San Siro, the Gallic striker toyed, teased and tormented the blue and blacks – and avenged, in outrageous fashion, a 3–0 reverse at Highbury just two months earlier.

In incessant rain Arsenal, for 90 minutes, showed that yes, on occasion, their domestic best was more than a match for the continent's finest. Henry swapped neat passes with Ashley Cole before side-footing in the opener after 25 minutes, only for Azzuri marksman Christian Vieri to level with a fortuitous goal when his effort took a wicked deflection off Sol Campbell and looped over Jens Lehmann eight minutes later.

There was little clue to what was to come.

Arsenal took the lead for a second time early in the second half, sparking 45 minutes of fantasy football for the travelling Arsenal fans packed behind Francesco Toldo's goal. Henry this time turned provider with a pinpoint left-wing cross that left Freddie Ljungberg with the simple task of slotting home from close range.

Could Arsenal hold on for a famous win? They did even better.

With Inter piling forward – their vociferous support demanding nothing less – they left gaping holes at the back and Henry twice could, and perhaps should, have put the tie beyond doubt, while Ljungberg somehow contrived to miss with the goal gaping.

But Henry finally made it 3–1 nine minutes from the end when he raced through from the halfway line, twice teasing Javier Zanetti who was in close attendance, before finding an extra yard of space to fire past Toldo with aplomb from an acute angle.

And Arsenal weren't finished.

Ljungberg's goal puts Arsenal 2–1 ahead just after the break.

With the vast stadium emptying fast, Brazilian Edu side-footed a fourth with three minutes to go. Dispirited Inter had been run ragged and Robert Pires was alert enough to make it five in stoppage time, rubbing salt into the Italians' deep wounds.

It was remarkable stuff, and the usually unflappable Arsène Wenger failed to put a lid on his emotions afterwards. 'Not in my wildest dreams could I have predicted a result like that,' he gushed. It was the first time an English side had beaten Inter on their own pitch for more than 40 years.

The giant German Jens Lehmann, strolling through the press area in the bowels of the stadium afterwards, admitted he had made an emotional speech to his team-mates, displaying his gratitude at being part of a special Arsenal team, with a special Arsenal spirit.

Henry's second goal and things are starting to go very well for Arsenal.

The next morning's front page of the *Gazzetta Dello Sport* was dominated by the grinning Frenchman. 'Henry umilia l'Inter' screamed the disbelieving headlines. Alberto Zaccheroni's side had been just that – humiliated.

Arsenal players celebrate their magnificent victory with the travelling fans at the end of the game.

Manchester United 0
Arsenal 1 Wiltord

8 May 2002

Manchester United
Barthez, P Neville, Blanc, Brown, Silvestre, Veron (van Nistelrooy), Keane, Scholes, Giggs, Forlan (Fortune), Solskjaer

Arsenal
Seaman, Lauren, Keown, Campbell, Cole, Parlour, Vieira, Edu, Ljungberg, Kanu (Dixon), Wiltord

Attendance: **67,580**

A perfect four days for Arsenal in the spring of 2002 ended with them securing their 12th league title – and third 'double' – with a fantastic win at the ground of their main rivals. It was a victory that gave rise to the thought that there had been a 'shift of power' in English football from the north-west to the south-east.

Manchester United may have ended the season dispirited in third place, Liverpool pipping them for runners-up spot, but make no mistake the title race was still between them and Arsenal, Liverpool never really threatening to challenge Arsenal despite a fine end-of-season run seeing them beat the Red Devils to second spot.

It was Sylvain Wiltord who was to score the vital winner for Arsène Wenger's golden-clad team for a result that also confirmed they were unbeaten away from Highbury for an entire season, the first top flight team to achieve this for more than a century. That in itself was a remarkable feat, but this win was also Arsenal's 12th league success on the trot – a new club record that would be extended to 13 with a 4–3 home win over Everton three days later – as they finished the season in championship-style.

It doesn't get much better than that, but United were determined from the off to disrupt Arsenal's fluid, attacking play. Sir Alex Ferguson's side adopted an aggressive attitude – three of their players getting booked in the opening 26 minutes – as the pace of the game remained relentless throughout.

Arsenal eventually settled and found their passing game as referee Paul Durkin attempted to keep the match flowing, despite the 100 mph pace. In fact, the Gunners could have grabbed a precious goal inside the opening 90 seconds, Kanu leaping to head the ball down to Ray Parlour who foraged down the right and crossed for Wiltord to fire the ball against Laurent Blanc and away to safety.

However much United tried to break through the gold defence they found it impossible, David Seaman barely being called into action as the hosts found themselves in the unusual position of being pinned back in their own half for long periods.

Sylvain Wiltord beats Fabien Barthez in the United goal for the winner.

But Arsenal had been boosted before kick-off when Fergie had inexplicably decided to leave striker Ruud van Nistelrooy on the bench. And with the hosts' attacking options running out, Arsenal finally made the breakthrough at the other end in the 56th minute to stun Old Trafford. Mikael Silvestre gifted the ball to Parlour, who earned the man-of-the-match champagne with another typically combative performance, and he found Ljungberg who held off Blanc to fire in a shot. United goalkeeper Fabien Barthez parried and Wiltord, racing in on the left, side-footed the ball past his France team-mate for the winner.

From then on it was comfortable as United again failed to make any inroads into the Arsenal backline and Durkin's final whistle was greeted with jubilant scenes from the players, staff and 3,000 travelling fans tucked away in the corner behind the goal. Boss Wenger said afterwards: 'To win it at United and bring the title home to Highbury is fantastic... We want tonight to be a shift in power.' Even Sir Alex had to admit: 'Arsenal are worthy champions.'

Life doesn't get much sweeter…

Above: Man-of-the-match Ray Parlour challenges for possession with United's Roy Keane

Below: Winning the championship on the ground of your main rivals – Arsenal players agree, things can't get much better than that.

4

Arsenal 3 Talbot, Stapleton, Sunderland
Manchester United 2 McQueen, McIlroy

12 May 1979

Arsenal
Jennings, Rice, Nelson,
Talbot, O'Leary, Young,
Brady, Sunderland, Stapleton,
Price (Walford), Rix

Manchester United
Bailey, Nicholl, Albiston,
McIlroy, McQueen, Buchan,
Coppell, J Greenhoff, Jordan,
Macari, Thomas

Attendance: **100,000**

Despite all the hype, FA Cup finals rarely live up to fans' expectations, and for the majority of this affair on a stifling hot Wembley day, the game plodded towards an unremarkable 2–0 win for Arsenal. But a late burst from Manchester United and a match-winning gamble from Alan Sunderland ensured it would go down in Wembley folklore as the one of the greatest ever.

The country was on a high after Margaret Thatcher's victory in the General Election earlier in the month, and the feelgood factor swept through Wembley on a perfect day for football's oldest cup final.

Like the famous 'Matthews final' of 1953, the best player on the pitch failed to score. But for Republic of Ireland international Liam Brady, now Head of Youth Development

and Academy Manager at Highbury under Arsène Wenger, this was his finest hour in a Gunners shirt. The Dubliner was the architect of all three Arsenal goals, confirming that his classy talents would, at some stage of his career, need to move to a club showing greater ambition.

For United this was their third cup final in four years, while Arsenal were desperate to make up for the disappointment of losing the previous year to Bobby Robson's rising Ipswich side. And the Londoners controlled most of the opening half, scoring twice without reply before the change of ends. Brady, with a jinking run, combined with Frank Stapleton to free David Price down the right and his drilled cross was met by the onrushing Sunderland and Brian Talbot. Sunderland wheeled away in delight, claiming the goal, but it was rightly credited to the hard-working Talbot, a cup-winner the year before with Ipswich Town.

Two minutes before the break Stapleton made it 2–0 against his future employers – a move later deemed unforgivable by the Arsenal faithful – when Brady skipped past two tackles to place a perfect centre on his head. And that seemed to be that. The second half petered out as the hot

Liam Brady, the supreme performer on the day, evades United's Joe Jordan and Lou Macari.

A jubilant Alan Sunderland (far right) wheels away in celebration after turning in Graham Rix's last minute cross for the fifth and final goal of the game. Just seconds earlier Arsenal had looked dead and buried.

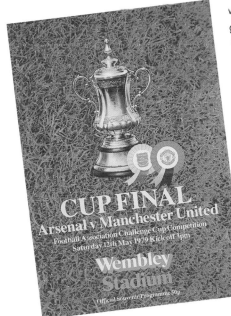

weather took its toll and when, with a few minutes to go, Arsenal boss Terry Neill gave substitute Steve Walford a taste of the action, he appeared to accept United were dead.

But there was a sting in the tail when first Gordon McQueen steered the ball past Pat Jennings for a soft goal, and two minutes later – and with only a couple of minutes of the match remaining – Ulsterman Sammy McIlroy skipped past two challenges and slid the ball under Jennings.

Brady, dripping with sweat afterwards, admitted, 'When United pulled level I was dreading extra time because I was knackered and our substitute was already on'. It was a hammer blow, but Arsenal had the final say when, with one final burst at the heart of a retreating United defence, Brady fed the ball wide to Graham Rix on the left. The young midfielder swung over a deep cross, goalkeeper Gary Bailey realised in horror that he wasn't going to reach it and flapped at thin air, and Alan Sunderland, who had made a blistering run down the right, steered the ball in.

At the end of what has become known as the 'five-minute final' it was Arsenal's cup, but it was a close run thing.

5

Arsenal 4 Bilic (o.g.), Overmars (2), Adams
Everton 0

3 May 1998

Arsenal
Seaman, Dixon, Winterburn,
Keown, Adams, Parlour,
Vieira, Petit (Platt),
Overmars, Anelka (Wright),
Wreh (Bould)

Everton
Myhre, O'Kane (Madar),
Short, Watson, Tiler,
Ball, Barmby, Hutchison,
Bilic (Farrelly), Beagrie (Oster),
Ferguson

Attendance: **38,269**

If one single passage of play could act as a microcosm of Arsène Wenger's impact on Arsenal Football Club, it came with two minutes to go of a game against Everton at Highbury that sealed the Frenchman's first Premiership title. And it really did happen, and Arsenal really were champions in front of another adoring sell-out crowd on a gloriously sunny afternoon.

Steve Bould, an old school bruiser of a centre-half, dinked a delightful chipped ball over the advancing Everton defensive line. Tony Adams, a wholehearted never-say-die centre-half, bent his run with perfection to cleverly stay onside, chested down the ball and finished with complete confidence.

It was a perfect, crazy way to end a title-winning 90 minutes, after a season in which from March onwards Arsenal had led the way to wrestle the trophy from Manchester United. If a writer had penned this ending – Bould and Adams evolving into Bergkamp and Wright in the final seconds of this perfect Highbury day – it would have been dismissed as far-fetched, sentimental rubbish and thrown in the wastepaper basket.

Adams had helped start this rout of an Everton team, who at times seemed to lose all sense of discipline as they chased shadows in the heat. The skipper put enough pressure on Slaven Bilic to force the Croat to head Manu Petit's cross into his own goal after just four minutes, with Arsenal needing a win to confirm the title.

Marc Overmars, who had enjoyed an astonishing first season in English football, all but put the red and white ribbons on the trophy 24 minutes later. Nigel Winterburn – on his 500th appearance for the Club – had already set up chances for Overmars and Nicolas Anelka as Everton

Marc Overmars stretches to score Arsenal's third as Toffees defenders Dave Watson and Michael Ball watch on helplessly.

struggled to compete with Arsenal's incessant attacking tide. But the Dutchman finally scored the second when he sprinted through from his own area, and even though Thomas Myhre partially blocked his shot, it still had enough to roll over the line.

The Merseysiders were lucky to have 11 men at the break after Don Hutchison's horror tackle on Petit saw the

French midfielder, like Overmars a revelation in his first year in London, stretchered off.

But there was no stopping Arsenal, by now in total command, and Overmars scurried away for his 15th goal of the season early in the second half, when he netted from an acute angle after Michael Ball lost possession.

With time running down Ian Wright, like an overeager schoolboy, entered the fray to a tumultuous welcome from the crowd, but the biggest cheer was reserved for another substitute, Steve Bould. As if to justify the cheers he and Adams then conjured up their moment of magic to confirm a 10th successive league win and the championship in an almost surreal fashion.

As captain Adams collected the Premiership trophy, Bob Wilson and Pat Rice, two members of the 1971 'double' winners, joined the present squad on the pitch for some raucous celebrations, as did a hobbling, heavily bandaged Petit, much to the fans' relief.

Tony Adams – Mr Arsenal – laps up the adulation of the Highbury masses after drilling home the fourth goal.

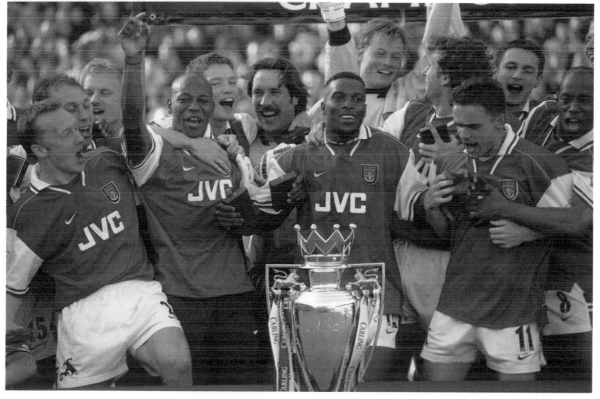

And the celebrations begin… Arsenal's players get the party started with the FA Premier League trophy in the foreground. It was Arsène Wenger's first English title.

Tottenham Hotspur 0
Arsenal 1 Kennedy

3 May 1971

Tottenham Hotspur
Jennings, Kinnear, Knowles,
Mullery, Collins, Beal,
Gilzean (Pearce), Perryman,
Chivers, Peters, Neighbour

Arsenal
Wilson, Rice, McNab,
Kelly, McLintock, Simpson,
Armstrong, Graham, Radford,
Kennedy, George

Attendance: **51,992**

History was made at White Hart Lane as Arsenal surpassed Manchester United, Everton and Liverpool to become the first club to win the First Division championship eight times. Ray Kennedy's late, late header earned the Gunners their first title since Joe Mercer's men had lifted the trophy in 1953.

There was no doubt 18 years had been far too long, but what a way to finally be crowned champions of England. Defeat would have given Leeds the title, a win or scoreless draw and the trophy would be Highbury-bound. But it was important for Spurs, too, as they sought qualification for the UEFA Cup.

The two sides went at it hammer and tongs, giving little away, as this 90 minutes on a balmy Monday evening turned into an epic struggle. Islington's own Charlie George, who understood the rivalry between Arsenal and Spurs more than most, relished the occasion and forced Pat Jennings into an athletic save in the opening minute,

Arsenal goalkeeper Bob Wilson rises above his captain Frank McLintock (centre) and Tottenham's Martin Peters and Alan Gilzean to pluck another cross out of the air. Wilson had enjoyed an almost faultless league campaign.

Ray Kennedy (centre) heads the winning goal in the closing minutes to clinch the League Championship for Arsenal.

setting the tone for a frenetic contest. But Arsenal didn't have it all their own way.

Martin Peters saw his 25-yard volley flick off the Arsenal crossbar and then he went close with a header, while Bob Wilson had to be alert to save at the feet of Alan Gilzean. But Arsenal edged the first half play, as was reflected in the corner count, 7–1 in favour of the visitors.

If anyone thought the second half would have seen both sides settle back, they were sorely mistaken. Arsenal, who had been derided for their defensive approach all season, flooded forward in search of a winner – but so did Spurs. Gilzean nearly sent the home fans – roughly numbering only half the 52,000 present – wild but failed to connect with Cyril Knowles' first-time cross. Pat Rice was then called upon to clear Peters' effort off the line. George Graham then went close for Arsenal, only to see his header drop on the top of Jennings' bar and Joe Kinnear's overhit back pass just went wide of a post, as the game ebbed and flowed.

But with a goalless draw enough, Arsenal went one better three minutes from the end when Kennedy, a revelation in his first full season as a first-team regular, scored a classic winner. George took advantage of Kinnear's dithering to take possession and screw the ball on to the head of John Radford. The big Yorkshireman must have thought he had scored, but Pat Jennings stretched full-length to punch the ball away. George Armstrong, joining the attack on the left, chipped the ball back into the area and Kennedy rose above Alan Mullery to send his header in, clipping the underside of the bar on its way to the back of the net.

Arsenal were almost home but had to survive a fanatical onslaught in the final minutes as Spurs threw everything at the Arsenal goal, knowing an equaliser would send the title up to Leeds.

But when referee Kevin Howley, officiating his last ever league match, finally blew the whistle to end a titanic contest, the first stage of an historic 'double' was completed and the scenes at the end were astonishing, as Arsenal fans invaded the pitch to chair off skipper Frank McLintock. However, the celebrations had to be cut short, as the players now had to prepare for a trip to Wembley five days later.

An emotional Frank McLintock is mobbed at the final whistle.

Arsenal 3 Kelly, Radford, Sammels

28 April 1970

Anderlecht 0

Arsenal
won 4–3 on
aggregate

Arsenal
Wilson, Storey, McNab,
Kelly, McLintock, Simpson,
Armstrong, Sammels, Radford,
George, Graham

Anderlecht
Trappeniers, Heylens, Maartens,
Nordahl, Velkeneers, Kialunda,
Desanghere, Devrindt, Mulder,
van Himst, Puis

Attendance: **51,612**

Despite being 3–1 down after the first leg of this European Fairs Cup Final, Arsenal won their first trophy in 17 years on a dramatic night at Highbury. The architects of this memorable success were two home-grown teenagers – Ray Kennedy and Eddie Kelly – who were to help drag the Club out of the dark ages.

Ray Kennedy, still only 18, had climbed off the bench to head a late consolation in the first leg in Brussels. 'Arsenal's Ray of Hope' screamed the back page headlines the day after that game, and how right it was to be as the Gunners bossed the Belgians in the return match. But it was another teenager, Eddie Kelly, who was to break the deadlock and turn the second leg tie on its head.

The Glaswegian midfielder, fast making a name for himself with his effective, if unspectacular, performances, controlled the ball outside the box, cut inside and curled

Anderlecht goalkeeper Jean Trappeniers is left exposed as John Radford heads in the second goal of the night to haul Arsenal level on aggregate at 3–3. The Gunners now led on away goals.

The 17-year wait is nearly over as Jon Sammels thumps a magnificent third past the helpless Trappeniers.

a 25-yard shot beautifully into the net to make it 2–3 on aggregate and bring Anderlecht within touching distance.

Inspirational skipper Frank McLintock had been convinced this final could still be turned around and he urged his team to continue to take the game to the Belgians. The crowd had certainly heeded his call. Goalkeeper Bob Wilson recalled: 'The noise, it was nearly frightening, even though you were the home side. I thought "God! This is unreal."'

But the fans were nearly silenced 15 minutes after the change of ends, when a flowing Anderlecht move involving the magnificent Jan Mulder ended with Thomas Nordahl striking an upright from Wilfried Puis' near-post cross.

At 2–4 down it would surely have been lights out for the Gunners. Instead, grateful for their stroke of luck, they poured forward again. And fortune certainly favoured the brave on this wet night. The Belgian defence was at breaking point and it finally caved 15 minutes from the end when George Graham and Bob McNab combined on the left and John Radford was in total isolation to head down past Jean Trappeniers.

Kennedy's goal in Brussels' Parc Astrid meant Arsenal now led on away goals, but within a minute they went one better. Jon Sammels chested down Charlie George's magnificent crossfield ball and drove it into the net to the delight of the North Bank. Arsenal held on till the final whistle and won the tie 4–3 on aggregate.

McLintock, whose belief had driven his team-mates along, picked up the trophy from FIFA president Stanley Rous amid unprecedented scenes. Forgotten was the humiliation of the year before when Third Division Swindon Town had won in extra time in the League Cup Final.

Bob Wall, the secretary who had worked for the Club for more than 40 years, from the Herbert Chapman days, admitted: 'I've witnessed many wonderful occasions here in the past, particularly in the pre-war days, but I must say I've never seen anything quite like these scenes at Highbury before.'

Ask most fans who were fortunate enough to be there that night and they will tell you, without hesitation, this was the greatest game ever played at Highbury.

But for boss Bertie Mee, his calm voice in the pressroom afterwards pointed at even bigger fish to fry. 'The players realise this is only an interim step,' he said. 'The First Division is the toughest competition in the world and no club, whatever they achieve outside it, can call themselves great until it has been won.'

He had signalled his intent for the 1970/71 season…

Arsenal's Frank McLintock holds the trophy aloft as he and his team-mates are mobbed by ecstatic fans.

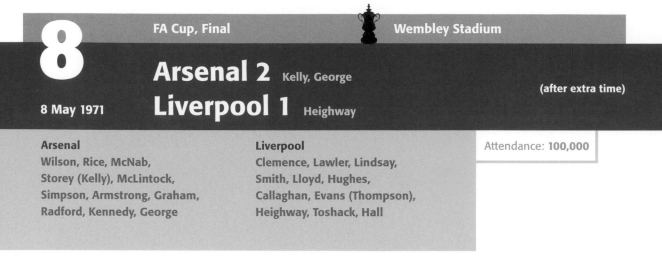

Arsenal 2 Kelly, George
Liverpool 1 Heighway

8 May 1971

(after extra time)

Arsenal
Wilson, Rice, McNab,
Storey (Kelly), McLintock,
Simpson, Armstrong, Graham,
Radford, Kennedy, George

Liverpool
Clemence, Lawler, Lindsay,
Smith, Lloyd, Hughes,
Callaghan, Evans (Thompson),
Heighway, Toshack, Hall

Attendance: **100,000**

It's difficult to think of many better or more dramatic cup-winning goals than the one that completed a dream journey from North Bank to Wembley hero for one sullen Holloway youngster. But Charlie George's goal is remembered as one of the finest and the boot with which he scored it now rests in pride of place in the Arsenal museum.

Arsenal had secured the first stage of the 'double' on a dramatic Monday night at, of all places, White Hart Lane. But once the euphoria of that magnificent night had died down, Mee's men had to knuckle down and prepare for Saturday's Wembley appointment with an emerging Liverpool side who would go on to dominate the English game for the next two decades.

The odds were stacked against Arsenal as only four title winners had also played in the FA Cup Final during the twentieth century, and for all but Spurs their 'double' hopes had been dashed at the final hurdle. But then Arsenal loved playing with the odds stacked against them. In September Stoke had thrashed them 5–0 at the Victoria Ground, hardly the

Holloway's finest – Charlie George – unleashes the winner. It was his finest hour for his beloved Gunners.

form of champions, but they slowly ground out the results to remain in the running.

Leeds United had led the way by seven points with March approaching before Arsenal embarked on a run of 11 wins in 12 league games to turn the championship race around, and even in the semi-final it was Stoke again who looked to have the beating of the Gunners before surrendering a two-goal lead to draw at Hillsborough.

Against Liverpool a tight contest, not helped by a searing heat, had failed to produce a goal in normal time, although Ray Kennedy missed from three yards and George Graham had a header cleared off the line as the Gunners had the better of the play.

But a rare error by Bob Wilson was to gift Liverpool the opener two minutes into extra time. The fleet-footed Steve Heighway sped down the left, and shaping to cross he instead fired the ball inside the near post, Wilson leaving too tempting a gap for the Eire winger to take full advantage.

They now had a monumental task as Liverpool boasted one of Europe's tightest defences, and had conceded just one goal in the competition that season. Arsenal had to pull on all their reserves but managed to conjure an equaliser nine minutes later when substitute Eddie Kelly scrambled a goal from close-range, though George Graham was initially credited as the scorer.

Liverpool looked broken and the stage was set for George's moment of magic. John Radford found the 20-year-old striker, who took a touch before unleashing a scorching drive from the edge of the box with Clemence given no chance. 'As soon as it left my foot I knew it was a goal,' he claimed afterwards with characteristic confidence.

His immortal celebration – lying down on the lush turf in a state of near exhaustion – has been copied on north London playgrounds ever since.

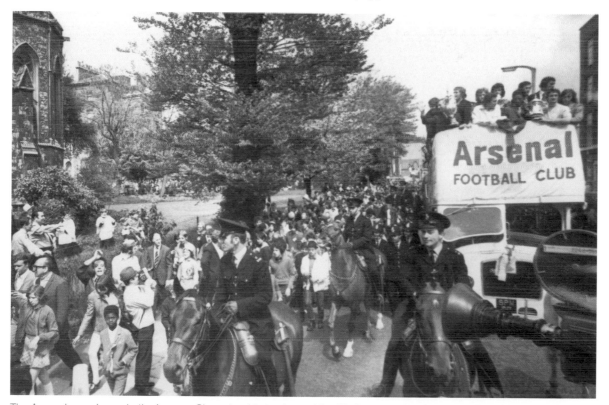

The Arsenal squad parade the League Championship trophy and the FA Cup through the streets of Islington.

9

FA Premier League — Stamford Bridge

Chelsea 2 Flo, Petrescu
Arsenal 3 Kanu (3)

23 October 1999

Chelsea
De Goey, Ferrer, Le Saux (Poyet), Deschamps, Leboeuf, Desailly, Petrescu, Babayaro, Sutton, Flo (Zola), Wise

Arsenal
Seaman, Dixon, Adams, Keown, Silvinho, Parlour, Ljungberg (Henry), Petit (Vivas), Overmars (Vernazza), Kanu, Suker

Attendance: **34,958**

For the bulk of this game Arsenal, it appeared, had forgotten to turn up. Arsène Wenger's team had been uncharacteristically sloppy, conceding possession alarmingly, and at times being overrun by a mightily impressive Chelsea side, full of passion and desire. The Blues led 2–0 early in the second half and seemed most likely to to take the three points on offer.

It was a stark contrast to the previous week when Arsenal had blown away a spirited Everton team at Highbury, Davor Suker impressing in particular that day with a double strike.

In recent years encounters between Arsenal and Chelsea had been powder-keg affairs, with Arsenal more often than not coming out on top. But a looping first-half header from Norwegian Tore Andre Flo had beaten David Seaman to give the Blues an early advantage. And when Dan Petrescu headed home Graeme Le Saux's superb centre minutes into the second half, it looked like it was game over for the Gunners, especially as the hosts' defence had not conceded a league goal at home since the previous spring.

Marc Overmars and Ray Parlour congratulate Kanu after the Nigeria striker's second goal at Stamford Bridge.

Kanu (far left) cranes his head to see his outrageous shot evade the stretching Frank Leboeuf on the line for his third of the afternoon, and hands Arsenal one of their greatest wins over their west London neighbours.

So what possessed Kanu to suddenly, inexplicably, brilliantly, turn this game on its head in 15 breathtaking minutes, with a personal display that was to brand his name into Arsenal legend? Only the man himself could tell you.

New signing Thierry Henry, who had started the game on the bench, watched in awe. As the game petered out on a heavy pitch, getting heavier due to the ceaseless rain, Kanu got to work. First he pulled one back when he controlled Marc Overmars' tame effort on goal, swivelled and stabbed the ball past Ed de Goey with a swing of his size 16 boot. Chelsea, for whatever reason, visibly wilted.

With seven minutes remaining and Arsenal growing in confidence by the second, the Nigerian magician equalised when he collected an Overmars cross, wrong-footed Marcel Desailly and slammed the ball inside the near post. One point saved? But Kanu hadn't finished yet, and his third, deep into injury time, summed up what a precocious talent Wenger had acquired the previous February from Italian giants Internazionale.

First his telescopic legs, by now looking to have a life of their own, raced him to the corner flag, where he charged down a clearance and found de Goey well out of position between the corner flag and penalty area. With a shake and a wriggle in his now customary lackadaisical manner, Kanu dumped de Goey's backside in the Stamford Bridge puddles as his rubbery legs rounded the keeper with consummate ease.

But the striker was still on the byline, and he faced the formidable barrier of France's World Cup-winning central defence of Desailly and Frank Leboeuf. He looked up for support, but his tired team-mates were nowhere to be seen. No matter. He simply fired an unstoppable bending shot around Desailly and over Leboeuf's straining head to send the travelling Arsenal fans into heaven. It was an impossible goal.

Poor Chelsea had simply been out Kanu'd!

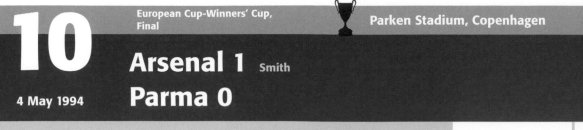

European Cup-Winners' Cup, Final

Parken Stadium, Copenhagen

Arsenal 1 Smith
Parma 0

4 May 1994

Arsenal	Parma	Attendance: 33,765
Seaman, Dixon, Winterburn, Bould, Adams, Davis, Selley, Morrow, Merson (McGoldrick), Campbell, Smith	Bucci, Benarrivo, Di Chiara, Minotti, Apolloni, Sensini, Brolin, Pin (Melli), Crippa, Zola, Asprilla	

Arsenal snuffed out the multi-talented Italians and won their second European trophy thanks to a brilliant goal from Alan Smith. In one of the most disciplined performances by any English side on the European stage, Parma simply ran out of ideas as they desperately tried to break down Arsenal's rock hard red-and-white defence.

Wonderful, wonderful Copenhagen had become a huge Arsenal enclave in the days leading up to this match in the imposing Parken Stadium. It seemed everyone in north London wanted to be there, despite the fact that the odds were stacked heavily against Arsenal.

Parma boasted the likes of Tino Asprilla, Tomas Brolin and Gianfranco Zola, all of whom would become more familiar to British football fans in later years. Arsenal were missing leading scorer Ian Wright, suspended after picking up a yellow card in the semi-final against Paris St-Germain. This was a big enough blow, but Johnny 'Faxe' Jensen, David Hillier and Martin Keown – all perfect for this type of game – were also out, to leave them with an even bigger uphill struggle. With David Seaman also having painkilling injections for a long-standing rib injury, Arsenal surely stood no hope.

They struggled early on as Parma's yellow shirts swarmed all around the Arsenal area, prompting and probing for an early break. The Italians, holders of the cup after beating Royal Antwerp 3–1 a year before, nearly took the lead when Brolin shot against a post, the ball flying across the face of the goal before going out of play.

Zola also had Seaman stretching – testing his battered ribs – before Smith made the most significant impact on the game with the only goal after 21 minutes. Parma skipper Lorenzo Minotti attempted to clear Lee Dixon's long throw with an elaborate overhead kick, but instead he deflected the ball into Smith's path. The former Leicester striker allowed the ball to bounce once and then unleashed a stunning volley inside Luca Bucci's near post.

The vast majority of the crowd were supporting Arsenal and the newly revamped stadium exploded as Smith wheeled away in celebration. But there was a long way to go, not that Arsenal seemed too bothered. From then on Parma had the lion's share of possession, but facing an Arsenal defence who were completely confident in their ability to keep a clean sheet – and man-of-the-match Steve Bould in imperious form – they just could not get through.

Arsenal played out the game with Parma, despite all their flair, not creating one clear-cut opportunity. With the

Alan Smith – one of the most popular players to have represented Arsenal – volleys in the only goal of the game in Copenhagen. Injury would prematurely end the career of 'Smudger' the following year.

final whistle came confirmation of Arsenal's first European trophy for 24 years, in the city in which they had made their European bow against Staevnet in 1963. The travelling North Bank sang their new anthem – 'One-Nil to the Arsenal' – long into the Danish night.

Proud manager George Graham was ecstatic his team's stubbornness had paved the way for victory. 'We're a club with a marvellous team spirit and everyone – including the guys who couldn't play – was involved,' said the Scotsman, echoing his all-for-one, one-for-all mentality.

He now held a unique place in the Club's history, having been involved in both of their European successes, playing against Anderlecht in the European Fairs Cup win in 1970, and managing the 1994 winners of the Cup-Winners' Cup.

The Arsenal squad poses with the Club's first European trophy for 24 years.

Tottenham Hotspur 2 Redknapp, Keane (pen)
Arsenal 2 Vieira, Pires

25 April 2004

Tottenham Hotspur	**Arsenal**	Attendance: **36,097**
Keller, Kelly (Poyet), Gardner, King, Taricco (Bunjevcevic), Davies, Brown, Redknapp, Jackson (Defoe), Keane, Kanoute	Lehmann, Lauren, Cole, Toure, Campbell, Vieira, Pires, Gilberto, Parlour (Edu), Bergkamp (Reyes), Henry	

It wasn't quite Ray Kennedy in 1971, but if you polled a hundred fans, most would take a draw at White Hart Lane over most other results to seal the title. Surprisingly, this pulsating encounter ensured Arsène Wenger became the first manager in the Club's history to win three titles, Herbert Chapman's premature death preventing him doing so 70 years before.

The excitement around the red half of north London was mounting in the preceding weeks, as the games slipped by and slow realisation kicked in that Sunday 25 April would be the day Arsenal could clinch the title. For Spurs fans it was the unthinkable, 33 years after Arsenal's 1–0 White Hart Lane win had sealed the first stage of the 'double'.

And the home side appeared to freeze in the opening exchanges as Arsenal produced some of their most thrilling football of the season to stretch Tottenham's defence to breaking point. With just three minutes gone, and Arsenal already toying with the hosts, skipper Patrick Vieira drew first blood with a goal that characterised the Gunners' footballing strengths, turning defence into attack in seconds. Much like Chapman's team, this side had mastered the art of counter-attacking.

Tottenham defender Anthony Gardner headed Johnnie Jackson's corner straight to the lightning feet of Thierry Henry. He sped away on a 50-yard run deep into Spurs territory before feeding the ball wide to Dennis Bergkamp. With Spurs' defence gaping wide, the Dutchman delivered an inviting ball into the centre and Vieira, who made up virtually the entire length of the pitch in seconds, stuck out a telescopic leg and steered the ball in.

Tottenham were on the ropes, but Frederic Kanoute and Mauricio Taricco rallied the home fans with a couple of useful efforts that had Jens Lehmann stretching. However, Arsenal doubled their lead ten minutes before the interval when a flowing move ended with Pires converting after a delightful one-two with Vieira for his 19th of the season.

The title was all but in the bag, and for Spurs, after another disappointing campaign, this was the final indignity.

Skipper Patrick Vieira races away after netting the opener.

Spurs goalkeeper Kasey Keller is beaten by 'Bobby' Pires.

Home skipper Jamie Redknapp matched his Arsenal counterpart just past the hour mark when he drilled home a fine effort inside Lehmann's right-hand post from 25 yards. Pires nearly restored the two-goal advantage but saw his effort clip the bar, while Henry should have made it three but instead poked the ball wide.

Spurs' spirited second half brought them a deserved point, just as Arsenal seemed to have won all three, when referee Mark Halsey harshly adjudged Lehmann to have impeded Robbie Keane at a corner, and the Irishman slotted home the resultant penalty.

What followed was Spurs fans raucously celebrating an equaliser, while the travelling North Bank roared at the final whistle to hail the new Premiership champions.

It was a day when both sets of fans went home happy… well, one maybe happier than the other!

They needed three to win the game – and more importantly, delay Arsenal's celebrations. The champions-elect took their foot off the gas in the second half, comfortable they wouldn't concede thrice, and Spurs took advantage.

Does it get any better than this? The players celebrate on the White Hart Lane turf.

12

Tottenham Hotspur 0
Arsenal 5   Sunderland (3), Stapleton, Brady

23 December 1978

Tottenham Hotspur
Kendall, Naylor, Gorman, Holmes, Lacy, Perryman, Pratt (Jones), Ardiles, Lee, Hoddle, Taylor

Arsenal
Jennings, Rice, Walford, Price, O'Leary, Young, Brady, Sunderland, Stapleton, Gatting, Rix

Attendance: 42,273

For the 10,000 Arsenal fans who had made the short trip up the Seven Sisters Road two days before Christmas, even Santa himself couldn't have brought them a better Yuletide present. Tottenham were humiliated on their own pitch with Liam Brady putting on a world-class display and Alan Sunderland claiming a hat-trick.

The Spurs faithful had been desperate for this game after bouncing back to the First Division following relegation in 1977, but a ruthless Arsenal dominated, with the home stands emptying long before the final whistle.

It was a game in which Brady was to find himself in direct battle with World Cup-winning star Osvaldo Ardiles. And while the little Argentinian had an impressive game, even with his wonderful ability he struggled to keep up with the Irishman's rare footballing brain.

The rout started in the first minute, Spurs unintentionally setting up the opener for their neighbours. John Pratt clattered into Arsenal's David Price but saw the ball ricochet back towards his goal. Sunderland beat Tottenham defender John Lacy, took a touch and fired into the roof of the net, the ball flicking off the advancing Mark Kendall on its way in.

Pat Jennings, making his first return to White Hart Lane since his controversial move to Arsenal in the summer of 1977, barely had a save to make as his old team tried to fight back without any shot of note.

Brady decided to take charge and drilled a spectacular crossfield pass to Sunderland, who belted in a second with seven minutes of the half remaining.

Spurs' defence are asking questions – but Alan Sunderland gets on with celebrating another goal.

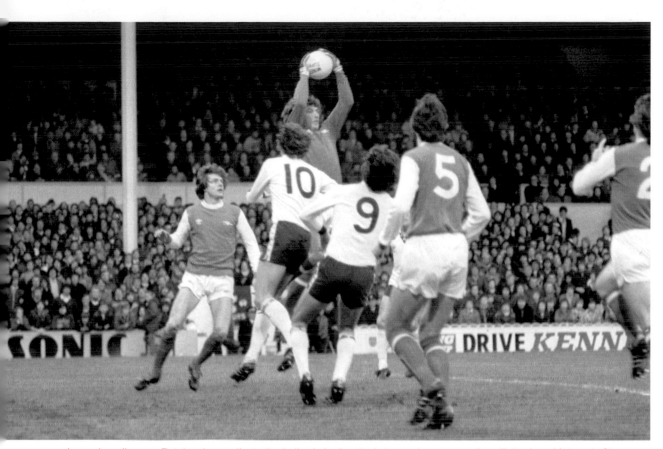

Arsenal goalkeeper Pat Jennings collects the ball calmly, despite being under pressure from Tottenham Hotspur's Glenn Hoddle (10) and Colin Lee (9).

Arsenal tightened their grip on the game with Spurs chasing shadows after the change of ends, Brady showing off his full repertoire of skills.

Sunderland nearly got his hat-trick when he thumped a header against the underside of the bar, while Price contrived to miss from point blank range with the goal at his mercy. But a third arrived in the 62nd minute when Brady found space to send over a perfect cross and Frank Stapleton sent his downward header into the bottom corner.

Then came a moment of true Brady magic, with a wonder goal still replayed on TV years on. He won possession on the edge of the box and looked up before arrowing an absolute corker into the far top corner with Kendall helpless. It was a breathtaking goal that sent the massed Arsenal fans behind the goal into ecstasy.

And their team was still not finished. Sunderland completed his first treble for the Club since moving from Wolves the year before when he collected Stapleton's neat flick and scored into the corner with a crisp drive.

The travelling support chanted, 'We want six!' and Arsenal tried their utmost to equal their record win in N17 – a 6–0 drubbing back in 1935. But five would have to do, still the highest number of goals Tottenham have conceded at home since the war.

As for Ardiles, he didn't even have the consolation of heading back to his new home in Hertfordshire to forget a thoroughly miserable afternoon. His new neighbour was none other than a certain Mr Alan Sunderland!

TOPPS ALL★STARS

LIAM BRADY
MIDFIELDER • EIRE

Arsenal 2 Overmars, Anelka

16 May 1998

Newcastle United 0

Arsenal
Seaman, Dixon, Winterburn,
Vieira, Keown, Adams,
Petit, Overmars, Parlour,
Wreh (Platt), Anelka

Newcastle United
Given, Pistone,
Pearce (Andersson), Batty,
Dabizas, Howey, Lee,
Barton (Watson), Shearer,
Ketsbia (Barnes), Speed

Attendance: 79,183

Imports Marc Overmars from Holland and Nicolas Anelka from France scored the goals that sealed Arsenal's first 'double' since 1971, but it was the home-grown talent of Ray Parlour, all the way from Romford, that earned Arsenal victory over Newcastle United in the FA Cup Final at Wembley.

Parlour worked like a Trojan and responded magnificently to manager Arsène Wenger's decision to stick with the Essex-born midfielder. He constantly outmuscled Newcastle's lively midfield and could have scored at the end of a fine display as he staked a claim for a place in Glenn Hoddle's squad for the forthcoming World Cup in France.

Coupled with the pace of Overmars and Anelka, and the rock-like central midfield of Patrick Vieira and Emmanuel Petit, Arsenal were simply too strong for Newcastle, even without Dennis Bergkamp who was forced to miss the match through injury.

With Arsenal carving through the Geordies almost too easily in the first half, the opening goal had an air of inevitability about it when it finally came through the lightning quick feet of Overmars. Manu Petit chipped the ball over the Newcastle back line, the flying Dutchman

Holland international Marc Overmars bravely beats Shay Given for the opener.

wrestled in front of Alessandro Pistone and his speed allowed him to pull away and bravely toe-poke the ball under the oncoming frame of Newcastle goalkeeper Shay Given.

It was a long way from Overmars' ineffective debut at Leeds the previous August, and proved in an instant just how quickly he had repaid Arsène Wenger's faith in him – and how he had come to terms with the physical demands of English football.

Newcastle fought back with plenty of spirit in the second half, with England striker Alan Shearer beginning to free himself from the shackles of Tony Adams and Martin Keown. Shearer, desperate to help his hometown club to their first major trophy since the Fairs Cup in 1969, amazingly spurned a great opportunity to pull Newcastle level after Keown made a horrendous error. He pounced as the Arsenal man trod on the ball in the area, but scuffed his shot against the post.

Another 'double' for Arsenal: Nicolas Anelka makes it two.

With the Wembley crowd still in shock at having witnessed a rare Shearer error, he astonishingly did it again within minutes. All alone facing David Seaman, he fatally hesitated as he expected the offside flag and allowed Nigel Winterburn to charge back and boot the ball away off his toes for a corner.

They were two very lucky escapes for Arsenal and the Londoners took full advantage within minutes by taking a 2–0 lead through Anelka. Parlour turned the ball to Anelka who checked his run before racing through a static Newcastle defence that was failing abysmally to deploy the offside trap. Before Given could react, he dispatched the ball into the net with a finish bordering on arrogant, unwisely celebrating in front of the travelling Toon Army who had targeted him for abuse throughout.

Despite cries to bring Ian Wright on to the pitch to share in the glory, the Club's all-time leading scorer was not allowed to take part, staying on the bench for the final minutes as Arsène Wenger shut up shop to ensure victory and a historic 'double'.

And for captain fantastic Tony Adams, it completed his remarkable journey through two decades to become a 'double'-winning skipper.

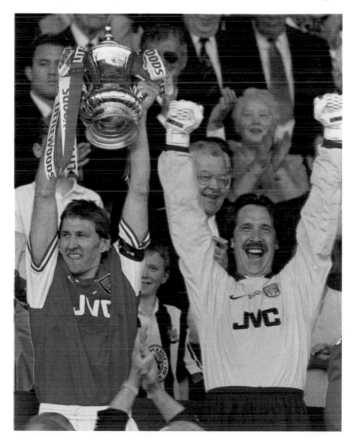

Tony Adams lifts the famous old cup, flanked by a delighted David Seaman.

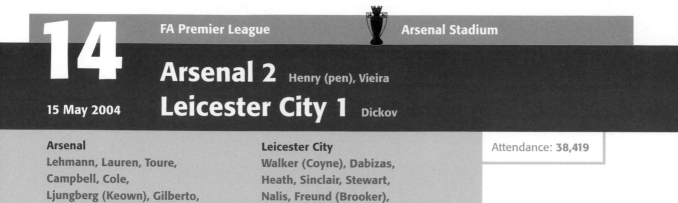
Arsenal
Lehmann, Lauren, Toure,
Campbell, Cole,
Ljungberg (Keown), Gilberto,
Vieira, Pires (Edu),
Bergkamp (Reyes), Henry

Leicester City
Walker (Coyne), Dabizas,
Heath, Sinclair, Stewart,
Nalis, Freund (Brooker),
McKinlay, Scowcroft,
Dickov (Benjamin), Bent

Attendance: **38,419**

Since the championship had been sealed two weeks before with a point from a 2–2 draw against Spurs at White Hart Lane, the talk had turned to the unbeaten league run. With the final match of the season at home to Leicester City could the Gunners become the first side in modern history to go through an English league season unbeaten?

Preston North End's 'Invincibles' were the only team in top-flight football to do it back in 1888/89 – the first season of the Football League – when it was still an amateur sport, the league season barely consisting of half the games played now.

Arsenal had been the side closest to achieving it when, in 1991, George Graham's title-winning side lost only one league game all season, a narrow 2–1 defeat at Chelsea in the 24th First Division game putting paid to their unbeaten aspirations.

With the trophy in the bag, Arsenal's form had slipped a little – a Highbury draw with Birmingham and another at Portsmouth before an unremarkable win at Fulham. So

with the visit of the Foxes, their 38th and last game, they were just 90 minutes away from immortality.

Leicester had provided the very first opposition on another significant Highbury occasion – the Club's first-ever home game in north London back in 1913. Arsenal won that day 2–1, and were to do so again here, but they were to prove dogged, spirited adversaries, despite being already relegated, and even managed to shake Highbury by taking an unexpected half-time lead.

It was former Gunner Paul Dickov, a fiery little striker never one to bow to big reputations, who was to break the deadlock with the Foxes' first meaningful attack midway through the first half. Frank Sinclair floated a super ball to the far post, and the 5ft 5in striker somehow managed to climb high enough to nod the ball past Lehmann.

He celebrated with gusto in front of a shocked North Bank – could Arsenal blow it at the final hurdle? They reacted as expected, wave after wave of attack being repelled by a well-organised Leicester defence as Arsenal drew a first-half blank.

But just 60 seconds after the restart, those anxieties were to be dispelled. Ashley Cole made a thrust into the box but found his progress halted when he was bundled to the ground. Thierry Henry immediately grabbed the ball for the penalty and sent former England goalkeeper Ian Walker the wrong way

Thierry Henry strokes home from the spot to level the scores.

Patrick Vieira rounds former Spurs keeper Ian Walker for the winner. Arsenal had created history.

for his 30th league goal of the season. Significantly, the PFA and Football Writers' Footballer of the Year Henry became the first Arsenal player since Ronnie Rooke in the 1948 title-winning season to break the 30 league goals in a season barrier.

Leicester sat back for the expected onslaught, Kolo Toure and Gilberto both going close, but how fitting that it was to be the skipper, a rock all year, who was to score the final, 73rd goal of the campaign. With a wall of blue shirts in front of him, Dennis Bergkamp somehow played in Patrick Vieira, who rounded Walker to score. Walker was later subbed due to injury and his replacement Danny Coyne pulled off a remarkable save to stop Freddie Ljungberg making it three.

But Arsenal held on to their advantage, and the final whistle sparked riotous celebrations from players and fans, led by Leicester-bound Martin Keown, whose late substitute appearance earned him a title medal.

Arsenal's 'Invincibles' line up for the trophy presentation (left) and manager Arsène Wenger raises the cup with pride (right).

White Hart Lane

Tottenham Hotspur 4 Naybet, Defoe, King, Kanoute

13 November 2004 ## Arsenal 5 Henry, Lauren (pen), Vieira, Ljungberg, Pires

Tottenham Hotspur
Robinson, Paramot, Naybet,
King, Edman, Mendes (Davies),
Brown (Kanoute), Carrick,
Ziegler, Keane (Gardner),
Defoe

Arsenal
Lehmann, Lauren, Toure,
Cygan, Cole, Ljungberg,
Vieira, Fabregas, Reyes (Pires),
Bergkamp (van Persie),
Henry

Attendance: **36,095**

Was it poor defending or super attacking? Who cares. This high-noon encounter will go down in history as one of the greatest derby games in north London's rich footballing history. Both sides abandoned any ideas of defensive dourness to put on a truly entertaining encounter that even the Spurs faithful will have enjoyed – to an extent.

The purists questioned the quality of some of the nine goals a sold-out White Hart Lane was treated to, but would they rather have had a 0–0 draw? Surely not.

There was little clue to what was to come when Moroccan defender Noureddine Naybet stayed forward to hook in Michael Carrick's 37th minute free-kick and give Spurs the lead for the only time in the game.

Arsenal had controlled much of the half, but had rarely threatened against a Tottenham side rebuilding again under highly rated Dutch manager Martin Jol. However, it was all square at the break as Thierry Henry collected Lauren's angled pass, dummied his marker and slotted the ball past Paul Robinson with the last kick of the half.

Cameroon defender Lauren then gave Arsenal the lead from the penalty spot in the 55th minute after Freddie Ljungberg was hauled down in the area by Noe Paramot, and before Spurs could recover Patrick Vieira appeared to wrap things up on the hour when he strolled purposefully through after stealing the ball in midfield to clip it over the exposed Robinson.

But with Arsenal still celebrating, Spurs hauled it back to 2–3 within a minute when England striker Jermain Defoe scored the best goal of the game. The little forward collected a throw-in from the left, wriggled past two challenges and curled a brilliant effort into the far corner, the ball fitting snugly between crossbar and upright in front of watching England manager Sven-Goran Eriksson. Jens Lehmann did not stand a chance of keeping it out.

By now the match was a breathless affair. With all thoughts of defending long since forgotten on both sides, more goals were inevitable. Spanish teenager Cesc Fabregas, playing in his first north London derby after an extremely impressive start to his Arsenal career, took a crucial role in the next when he won the ball, played a one-two with Thierry Henry, and put in Ljungberg with a remarkable reverse pass and the Swede poked the ball home for 4–2. But Arsenal could not find the knockout blow as Spurs, like a brave boxer against the ropes,

Thierry Henry and Lauren celebrate the Cameroon defender's penalty success.

Patrick Vieira's emphatic finish beats England goalkeeper Paul Robinson.

Popular Swede Freddie Ljungberg gets in on the act with Arsenal's fourth.

kept coming back, and it was soon 3–4 when England defender Ledley King moved forward to plant a fine header past Lehmann.

There were still 16 minutes left and the game was in the balance. But substitute Robert Pires, who had replaced José Antonio Reyes, finally scored the goal that put the game beyond Spurs in the 81st minute, when he wriggled his way to the byline with a shake of the hips and fired through Robinson from an acute angle.

Now Arsenal felt as though they could relax, but when the defence went to sleep two minutes from time Mali international Frederic Kanoute punished the mistake and slid in the home side's fourth before referee Steve Bennett finally found just enough breath left to blow the full-time whistle and end an extraordinary match.

Nine goals, nine different scorers – but most importantly for the somewhat stunned but ultimately triumphant Gunners fans, three points to Arsenal.

Substitute Robert Pires scores the pick of the Arsenal goals with a cheeky finish under Robinson from a difficult angle.

Leicester City 3 Heskey, Elliott, Walsh
Arsenal 3 Bergkamp (3)

Leicester City
Keller, Kaamark, Guppy,
Elliott, Prior, Walsh,
Izzet (Cottee), Lennon,
Salvage (Parker),
Claridge (Fenton), Heskey

Arsenal
Seaman, Dixon, Winterburn,
Vieira, Bould, Wright (Anelka),
Bergkamp, Overmars (Hughes),
Parlour (Platt), Petit,
Grimandi

Attendance: **21,089**

An individual performance of such stunning quality ensures this game stands out like a beacon. It tells you just how good Dennis Bergkamp was at Filbert Street that Arsenal fans still remember this game with such pleasure, even though they saw their side lead 2–1 in injury time – and score another – but still only manage a draw against Martin O'Neill's battling Foxes.

The Dutchman's hat-trick – and his third goal in particular – was as close to footballing perfection as any Arsenal fan has surely seen. It even softened the blow for the thousands of Arsenal fans who had travelled to the East Midlands to see Ian Wright, as had been expected, beat Cliff Bastin's Club goalscoring record. Wright, as it turned out, had to wait a few more weeks to overtake 'Boy' Bastin's milestone after drawing a blank. In fact his only notable contribution was to end the game berating referee Graham Barber, along with several of his angry team-mates, demanding to know why he had allowed more than six minutes of injury time.

But Bergkamp's brilliance meant that those few unsavoury scenes at the end would pale into insignificance. He had opened the scoring on a remarkable night in the ninth minute when he collected Marc Overmars' short corner on the edge of the box and curled a majestic effort into the far top corner, as Leicester goalkeeper Kasey Keller stood rooted to the spot.

That was a contender for goal of the month in itself, but even better was to come. His second goal wasn't bad either; racing through on to Patrick Vieira's perfectly weighted pass and then lifting the ball beautifully over Keller, who had got a touch but not enough to stop its inevitable progress.

But when Emile Heskey pulled one back seven minutes from the end, Arsenal looked wobbly. And O'Neill's resourceful side seemed to have completed the scoring with 90 minutes on the clock when Matt Elliott's deflected effort found the net.

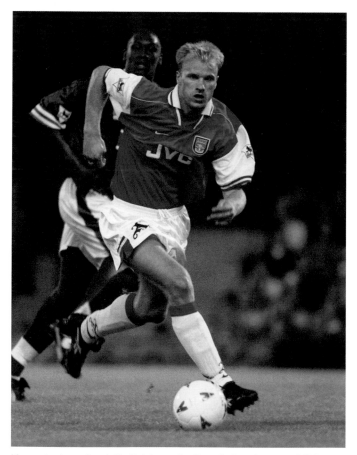
It's poetry in motion with Dutch master Dennis Bergkamp in full flow.

Dennis Bergkamp lifts the ball over the head of Leicester defender Spencer Prior in injury time to score his magnificent third of the game at Filbert Street.

Now was time for the Iceman to complete his treble, with the goal of the season. David Platt arrowed an excellent diagonal cross to the far post. Bergkamp controlled it dead in an instant, as if the ball had gone flat, and lifted it over Spencer Prior's challenge with his left foot, which gave him enough time and space to side-foot it powerfully past Keller with his right, before the American could even react. Filbert Street gasped as one, and if any goal was worthy of winning a football match, this was it.

But incredibly there was no final whistle and Foxes skipper Steve Walsh still had time to head a second equaliser past David Seaman, after a game of head tennis in the Arsenal box, for the final action of a frenetic five minutes.

Whether there should have been so much injury time is open to long, hard debate. But then the best hat-trick the Premiership has ever seen would never have been scored.

Bergkamp would, incredibly, repeat that third goal with a virtual carbon copy, again with the game almost at its conclusion, in the Netherlands' 2–1 World Cup quarter-final win over Argentina the following summer.

Below: Arsène Wenger lets his emotions get the better of him after witnessing Bergkamp's brilliance.

Roma 1 Cassano

27 November 2002 # Arsenal 3 Henry (3)

Roma
Antonioli, Zebina, Samuel,
Panucci, Cafu, Emerson,
Lima (Batistuta), Candela,
Totti, Cassano (Montella),
Delvecchio (Guigou)

Arsenal
Shaaban, Luzhny, Cygan,
Campbell, Cole, Ljungberg (Edu),
Gilberto, Vieira, Wiltord (Keown),
Pires (van Bronckhorst), Henry

Attendance: **49,860**

**Injuries in the warm-up, a rookie keeper drafted in, a goal down inside four minutes…
what was to become Arsenal's greatest Champions League performance to date initially
had all the ingredients of being an unmitigated disaster.**

Thierry Henry, as he has done so many times before, proved the difference, his deadly finishing ripping apart a bewildered Roma side to give the Londoners a perfect start to the Second Group Stage. This, we should remember, is the man who, we are constantly told by certain sections of the media, doesn't perform in the big games, a view that seems eccentric to say the least after displays like this.

The Gunners were dealt a blow before the game had even started, David Seaman pulling out with a recurrence of a long-standing groin strain. It meant a third successive start for Swedish-Egyptian Rami Shaaban, who had still to concede a goal after clean sheets against Tottenham and PSV Eindhoven. But that record was to end within four minutes of the first whistle when Italy striker Antonio Cassano capped a lively opening by Roma to give them the lead. He turned Sol Campbell inside and out before shooting inside Shaaban's near post, the ball clipping the woodwork and running along the line before spinning over.

But the Gunners responded in the perfect manner, Henry scoring his first of the night within 100 seconds. Brazilian Gilberto played in the Frenchman and he showed ice-cool composure to stroke the ball past Francesco Antonioli to make it all square again with only six minutes on the stadium clock.

Arsenal's defence had been criticised for its lack of concentration previously, but a makeshift central defensive partnership of Sol Campbell and Pascal Cygan – along with Oleg Luzhny and Ashley Cole as full-backs – continued to keep Roman hero Francesco Totti at bay, as the game ebbed and flowed in a highly competitive first half. Cygan, in particular, excelled with one goal-line clearance while Antonioli at the other end did well to hold on to another Henry effort.

As the second half wore on, the 'Giallorossi' began to ask all the questions, substitute Gianni Martinez Guigou nearly earning them a penalty

*Thierry Henry points the way after netting
his first of the night in Rome.*

Roma defenders Christian Panucci and Cafu watch Thierry Henry give Arsenal the lead.

when he appeared to be fouled by Shaaban, only for referee Michel Lubos to wave play on. But with 20 minutes remaining, it was time for Henry to make his mark again, displaying a true striker's instinct to fire Arsenal ahead. After contesting Luzhny's floated cross, he reacted to the second ball ahead of Roma's international defenders Cafu and Christian Panucci and buried it past Antonioli in a flash with his left foot.

Roma coach Fabio Capello, who had won them their first Serie A title for 18 years in 2001, introduced Argentinian striker Gabriel Batistuta into the fray in a desperate bid to salvage a point. But he made little impact as Henry searched for a third. And with Roma reeling, he capped a brilliant display with a perfect curling 20-yard free kick over the wall and into the top corner to ensure the locals made for the exits long before the final whistle.

Number three duly arrives with a textbook free-kick from the Gallic magician.

Manchester United 0
Arsenal 1   Overmars

14 March 1998

Manchester United
Schmeichel, Curtis (Thornley), Irwin, G Neville, Johnsen (May), Berg, Beckham, P Neville (Solskjaer), Cole, Sheringham, Scholes

Arsenal
Manninger, Dixon, Winterburn, Keown, Adams, Parlour (Garde), Vieira, Petit, Overmars, Wreh (Anelka), Bergkamp

Attendance: 55,174

The fate of the Premiership was now in Arsenal's hands after Marc Overmars scored the only goal of an exhilarating battle royale at Old Trafford. The Dutchman's second-half strike secured three points to bring the Gunners to within six points of the league leaders – but crucially with three games in hand.

Arsenal now knew that if they won those three matches, they would be three points clear at the top of the league and Alex Ferguson's team would be powerless to stop them taking their title. The psychological damage it had done to a United side who had had it their own way for too long could not be underestimated.

But while Overmars' goal capped a fantastic solo display – at times he appeared to single-handedly take on United's defence – mention has to go to a brilliant goalkeeping display by young Austrian Alex Manninger, in the middle of a run of eight consecutive clean sheets after replacing injured No. 1 David Seaman. Twice he denied United certain goals in the first half – from Teddy Sheringham and Andy Cole when both were through on goal – and generally he didn't put a foot wrong in the most intense game of a gruelling season.

For Overmars, his pace constantly opened up United and he could have had two goals and earned a penalty in the first half alone. First he sprinted wide of the goal, leaving United's defenders in his wake, then rounded Peter Schmeichel with embarrassing ease, only to see his delicate chip run across the face of the goal and away to safety.

With the home defenders clearly wary of his pace, Overmars was given plenty of space in the middle third of the pitch, but he soon found his way through again, cutting inside from the left only for John Curtis to crudely trip him. But the referee somehow missed what 55,000 people had clearly seen and waved play on.

Austrian goalkeeper Alex Manninger put up superb resistance at Old Trafford.

So it was only fitting that Overmars would score the only goal of the game with just 11 minutes remaining, when he scampered on to Nicolas Anelka's flick on and shot through Schmeichel's legs for a brilliant winner. His direct running had paid off against a United team that looked almost content to settle for a point from the first ball, while Manu Petit and Patrick Vieira had been nothing short of colossal in the centre of the park, with Arsenal playing like the home team for huge swathes of the game.

Finally United had to search for a goal, but they only did themselves more damage when Schmeichel went up for a late corner and, when Arsenal regained possession, sprinted back to his own goal only to pull up with a snapped hamstring.

Curtis was withdrawn for his own good minutes into the second half after being relegated to the relative safety of the left wing. But not before Overmars cut inside him and Henning Berg again, but toe-poked the ball into the side netting with Schmeichel beaten.

The Arsenal players went wild at the final whistle, their delight obvious as the title swung their way. They had also completed a rare double against the most successful English team of the decade.

Gary Neville chases back but it is too late as Marc Overmars' neat finish eludes Peter Schmeichel for the winner.

Arsenal 3   Pires (2, 1 pen), Henry

16 October 2004   # Aston Villa 1   Hendrie

Arsenal
Lehmann, Lauren, Cole,
Campbell, Toure, Pires (van Persie),
Fabregas, Vieira (Flamini),
Reyes (Pennant), Bergkamp,
Henry

Aston Villa
Postma, Delaney, Samuel,
Mellberg, Barry (Whittingham),
Hendrie, De La Cruz, McCann,
Hitzlsperger (Davis), Vassell,
Cole (Angel)

Attendance: **38,137**

The unbeaten run rolled on to 49 – a record in English football – as the final game of a remarkable sequence produced a display that showed all the qualities that had made Arsenal the 21st-century 'Invincibles'. It was all the more impressive as most of the Gunners squad has just returned from a tiring international week.

Even though Villa scored after only three minutes it could have been Arsenal celebrating the opening goal, but Sol Campbell saw his header smack off the Villa crossbar with many fans still taking their seats. But just a couple of minutes later Jens Lehmann, still to lose a Premiership game after more than a year, was picking the ball out of his net. Carlton Cole's pass bobbled to Lee Hendrie and he took a touch before scoring with a stunning shot.

Thierry Henry grabbed the ball and sprinted to the halfway line for the restart, impatiently watching the Villa players celebrate. The Frenchman was clearly in no mood to see his side relinquish their unbeaten run. His teammates were also not perturbed by their early setback and Villa's Dutch goalkeeper Stefan Postma had to be alive to halt a number of home attacks, twice saving brilliantly as Arsenal poured forward in search of the equaliser.

The hosts were playing at the height of their attacking game, mixing passion with sublime technique, and deservedly hauled themselves level in the 19th minute after a sustained period of pressure. Henry burst through,

Robert Pires is a picture of concentration as he converts his spot-kick.

Spaniard José Antonio Reyes evades Gavin McCann's challenge.

Thierry Henry turns the game on its head in first-half injury time.

evading Ulises De La Cruz's challenge and hitting the byline, only to be illegally halted by Wales defender Mark Delaney. Robert Pires converted the resultant spot-kick in his usual clinical manner.

And Henry was in the mood to torture and torment the Villa defenders even more, always probing in and around the 18-yard box in an attempt to find another opening. First he released Dennis Bergkamp, only for Postma to save, and then the keeper – performing heroics in the visitors' goal – denied Henry with a brave block. But in first-half injury time Henry turned the game around when José Antonio Reyes sent him clear and the Parisian marksman did the rest with total confidence. After starting so brightly the half ended with Villa 2–1 down and on the back foot.

Arsenal continued to boss proceedings after the break as Villa dropped further back, hoping to catch the home side on the break in the last ten minutes. But the unbeaten run was assured to last at least one more week when, with 18 minutes remaining, the Gunners made sure of the three points. Fed by Flamini, Henry turned the ball on to his unmarked international team mate Pires, who swept the ball emphatically past Postma in an instant with his right foot.

The run – starting on 7 May 2003 with a 6–1 win over Southampton – was now one shy of the half-century. It beat the previous top-flight record of 42, achieved by Nottingham Forest in December 1978 and featured: 36 wins, 13 draws, 108 goals scored and 34 against.

Villa custodian Stefan Postma lies prostrate as Pires rolls in the decisive third.

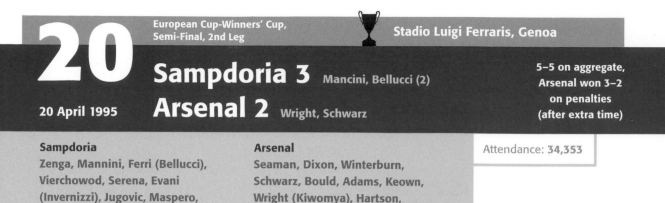

20

European Cup-Winners' Cup, Semi-Final, 2nd Leg

Stadio Luigi Ferraris, Genoa

20 April 1995

Sampdoria 3 Mancini, Bellucci (2)

Arsenal 2 Wright, Schwarz

5–5 on aggregate, Arsenal won 3–2 on penalties (after extra time)

Sampdoria
Zenga, Mannini, Ferri (Bellucci), Vierchowod, Serena, Evani (Invernizzi), Jugovic, Maspero, Lombardo, Mihajlovic, Mancini

Arsenal
Seaman, Dixon, Winterburn, Schwarz, Bould, Adams, Keown, Wright (Kiwomya), Hartson, Merson, Hillier (McGoldrick)

Attendance: **34,353**

Rarely have Arsenal fans, players and management been forced to endure such a turbulent few months as those that led up to the thrilling events in north-west Italy in late April 1995. But as in previous years, knockout football had kept Arsenal's season alive and the reigning Cup-Winners' Cup holders had got through to a semi-final meeting with Italian giants Sampdoria.

The talismanic Paul Merson had missed much of the season after publicly facing huge personal problems. Manager George Graham, in the Highbury hot-seat since May 1986, had departed, leaving assistant Stewart Houston to steer the Club through to the end of the campaign. And with the season's end approaching rapidly, the Gunners were still in danger of the unthinkable: a relegation scrap.

But Houston, to his credit, had engineered an improvement in results and crucially united a seemingly divided squad. Arsenal had overcome Cypriot, Danish and demanding French opponents in the form of Auxerre – Ian Wright netting a brilliant season-salvaging winner in France – to get through to a last-four meeting with Sampdoria.

Two Steve Bould headers and a customary Wright strike past Walter Zenga gave Arsenal a slender, vulnerable 3–2 advantage going into the second leg. But Sven-Goran Eriksson's Sampdoria, seeing several key players returning from injury, were overwhelming favourites to progress to

Ian Wright keeps his remarkable scoring run going with an instinctive finish past Walter Zenga in the Sampdoria goal.

Paris' Parc des Princes stadium for May's final. And more so when Robert Mancini sprung Arsenal's offside trap and lobbed David Seaman with ease just 13 minutes in.

Both sides were committed to scoring, in an unexpectedly open contest, but even Arsenal were surely surprised to find themselves level just after the hour mark. John Hartson nudged on a Paul Merson corner and Ian Wright – all alone six yards out – reacted with characteristic striker's instinct, to force the ball home and maintain his remarkable record of scoring in every European tie that season.

If the result stayed the same Arsenal, somehow, were through.

Wright, targeted by the tough Italian defenders, departed proceedings with ten minutes remaining, and things deteriorated when substitute Claudio Bellucci restored Sampdoria's advantage immediately. And when the same player netted again minutes later, Arsenal looked buried.

Attilio Lombardo watches in despair as David Seaman stretches magnificently to keep out his penalty and put Arsenal through.

But with just three minutes remaining, Arsenal won a free-kick 35 yards out. Swede Stefan Schwarz a bright light in a season of turmoil – drilled the ball low and hard; it deflected off the wall and squirmed past Zenga. That goal made it 3–2 to Sampdoria and 5–5 on aggregate, sending the game into extra time. The hosts, predictably, led the charge for the sixth goal of the evening, but could not break through a resilient red-and-white rearguard. Penalties it was and Sampdoria – who had made disparaging comments towards their English counterparts before the game – looked broken.

Lee Dixon gave Arsenal the lead and then David Seaman – forging a reputation for saving penalties – kept out Sinisa Mihajlovic's effort. Eddie McGoldrick missed and Seaman – again – saved brilliantly from Vladimir Jugovic, who had netted Sampdoria's two Highbury goals. John Hartson blasted his penalty in but Sampdoria pulled one back, only for Tony Adams to expertly net.

The home side kept the tie alive to make it 3–2 but if Paul Merson – outstanding all evening – was to score, Arsenal were through. Zenga beat out his effort leaving Attilio Lombardo with the task of keeping the Italian's hopes intact. The bald winger stepped forward and side-footed to Seaman's left, but the big Yorkshireman expertly flung himself across and reached high to keep the ball out and put Arsenal through.

Seaman's star was rising, and would reach new levels at the following year's Euro 96.

'Safe Hands' is the hero!

1893

2 September

Woolwich Arsenal 2 Shaw, Elliott
Newcastle United 2 Crate, Sorley

Woolwich Arsenal
Williams, Powell, Jeffrey,
Devine, Buist, Howat,
Gemmell, Henderson, Shaw,
Elliott, Booth

Newcastle United
Ramsey, Jeffery, Miller,
Crielly, Graham, McKane,
Bowman, Crate, Thompson,
Sorley, Wallace

Attendance: **10,000**

Woolwich Arsenal played the first ever professional football match in London and justified their decision to embrace professionalism. They swept into a 2–0 lead against Newcastle, another side making their league bow, before the Geordies recovered to earn a draw and make their long journey back to the north-east far more bearable.

But the result was not the most important thing to the Gunners. By far the most forward-thinking club in the south of England, their ambitions had made them the pariahs of London football. The London FA had banned them from all of their competitions after the Club's 1891 AGM carried a motion to adopt professionalism. Two seasons of friendlies, punctuated with FA Cup games, followed as Arsenal desperately yearned for league football. They had sparked several meetings with other clubs in the Greater London area who had toyed with the idea of a south of England league, but the London FA made noises again and Arsenal decided to drop their interest in it.

But when the Football League, which had no members south of Birmingham, extended the second division from 12 to 15 clubs for the start of the 1893/94 season, Arsenal put in an application. Two more places were created when Bootle resigned and Accrington refused to play in Division Two following relegation from the top-flight, so the Club's hopes were bolstered further.

Seven clubs applied for the five places available and the Gunners, as expected, were chosen to be the only southern side in professional football, elected alongside Newcastle, Rotherham United, Liverpool and Middlesbrough Ironopolis.

It was a bold move to elect Woolwich Arsenal, more than 120 miles from their nearest opponents, but it invigorated the Club, which founded a limited company to raise the money to buy their own ground. The team had been playing at the Invicta Ground in Plumstead, but due to a rise in rent they decided to repurchase their old Manor Ground just across the High Street where they had played

between 1888 and 1891 – 862 shareholders raising £1,552 for the coffers of the newly professional outfit.

With no recognised support, a ground having to be built from scratch and little money, they still managed to be ready to hit the ground running for the historic visit of Newcastle United.

After ten minutes they scored their first ever league goal, through centre-forward Walter Shaw, and doubled their lead in the 48th minute. But Newcastle were made of stern stuff and struck twice in the final quarter of an hour to make it all square.

Arsenal realised things weren't going to be easy, but relinquishing a two-goal lead was a trifling matter, a minor setback, after the pain of two years out in the cold being shunned by their neighbours. What was important was that they had stuck to their guns and, as they would do throughout the next century, they had shown innovation and courage to lead the way as the biggest and most important club in London.

Joe Powell captained Arsenal during their first season of professional football.

1913

6 September

Woolwich Arsenal 2 Jobey, Devine (pen)
Leicester Fosse 1 Benfield

Woolwich Arsenal
Lievesley, Shaw, Fidler,
Grant, Sands, McKinnon,
Greenaway, Hardinge, Jobey,
Devine, Winship

Leicester Fosse
Brebner, Clay, Currie,
McWhirter, Harrold, Burton,
Douglas, Mills, Sparow,
Benfield, Waterall

Attendance: **20,000**

Arsenal kicked off at their new Highbury home with a winning start, battling back from a goal down to give their fans – many watching them for the first time – something to cheer in a setting that resembled a building site more than a top-class football arena.

The Club's last season at the Manor Ground, Plumstead, had ended in relegation from the top flight with only three wins all year, and with crowds regularly dipping below 10,000 there was much soul-searching before the decision was made to move lock, stock and barrel and lay down new roots elsewhere.

Henry Norris, the dazzling chairman of Fulham who had masterminded a takeover of a virtually bankrupt Woolwich Arsenal in 1910, was the man to decide they must vacate the Manor. He had remained a director at the Cottagers and even tried to merge the two clubs in a bid to increase crowds. When the Football League refused permission, he attempted to move Arsenal to Craven Cottage, allowing them to play alternate weekends with Fulham. But again the plan was rejected and in the end he decided the Gunners, with just £19 in the bank, needed a new home.

Sites in Battersea and Harringay were identified and rejected before one in the borough of Islington appeared to tick all the boxes. The playing fields of St John's College of Divinity were served superbly by public transport – a major bugbear in Plumstead. It was also heavily populated – with thousands of potential new fans – and available for development. Months of protracted negotiations eventually saw Norris pay £20,000 – an astronomical figure in 1913 – for an initial 21-year lease (the Club had to promise not to play games on Good Friday or Christmas Day due to the beliefs of the college students) and Arsenal, who would retain Woolwich in their title until the following April, had a new home.

A stand was hurriedly built on the east side of the land and terracing gradually constructed up around the rest of the pitch. The playing surface had to be levelled too, the entire work costing Norris a cool £125,000.

A large crowd of 20,000, made up of old fans from south-east London and curious locals, justified the move north of the river but were soon disappointed when Leicester Fosse took an early lead through Tommy Benfield. But Geordie striker George Jobey had the great honour of becoming the first ever Arsenal player to score at Highbury when he headed his side level just before half-time. He would later be carried off injured, the sparse facilities meaning he would have to be transported away from the ground for treatment in a milk cart.

But, down to ten men, Arsenal rallied and Scottish international Archibald Devine fired home the winner in the latter stages of a keenly-contested game. The former Bradford player converted a spot-kick after a Fosse defender handled in the box to send the fans – some old, many new – home happy. Sadly Benfield, who would leave Leicester for east Midlands rivals Derby County the following season, would have his life cut short by a sniper's bullet on a French battlefield less than two months before the Armistice, in September 1918.

Jobey, Arsenal's first scorer at their new ground, would later move to Filbert Street, when Fosse changed their name to Leicester City, and would prove a popular figure in the east Midlands. But, even after a 16-year spell managing Derby County in his later years, he'd be best remembered for his historic goal.

1930

22 March

Hull City 2 Howieson, Duncan
Arsenal 2 Jack, Bastin

Hull City
Gibson, Goldsmith, Bell,
Walsh, Childs, Gowdy,
Taylor, Alexander, Mills,
Howieson, Duncan

Arsenal
Lewis, Parker, Hapgood,
Baker, Seddon, Jones, Hulme,
Jack, Lambert, James,
Bastin

Attendance: **47,549**

Generally recognised as one of the most important matches – or second-half performances to be precise – in Arsenal's history, it is still pondered by some today as to how the 1930s would have developed if they had lost this game. A fifth trophyless season may have proved too much for the great Herbert Chapman and he could have left.

Though the seeds of a great side had been sown, would they have stayed together had the manager fallen on his sword, so to speak? Would Arsenal have still gone on to become the most famous club side in world football for the decade leading up to the Second World War?

Struggling at 2–0 down with an hour to play, a disjointed Arsenal drew on resources they may have never known they had before to live to fight another day.

Arsenal's Wales international goalkeeper Dan Lewis will unfortunately always be remembered for his mistake in the 1927 FA Cup Final against Cardiff City when he allowed a weak shot to squirm under his body and over the line for the only goal of the game.

He certainly never forgot, and the usually reliable custodian was at fault again for Hull's opener with just 15 minutes gone at a partisan Elland Road, the majority of the crowd making the relatively short trip from Hull. Lewis had just saved well but allowed his confidence to slip and sent a poor clearance down the centre of the pitch straight to Cliff Howieson, roughly ten yards into the Arsenal half. Spotting Lewis out of his goal he immediately sent a well-struck lob arrowing straight back towards the Gunners' goal. Lewis, several yards off his own line, scuttled back desperately but the ball dropped right under the bar and in to send the crowd wild.

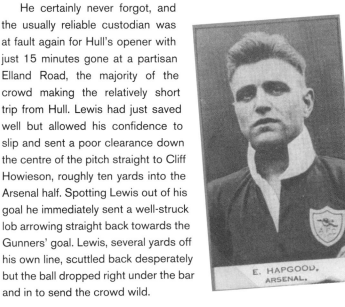

E. HAPGOOD,
ARSENAL.

The Tigers' rigid offside trap was further stunting a misfiring Arsenal side and to compound Chapman's problems he soon found his side 2–0 down a third of the way into the match. Scottish teenager Douglas 'Dally' Duncan found space on the left to send his shot across Lewis' outstretched hand and into the net, via a helpful deflection from the Arsenal full-back Eddie Hapgood.

Arsenal were in disarray, but they gradually rediscovered some defensive steel and started to ask questions, finally, of the Tigers' own defence, Alex James being denied on the stroke of half-time.

Arsenal found themselves probing further forward but, with just 20 minutes left, they had failed to break through.

That was about to change as Joe Hulme raced down the wing and his centre was met by David Jack to finally end Hull's dogged resistance.

Game on, as they say…

Hull sensed there would be no more goals at the other end and sat back waiting for the onslaught. With just eight minutes remaining youngster Cliff Bastin, who had impressed the Arsenal fans with his intelligent play and quick feet all season, finally conjured an equaliser when he picked up Alex James' pass, evaded several challenges, and fired a beauty into the top corner.

Hull's chance had gone and Jack was the scorer four days later as Arsenal won 1–0 in the Villa Park replay to earn a second Wembley appearance in four years.

1930

21 April

Leicester City 6 Lochhead (2), Adcock (2), Hine, Barry
Arsenal 6 Halliday (4), Bastin (2)

Leicester City
Wright, Black, Brown,
Duncan, Harrison, Watson,
Adcock, Hine, Chandler,
Lochhead, Barry

Arsenal
Lewis, Parker, Cope,
Baker, Haynes, John,
Hulme, Jack, Halliday,
James, Bastin

Attendance: **27,241**

With just five days to go before the FA Cup Final, Arsenal were expected to field a shadow side at Filbert Street. And if the game passed by without incident or injury all the better. Instead, a 27,000-strong crowd was to witness one of the most spectacular games of football ever played in England – and a new record for the highest ever scoring draw in top-flight football.

Several candidates in the Arsenal side were trying to grab a last-minute place for the Wembley date with Herbert Chapman's former club Huddersfield, and one in particular will have felt understandably aggrieved not to make the cut.

Reserve forward David Halliday revelled in a rare starting spot in this Easter Monday clash, hitting four goals to double his tally for the season on a prolific afternoon in the East Midlands. Alex James, who had scored in a 1–1 draw with City at Highbury three days earlier, returned to the side after missing a cup dress rehearsal with Huddersfield the next day, as did star striker David Jack.

Halliday, who would later go on to manage Leicester, struck Arsenal's first-half opener, but at the interval the Londoners were trailing 3–1. Arsenal goalkeeper Dan Lewis, back in the side after four games out, parried Leicester forward Hugh Adcock's shot, and although skipper Tom Parker cleared the ball, the linesman deemed it had already crossed the line. Arthur Lochhead's rasping drive gave them a second and Adcock hit a third to leave Arsenal reeling.

But the second half was a different story, Arsenal running into a 5–3 lead within 18 minutes of the restart with some devastating attacking. Youngster Cliff Bastin pulled one back quickly to make it 3–2 when he placed a header past Joe Wright in the home goal before Halliday took over with a five-minute treble – winger Joe Hulme having a hand in all three with Leicester failing to get to grips with his electric pace.

Leicester recovered sufficiently for Ernie Hine to make it 4–5 only for Bastin to trade passes with Jack and waltz

through to restore the two-goal lead and apparently seal an Arsenal win with 13 minutes remaining.

But Leicester, league runners-up in the previous season, were made of stern stuff and just two minutes later Len Barry set up a grandstand finish when he placed the ball wide of Lewis, and with the Filbert Street crowd roaring their team forward, Lochhead made it 6–6 less than two minutes later. It was rare for City to score six without main striker Arthur Chandler on target – he ended the season with 32 league goals to his credit – but Arsenal's defence maybe paid him a little too much attention at the expense of others.

And that was that – well, after James nearly sealed a 7–6 win only to see his shot cleared off the line, and Wright denied Halliday a fifth at full stretch with the crowd shrilling for the final whistle. But a point a piece from a 12-goal thriller was a fair result and one Arsenal would certainly have taken at half-time.

How Halliday must have wished he could play the Foxes every week – earlier in the season he netted five against their reserves. Maybe Chapman would have played him at Wembley the following Saturday if they had been the opposition!

14. C. S. BASTIN.

1930

26 April

Arsenal 2 James, Lambert
Huddersfield Town 0

Arsenal
Preedy, Parker, Hapgood,
Baker, Seddon, John,
Hulme, Jack, Lambert,
James, Bastin

Huddersfield Town
Turner, Goodall, Spence,
Naylor, Wilson, Campbell,
Jackson, Kelly, Davies,
Raw, Smith

Attendance: **92,488**

Arsenal won the first trophy in their 44-year history on an historic day at Wembley, which went some way to exorcising the pain of a Cup Final defeat to Cardiff three years before. It was an extra special occasion for Arsenal manager Herbert Chapman, who had previously managed Huddersfield for the first two of their three successive titles in the mid-1920s.

Chapman saw his Gunners side begin a period of domination that would last the entire decade and make them the most famous club in world football.

The two sides entered the field of play side-by-side in honour of the highly respected Yorkshireman, beginning a Cup Final tradition instigated by Chapman that lasts to this day. They had met seven days before at an icy Leeds Road, scrapping out an instantly forgettable 2–2 draw. But back in London, Arsenal looked hungrier from the first whistle, desperate to write themselves into the history books after a wretched league season had seen them briefly flirt with relegation before finishing in 14th place.

The opener was all down to the quick thinking of Alex James, one of the legendary Wembley Wizards of two seasons before when Scotland had crushed England 5–1 in the same stadium. 'Wee' Alex had planned the goal on the team coach, telling Cliff Bastin that if they won a free-kick in the Terriers' half he'd play it to him straight away, collect the return and have a shot at goal, all in a flash.

When the opportunity arrived 16 minutes into the game, that's exactly what he did, firing the ball into the bottom corner for the first goal of the 55th FA Cup Final. Despite the heated protestations of the Town players claiming they were not ready, referee Tom Crew pointed to the centre circle, indicating the goal was legitimate.

With Arsenal leading, one of the most famous Cup Final incidents of all time took place – hundreds of feet in the air – when the famous airship *Graf Zeppelin* droned over the stadium and apparently saluted the King, much to the crowd's bemusement, although some reportedly booed the German machine.

Alex James (left) scores for Arsenal in the first half of the game against Huddersfield at Wembley, in the 1930 Cup Final.

It did not put Arsenal off their stride though as they continued to attack with zest, although Huddersfield fought like tigers, not giving an inch in an evenly fought contest. Charlie Preedy in the Arsenal goal nervously dropped the ball three times before it was cleared, but redeemed himself with some brave saves at the Huddersfield forwards' feet.

After a first half described in *The Times* as 'at times unexpectedly brilliant', the second 45 minutes were not as fluid, but Huddersfield worked with added vigour for the equaliser that never came. And with the clock running down Arsenal sealed it, with James the architect of the deciding goal when he played a searching ball – or did he just boot it clear to relieve the pressure on his defence? – which forward Jack Lambert ran on to and shot past Huddersfield goalkeeper Turner.

Skipper Tom Parker proudly lifted Arsenal's first major trophy and Arsenal, nearly five years to the day after Chapman had arrived, were finally winners.

It will go down as possibly the most important of all Arsenal's successes. What would have happened to the Club if Chapman's fifth season had also ended without silverware? Would he have left? Maybe he'd have been shown the door. Regardless, had Huddersfield won Arsenal's entire history might have been so very different.

The famous bust of Herbert Chapman sits just inside the entrance to Arsenal's marble halls.

HERBERT CHAPMAN

Born in Kiverton Park, a small mining village in south Yorkshire, Herbert Chapman went on from humble beginnings to make Arsenal the most famous club in world football. His legacy is felt to this day, his influence as great as any other manager in history.

Whisper it, but Chapman was a former Tottenham Hotspur player of moderate ability, before starting his managerial career at Northampton Town. He moved on to the now defunct Leeds City and later took the reins of Huddersfield Town, building the foundations for their trio of league championships between 1924 and 1926.

By the time the last title had been won, Chapman was in north London, answering an advert in the *Athletic News* to manage Arsenal at a salary of £2,000 per annum.

A runners-up spot followed immediately before defeat to Cardiff in the Cup Final. Other honours came thick and fast; the cup in 1930 and the league a year later. A second title arrived in 1933, the first of three in succession, but in January 1934 he was struck down with pneumonia, which led to his premature death.

It was a huge shock. Chapman had been years ahead of his time, advocating floodlit football, artificial surfaces, numbered shirts, white footballs, television coverage, strict diets, enlightened training programmes, a single England manager rather a team of selectors; all things we take for granted in the 21st century.

He vowed to help build the finest stadium in the land and even persuaded London Underground to change the name of Gillespie Road station to Arsenal.

His bust still sits in Highbury's marble halls, a constant reminder of the greatest manager of the 20th century.

1930

11 November

Racing Club de Paris 2 Gailey, Delfour
Arsenal 7 Lambert (4), Jack, James, Parkin

Racing Club de Paris
Tassin, Capelle, Arratol,
Diague, Niko, Baron,
Gailey, Villaplane, Velmante,
Delfour, Veyssude

Arsenal
Preedy, Parker, Hapgood,
Parkin, Roberts, John,
Hulme, Jack, Lambert,
James, Bastin

Attendance: 35,000

Division One leaders Arsenal were fast forging a reputation as the best team in the land following their FA Cup win over Huddersfield – the team of the 1920s – in May. They had been in fantastic form since August, winning seven of their opening eight league games, hammering Aston Villa 5–2 at Highbury before flying to Paris.

The game had been set up to raise money for veterans of the Great War, but was to become a tradition, continuing almost every year until 1962. English touring sides had fared badly in France in recent times, but Arsenal, on the way to dominating the new decade, were to have a Harlem Globetrotters-type reputation abroad as news of their stunning success hit foreign shores. And in France, where 11 November had become a public holiday, a sizeable crowd gathered for what was a rare treat – a leading English club side visiting in the middle of the season.

Gailey shot low and hard in the opening minutes to fire the Parisians ahead, the ball going through third-choice goalkeeper Charlie Preedy in the Arsenal goal. Eddie Hapgood had hooked the ball off the line but the referee indicated that it had crossed and signalled a goal. The hosts were in the lead.

Arsenal took the game to the Paris side, Cliff Bastin unlucky not to equalise with several attempts on Tassin's goal. But Bastin had a hand in Arsenal's first when he set up David Jack to head the ball into the net for the equaliser. The English side attacked with more vigour but they were to go into the break 2–1 down when Delfour scored at the end of the half from a corner.

Arsenal decided that they would mean business after the break. Jack Lambert levelled from Alex James' free-kick seven minutes into the half and he was on hand to make it 3–2 just before the hour. Arsenal had now found their rhythm and were playing some of their best ever football under the guidance of Herbert Chapman, who interestingly agreed to run the line during the game, an unusual but sporting gesture even for the 1930s.

James, the Gunners' star man and a real object of curiosity for the French crowd, hit Arsenal's fourth with a brilliant burst through, scoring with a powerful drive, and within four minutes Lambert had a hat-trick.

Arsenal now played keepball, stringing together two dozen passes at a time as the famous Dutch 'total footballers' would do a few decades later. Parkin hit a sixth in the 82nd minute with a belter along the ground after clever work from Bastin and James, and with the large Paris crowd totally enthralled by a standard of football they had never seen before, Lambert stuck away his fourth – the visitors' seventh – with less than two minutes to play.

Arsenal were applauded off the pitch and afforded superstar status in the French capital, enjoying a magnificent reception after the game at the offices of the Parisian newspaper *Le Journal*.

But 'Les Rosbif's' exertions across the Channel did not affect their league form as they defeated reigning champions Sheffield Wednesday 2–1 away on their return.

The Jean Bernard-Levy trophy was awarded to the winner of this annual fixture.

1931

28 January

Arsenal 9 Jack (4), Lambert (3), Bastin, Hulme
Grimsby Town 1 Prior

Arsenal
Preedy, Parker, Hapgood,
Jones, Roberts, John,
Hulme, Jack, Lambert,
James, Bastin

Grimsby Town
Read, Bell, Bateman,
Priestley, Swaby, Buck,
Prior, Bestall, Coleman,
Coglin, Marshall

Attendance: **15,751**

Arsenal chalked up their biggest ever top-flight win with the annihilation of Grimsby Town on a freezing cold Wednesday afternoon in January. Absurdly, it was witnessed by one of the smallest ever league gates at Highbury with little more than 15,000 taking a half-day off work for a history-making match. Maybe the previous Saturday's result had also contributed.

Herbert Chapman's side were seeking to bring the title south of Birmingham for the first time ever, but the defence of the FA Cup they won the season before had ended with an insipid performance at Stamford Bridge. An easy away win was expected after a David Jack hat-trick had inspired Arsenal to a 5–1 win in front of 74,000 at the Bridge just six weeks before in the league. But the cup was a different matter and nearly 63,000 had roared Chelsea into a 2–0 lead inside the opening quarter of an hour before Arsenal, with a furious Chapman bellowing from the touchline, woke up. Cliff Bastin had pulled one back before the break and everyone sat back for the expected onslaught on the Blues' goal. But it failed to materialise with half the side in red and white looking worryingly out-of-sorts, talisman Alex James the only Gunner firing on all cylinders.

The speedy Joe Hulme – whose pace would have benefited even Arsène Wenger's lightning quick sides 70 years later – was particularly poor in west London. But he, like many of those underachievers angry at surrendering their trophy so easily, reacted exactly as Chapman demanded, with poor Grimsby blown away. The game was originally scheduled for 6 December but had to be abandoned – with Arsenal leading 1–0 – after 62 minutes, due to a dense cloud of fog enveloping north London, and played again, giving Arsenal a quick opportunity to get the cup disappointment out of their system.

Jack Lambert hit an early double as Arsenal got to work, James playing a part in both goals, but Grimsby's Jack Prior scored with the seasiders' first shot on target, past Charlie Preedy, making only his second appearance of the season in the Arsenal goal. Grimsby's cheek clearly annoyed Arsenal and Jack raced forward to score a third with Cliff Bastin sliding in a fourth before half-time.

The guile and cunning of James, coupled with Hulme's red-hot pace on the right, was destroying Grimsby, who could honestly claim to have had little or no chance with any of the Arsenal goals. Another characteristic burst from Hulme resulted in him drilling a fifth, while Lambert added another for his hat-trick.

James was enjoying one of his finest games in an Arsenal shirt, skilfully slipping some late Grimsby challenges as frustration crept into the visitors' midfield. His accurate balls were dropping over the Grimsby backline time after time, Hulme running on to them to send panic in their defence with a stream of dangerous crosses. And while Lambert may have thought the matchball was all his, Hulme was setting up three late goals for Jack who ended a profitable game with a personal haul of four.

The result meant that Arsenal leapfrogged Sheffield Wednesday – who had been beaten 24 hours earlier – into top spot on goal difference, and with three crucial games in hand.

The red and white machine rolled on.

DAVID JACK

1931

18 April

Arsenal 3 Lambert, Bastin, Jack
Liverpool 1 Roberts o.g.

Arsenal
Harper, Parker, Hapgood,
Jones, Roberts, John,
Hulme, Jack, Lambert,
James, Bastin

Liverpool
Scott, Jackson, Lucas,
Morrison, James, McDougall,
Barton, Hodgson, Wright,
McPherson, Gunson

Attendance: 39,143

Arsenal had been the leading professional outfit in the south since becoming London's first league club in 1893. And victory over Liverpool in the spring of 1931 earned both the Club – and London – their first ever championship trophy, with Aston Villa too far behind to catch them up with two games left to play.

Arsenal had won the FA Cup, their first major trophy in 44 years, the season before and Arsenal manager Herbert Chapman had immediately set his sights on the championship.

But at a tense Highbury, Liverpool did their utmost to upset the party and after winning the toss and making the champions-elect play into a strong wind, their bustling forwards went to work on a nervous Arsenal defence. Dave Wright had already gone close for Liverpool, shooting just wide of Ted Harper's post, before Herbie Roberts deflected Harold Barton's cross into his own net via his outstretched thigh, a gust of wind wrong-footing the big defender. Herbert Chapman looked on apprehensively from the bench as a wind-assisted Liverpool totally pinned the hosts in their own half.

But the visitors' onslaught died with the dropping wind, and Cliff Bastin showed the first sign that Arsenal were finally coming out of their shell when he picked up Alex James' clever pass and rattled the underside of the Liverpool crossbar from the edge of the box, Elisha Scott just getting his fingertips to the ball.

Arsenal suddenly found the initiative and David Jack scored the equaliser 25 minutes into the half when Liverpool failed to clear a corner and he booted the ball home, much to the relief of a crowd who had come to hail the champions but instead were becoming increasingly agitated as the game went on.

Arsenal started the second half with the wind on their backs and put the Merseysiders under intense pressure in search of that vital second. Liverpool defended stoutly but it was only a matter of time before Arsenal made the

breakthrough and their resistance was finally broken with only 25 minutes left to play. James was the instigator with a piece of crafty play, waving his forwards to push on and instead finding Jack Lambert in space nearby, who squared to Bastin and the Devonian fired past Scott in the Liverpool goal.

The crowd and team could sense that historic championship was finally coming to Highbury and a third, decisive goal came five minutes later. Harper's huge clearance bounced over the Liverpool defence and Joe Hulme sprinted clear and centred for Jack Lambert who finished with ease to put the game – and the Football League championship's destination – beyond doubt.

Arsenal's captain Tom Parker (centre) fights his way through the Highbury crowd to collect the league Championship trophy.

1932
10 December

Arsenal 4 Bastin (2), Coleman, Hulme
Chelsea 1 Russell

Arsenal
Moss, Male, Hapgood,
Hill, Roberts, John,
Hulme, Jack, Coleman,
James, Bastin

Chelsea
Woodley, Barber, Law,
Russell, O'Dowd, Ferguson,
Crawford, Rankin, Gallacher,
Miller, Prout

Attendance: **53,206**

Herbert Chapman's Arsenal side were on their way to a second league championship in three years – and during the course of this cold winter's day they would get the royal seal of approval as well as move five points clear at the top of the table. For months, supporters had seen the dominating £40,000 West Stand slowly rise from its skeletal beginnings.

Now it had grown into the plushest, most impressive structure in English football. No other ground in Europe could boast such a palatial environment for fans to view proceedings, with 4,100 seats suspended above terracing accommodating a further 20,000.

Less than 20 years before, when Arsenal had first moved to north London, bleachers had been laid down for fans in the same position. Many didn't want Arsenal in N5 back then, but just a month before this game even local underground station Gillespie Road had, through Chapman's dogged persistence, adopted the Club's name and been re-christened Arsenal station. It summed up just how far the Club had come in a short space of time, with money earned from their success ploughed back into the comfort of its fans, and residents appreciating the new sense of pride it had given the locality.

The Prince of Wales had accepted an invitation to officially open the new stand, which had been used by fans in the last home game, on a bitterly cold December day. *The Times* that day wrote: 'No finer stand is to be found on any football ground, and its opening marks the culmination of a series of improvements which make the ground probably the best equipped in the country.'

On the pitch, Arsenal had bounced back with two wins after a 5–3 defeat at Villa Park in November, and today they were to put on an exhibition of their attacking skills for the watching Prince. The speedy Joe Hulme didn't allow the freezing conditions to slow him down though, putting in a man-of-the-match performance full of invention and desire as Chelsea failed to contain him. Cliff Bastin had scored with a belter in the opening stages after David

Jack drew three defenders out of position; Alex James collected his pass and in turn found Bastin quickly to give him his chance.

The royal visitor greeted the players as they took to the field at half-time, and it clearly inspired Hulme who hit a second after Jack's clever play released him. Within a minute William Russell reduced the arrears with an expert free-kick into the top corner, but Hulme was enjoying the occasion and helped restore the two-goal cushion when he fed Tim Coleman to score.

Hulme hadn't finished yet and, with the Prince most probably looking at his watch, he set up Bastin to poke home a fourth and cement the league leaders' place at the top of the table.

Four years later a virtually identical stand was built to face it on the east side – costing

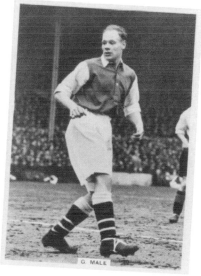

G. MALE

more than three times as much and putting Arsenal in a precarious financial position. It is a tribute to the Club that both still stand to this day.

1934
1 September

Arsenal 8 Drake (3), Bowden (3), Bastin, Crayston
Liverpool 1 Hanson

Arsenal
Moss, Male, Hapgood,
Crayston, Roberts, Copping,
Beasley, Bowden, Drake,
James, Bastin

Liverpool
Riley, Steel, Blenkinsop,
Savage, Bradshaw, McDougall,
Nieuwenhuys, Wright, Hodgson,
English, Hanson

Attendance: **54,062**

E. BOWDEN

Another bumper crowd of more than 54,000 packed into Highbury for the first home game of the season and were treated to a feast of goals. Arsenal had won the title for the past two seasons, chalking up 118 league goals in the first title-winning campaign, but only a lowly 75 in 1933/34.

A misfiring Gunners side set out to prove there was nothing wrong with an attack featuring the likes of Cliff Bastin, Ray Bowden and the irrepressible Ted Drake, possibly the finest, most consistent, centre-forward in the inter-war years. But Liverpool had for many the best goalkeeper in England, South African Arthur Riley, and the solid, dependable Ernie Blenkinsop, a no-nonsense full-back who was capped several times by England. Liverpool were no pushovers.

It was almost 21 years to the day since Woolwich Arsenal had played their first game at their new home, 2–1 victors over Leicester Fosse that September day in 1913. Before the game the Arsenal band entertained the fans with a rousing rendition of 'Twenty-One Today' – while George Allison's team set about entertaining them with goals. And lots of them.

Alex James was the conductor of his very own Arsenal orchestra, and on this day they were making very sweet music. It's a favourite pub debate to ponder which players from the past could make it in the modern game. James, it is generally agreed, would have been a superstar in any age. His speed of thought, extensive range of passing and ballerina-like balance were just too much for Liverpool. But, as in this game, he rarely scored, a constant mystery for the fans and constant annoyance to his managers.

James nearly set up an opener inside the first 60 seconds when his breathtaking dummy sent three defenders the wrong way and he found Ray Bowden who was tackled just as he shaped to pull the trigger. But 20 minutes in Bowden volleyed the first past Riley, Bastin squaring to him after James unlocked the visitors' defence for the umpteenth time.

Drake saw his hooked effort disallowed a minute later for a push, but made it 2–0 at the break with a low drive later in the half.

Any plans Liverpool had to fight back lay in tatters a minute after the change of ends, when James went on a mesmerising dribble, poked the ball through to Drake, who stopped, expecting the linesman's flag, but fortunately new signing Jack Crayston was right behind him and drilled home for a debut goal.

Drake hit his second from Pat Beasley's corner before Alfred Hanson pulled one back for Liverpool, Moss unsighted with full-back George Male obscuring his view of the shot until it was too late.

Arsenal were slicing through Liverpool at will, Bastin's efforts finally being rewarded with the fifth before he fed Drake for a simple sixth, James' vision again unlocking the Liverpool backline. The Highbury crowd were roaring with delight and Bowden completed his hat-trick before Drake's treble came up to complete a very fine afternoon's work for a team at the very peak of its powers.

Maybe if speedy winger Joe Hulme had not been injured, it could even have been double figures. But eight was enough. This win, their first of a third successive title-winning campaign, was one of three league games at Highbury in which Arsenal were to score eight.

Monday's edition of *The Times* opined: 'The result of this match will make the other clubs in the League Championship wonder what hopes they can have of finishing ahead of Arsenal.'

1935
6 March

Tottenham Hotspur 0
Arsenal 6 Kirchen (2), Drake (2), Dougall, Bastin (pen)

Tottenham Hotspur
Taylor, Channell, Watley, Phyners, Howe, Alsford, McCormack, Hall, G Hunt, D Hunt, Burgon

Arsenal
Moss, Male, L Compton, Crayston, Sidey, Copping, Kirchen, Davidson, Drake, Dougall, Bastin

Attendance: **47,714**

This still stands, unsurprisingly, as Arsenal's record win at White Hart Lane and indeed their biggest ever defeat of the old enemy. Local bragging rights may have been Arsenal's after this drubbing, but equally important was three points on the way to their third successive league title.

In previous weeks Sheffield Wednesday had ended the Gunners' hopes of becoming the first team in the 20th century to lift the coveted 'double', nearly 67,000 at Hillsborough seeing the Owls eliminate Arsenal from the FA Cup in the quarter-finals. And Ray Bowden had rescued a point in front of a mammoth 79,491 against a strong Manchester City side at Maine Road in the last league match, the game ending 1–1.

Since that game, Arsenal manager George Allison had finalised the transfer of winger Alf Kirchen, snapping him up from Norwich City for £6,000. And it was to prove an inspired piece of business by Mr Allison, who thrust him straight into the first team to meet the neighbours.

Arsenal, without Eddie Hapgood and star man Alex James, took a sixth-minute lead when they countered brilliantly after a Spurs attack had broken down, Ted Drake – on the way to 42 goals at season's end – racing past Howe to fire past Taylor in the home goal.

Midway through the first half, and with Tottenham's over-reliance on the offside trap failing miserably, Kirchen paid back part of his transfer fee when he cut in from outside right and swept the ball home. With Arsenal swarming around their Spurs counterparts – 'there always seemed to be more red and white on the pitch' claimed the following Monday's *Times* – Cliff Bastin helped produce a third. He went on a mazy run and held the ball up, expertly drawing in two Spurs' defenders, before playing in Peter Dougall for a simple third.

Kirchen, now thoroughly enjoying his first game in his new club's colours, raced down the right in the 68th minute before crossing for Drake to make it four. And a minute

later he added his second of the game with ease. All that was left was for 'Boy' Bastin to get his customary goal with only seconds remaining to humiliate the hosts, who had seen many of their faithful long since depart in disgust.

For Kirchen, it was a dream debut in a successful career that saw him net 44 times for the Gunners in 99 games, before leaving the Club in 1939. For Arsenal, it refocused their efforts after two disappointing results. They were to end the season with their third title in a row to match Huddersfield's feat in the 1920s, finishing four points ahead of closest rivals Sunderland. For Tottenham, the result was devastating. They never fully recovered and ended the season rooted to the bottom of the league and relegated to the second division.

Arsenal goalkeeper Frank Moss is called into rare action on an otherwise quiet afternoon for him at the Lane.

1935
16 March

Everton 0
Arsenal 2 Drake, Moss

Everton
Sagar, Jackson, Jones,
Britton, Gee, Thomson,
Geldard, Mercer, Cunliffe,
Stevenson, Coulter

Arsenal
Moss, Male, Hapgood,
Crayston, Roberts, Copping,
Kirchen, Davidson, Drake,
Dougall, Bastin

Attendance: **50,389**

The great England goalkeeper Frank Moss, tipped to be No. 1 for club and country well into the 1940s, was proving to be the finest custodian in Division One as his side led the table going into this tough trip to title rivals Everton. A first-half injury forced him to leave the pitch with Eddie Hapgood taking over in goal, but Moss reappeared to play out on the left wing.

The Toffees started the match strongly and looked to be the likeliest winners when Moss picked up an injury fisting away a corner kick from talented winger Jackie Coulter. In the days before substitutes, Arsenal manager George Allison was in a quandary. But after much discussion on the bench, the plucky Moss reappeared, opting to move out to the left wing with England colleague Eddie Hapgood having already taken the green jersey.

A lengthy reorganisation of the team saw several players swap positions and with an hour of the match still to play, Everton were relishing the prospect of testing both Hapgood and Moss whenever possible.

Moss drifted out to the touchline, holding his shoulder when play moved away from him, while Hapgood dealt competently with all Everton's attack could throw at him after receiving a stirring ovation from the Merseyside crowd. First he did brilliantly to turn away a Joe Mercer drive and shortly after denied the ever-dangerous Jimmy Cunliffe. George Male and Jack Crayston also gave ample protection at the back and, equally impressively, Arsenal were also causing problems at the other end.

Moss, in fact, went on several daring runs, much to the crowd's amusement, but the massed Evertonians soon became anxious when they realised the injury was not restricting him from proving an unlikely thorn in their side. A smart move involving Moss led to the opener when Ted Drake – as ever leading the charge from the front for his side – broke through and drilled home a long-range shot just before the interval. He had been unlucky in the opening minutes to see his smart lob hacked off the line, but now had got his goal.

Everton came back strongly but Arsenal had the look of a side on their way to a third successive title – and on a day of heroics, hardman Wilf Copping also defied a serious injury to remain on the pitch, having his damaged knee tightly bandaged so he could make it through the 90 minutes.

Moss by now had twice gone close to netting a second, but his deserved goal finally came with just 20 minutes left, when he sprinted on to Drake's pass and smacked a first-time shot past Everton's Ted Sagar.

At the last whistle, Moss slumped to the ground, the pain unbearable, while Copping did likewise, almost passing out as he clutched his throbbing knee. It was to be Moss' last game for the Club for nine months, a brief comeback aggravating his shoulder injury before he hung up his gloves at the age of just 26.

He went on to become one of the youngest ever professional managers when he moved to Edinburgh to take charge of Heart of Midlothian, becoming the club's first ever manager to have complete selection powers. But with the outbreak of war he moved back to England in 1940 – always remembered for his great goalkeeping talents, but rarely remembered for his dramatic goal on an incredible March day in Liverpool.

1935
19 April

Arsenal 8 Drake (4), Rogers (2), Bastin, Beasley
Middlesbrough 0

Arsenal
Wilson, Male, Hapgood,
Crayston, Roberts, Hill,
Rogers, Bastin, Drake,
James, Beasley

Middlesbrough
Hillier, Jennings, Stuart,
Brown, Griffiths, Baxter,
Williams, Bruce, Camsell,
Coleman, Warren

Attendance: **45,719**

Arsenal steamrollered relegation-haunted Middlesbrough to all but seal their fourth league championship in five years. Goal machine Ted Drake was enjoying his most profitable season in an Arsenal shirt on his way to a still standing Club record of 42 goals. But this match was as much about goal-maker Alex James than any of the goalscorers.

That Drake's record still stands to this day is even more impressive when you consider that players like Ronnie Rooke, David Herd, Joe Baker, Ian Wright and Thierry Henry have all tried and failed to emulate it. The Southampton-born striker struck four times in this match – the fourth and last time he was to do so that season. Incredibly, it was also his seventh hat-trick since September, when he had opened the Highbury season with a treble in an 8–1 win over Liverpool.

Boro's north-east neighbours Sunderland were Arsenal's closest title rivals and had been hoping the Teesiders, scrapping for their lives at the wrong end of the table, would do them a favour at Highbury.

Instead, they were hopelessly outclassed. With just ten minutes gone, many in the large crowd were debating what kind of cricket score the Gunners would have chalked up by 5 p.m. as realisation crept in that Boro were no match for an Arsenal side playing at their very best.

Inevitably Drake got the breakthrough goal with Alex James, as was so often the case that season, the provider. His cute ball escaped the Boro defence but not Drake and he ran through to score. Two minutes later devastating Drake added a second, eluding one of the best centre-halves in the interwar years in the form of Tom Griffiths, to touch home debutant Ehud Rogers' header.

James, despite yet another game without getting on the scoresheet, was running the game at whatever pace he fancied, but too often his rare footballing brain was too much for some of his own team-mates, as even the classy Drake failed to read his more ambitious flicks, passes and through-balls.

As for Rogers, just signed from Wrexham, he clearly loved playing with such a classy performer and weighed in with two goals to become an instant hit with the north London public. This also equalled Alf Kirchen's two-goal debut display in a 6–0 win at Spurs a few weeks earlier. Relishing the big stage, Rogers also set up Drake's hat-trick goal – the sixth of the game – with a smartly taken corner.

A. JAMES

Cliff Bastin was having increasing discomfort with a troublesome knee and at one stage had to depart proceedings to receive some extended treatment from trainer Tom Whittaker. But when he did return to the action he still managed to get on the scoresheet and set up another with an accurate cross headed in by Pat Beasley.

The game ended as it started with the best performer on the pitch James, nearing the latter stages of a glorious Highbury career, playing in a shrewd ball for Drake to make it eight and equal Arsenal's best win of the season. Sunderland were still fighting and kept the gap at the top to just three points with a 3–1 win over Preston North End at Roker Park. But on this form, even Sunderland must have known that the championship was only going to end up in one place.

1935

14 December

Aston Villa 1 Palethorpe
Arsenal 7 Drake (7)

Aston Villa
Morton, Blair, Cummings,
Massie, Griffiths, Wood,
Williams, Astley, Palethorpe,
Dix, Houghton

Arsenal
Wilson, Male, Hapgood,
Crayston, Roberts, Copping,
Rogers, Bowden, Drake,
Bastin, Beasley

Attendance: **58,469**

Villa Park, packed to the rafters, was to witness the greatest ever centre-forward performance in an English top-flight match, with a record that surely can surely never be beaten. The fearless Ted Drake scored seven times in an incredible afternoon of football, sealing his reputation as one of the best strikers in world football.

A former gas inspector from Southampton, he was boss George Allison's first signing following the death of Herbert Chapman in January 1934. Snapped up from his hometown club, Drake scored a debut goal in a 3–2 Highbury win over Wolverhampton Wanderers two months after Chapman's passing and he never looked back. Old Herbert would have approved of Allison's judgment and was believed to have been an admirer of Drake himself.

And Wolves' Midland rivals Aston Villa – fast building a reputation as the new Bank of England club for their buy-at-all-costs policy – were really put to the sword on their home patch as he plundered all of Arsenal's goals.

It's all the more remarkable as Drake was drafted in to the side despite having a cartilage problem in his knee and was to miss virtually the entire second half of a season that was to see Arsenal finish in a disappointing sixth place.

Ted Drake (left) on a training run around Highbury in the week before the match in Birmingham. His appetite for goals never floundered in an astonishing career.

The knee heavily strapped up, Drake brushed aside the pain to get to work on a Villa side who had, early on, enjoyed the bulk of possession. By half-time they trailed 3–0 thanks to Drake's superb finishing, Pat Beasley setting up the first a quarter of an hour into the game with a long ball and Drake running through to score at the near post.

Shortly before the half-hour mark it was two when Drake collected Cliff Bastin's pass, shrugged off two Villa defenders, and scored in the far corner. Six minutes later the Villans trailed by three, Drake reacting first to stab home after Beasley saw his effort parried.

Arsenal, missing the influential Alex James and Joe Hulme through injury, carried on where they left off within a minute of the restart when Drake chased a ball to the byline and drilled home from an acute angle. In the 50th minute he netted again and eight minutes later he had six to his name after the ball rebounded off a hapless Villa defender straight into his path. Poor Villa just couldn't cope.

Jack Palethorpe, who was to only make six appearance for the Villans before moving to Crystal Palace, tried desperately to stem the flow when he netted to make it 1–6, giving the Villa fans their only moment of joy in an otherwise miserable afternoon.

In the meantime Drake was to hit the bar with a stinging drive, but his seventh came a minute from the end, Bastin again the provider. Villa Park applauded Drake off the pitch, knowing they had seen the performance of a lifetime. Final score: Aston Villa 1 Ted Drake 7.

Ted Drake remained a popular figure for many years as the article below from a 1972/73 matchday programme illustrates.

WHAT HAPPENED TO THEM WHEN THEY LEFT ARSENAL?

TED DRAKE, 1934-1939

A Southampton schoolboy who played for Winchester City before joining Southampton in 1931 Ted Drake had already earned a reputation for goal-scoring long before he joined Arsenal. He quickly made his mark at Highbury and, in his second season here, created the club record for goal-scoring, which stands today—43 League goals in one season! In December, 1935, he equalled the Division 1 record for individual goal-scoring in a match by scoring all seven in a 7-1 victory over Aston Villa at Villa Park.

Amongst his many injuries he sustained a very bad one playing for England in February, 1936, but appeared for us in the Cup Final with his knee covered in bandages —to score the only goal of the game. In fact, Ted must have played more games as an "injured" player than a fit one! In 168 League games for us he scored 123 goals and won five International caps for England.

An unfortunate spinal injury brought an end to his playing career at Reading, during the War, and when hostilities ceased he joined Tom Whittaker's staff at Highbury. After a short time he became Manager of Reading and, subsequently, Manager of Chelsea. Ted gave up football once again and went into business but the game called him back after a few years when he joined Vic Buckingham at Barcelona. This was short-lived, however, for he found the climate of Southern Spain rather oppressive and, with a slight language problem, he set sail again for London where he is now based and working successfully in the life assurance business.

The Stop Press Football news on Ted is that he recently agreed to look after the Fulham Reserve XI.

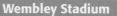

1936

25 April

Arsenal 1 Drake
Sheffield United 0

Arsenal
Wilson, Male, Hapgood,
Crayston, Roberts, Copping,
Hulme, Bowden, Drake,
James, Bastin

Sheffield United
Smith, Hooper, Wilkinson,
Jackson, Johnson, McPherson,
Barton, Barclay, Dodds,
Pickering, Williams

Attendance: **93,384**

The trusty boot of Ted Drake salvaged Arsenal's season with their second FA Cup success in six years against a fired-up Sheffield United side. Though Arsenal were seen as favourites, the second division side ran them close all the way, showing their attacking intent as early as the first minute. Arsenal's poor first-half performance saw the teams locked at 0–0 at half-time.

It had been a poor league campaign by Arsenal's now impeccable standards, with the side rarely in the championship race, which was won by Sunderland, a clear 11 points ahead of the sixth-placed Gunners. But manager George Allison clearly thought this was his side's year in the Cup after a 5–1 third round win over Bristol City in front of 24,234 at Ashton Gate.

From then on he rested some of his key players in an injury-plagued squad, only wheeling them out for the cup games. It was a policy that worked well, not that the FA were impressed, fining the Club £250 for fielding below-strength teams. But it was money well spent.

Bristol Rovers were thrashed 5–1 at Eastville in the third round, Liverpool were beaten at Anfield in the fourth, Newcastle were beaten in a replay at a sold-out Highbury in the fifth – sweet revenge for a controversial defeat in the 1932 final – and another 60,000 turned out for a 4–1 sixth-round beating of Barnsley. Grimsby Town, who were to avoid relegation from the first division by a point, were then dispatched 1–0 at Huddersfield's Leeds Road in the semi-final, Cliff Bastin getting the goal.

Drake, who scored seven in a league game at Villa Park in December, had played in the opening two ties at Bristol and Liverpool, before a knee cartilage operation sidelined him for most of the second half of the season. He returned to the team a week before Wembley, predictably netting in a 1–0 win over Villa again, to settle any fitness fears for the big day.

A media dispute saw the newsreels banned from the Empire Stadium – unthinkable now – with Arsenal made overwhelming favourites on the day. But it was United,

The Valiant Blades put up a spirited show but could not find a way past Arsenal's defence.

Left: Sheffield United goalkeeper Jack Smith looks back as the ball hits the net for the winning goal, scored by Arsenal's Ted Drake (out of picture).

Below: Arsenal captain Alex James shows off the FA Cup as he is held up by his victorious team-mates: (left to right) manager George Allison, Ray Bowden, Herbie Roberts, George Male, James, Eddie Hapgood and Joe Hulme.

who had gone 22 games unbeaten earlier in the season, that made all the running in the opening quarter of an hour before the second division side's early enthusiasm died down and Arsenal managed to control the game.

Ray Bowden should have scored when he was unmarked but rolled his shot wide of the post, much to the obvious dismay of Drake standing yards away. But Drake finally got his chance 16 minutes from the end of the match when Cliff Bastin created space and squared the ball to the unmarked Drake, who swung his left-foot quick as a flash to send the ball crashing into the roof of the net.

Job done for Arsenal? Well, not quite as the Blades sliced through Arsenal's rearguard and the last minute of the match saw their forward Jock Dodds crash a header against the bar.

It was a valiant effort by the underdogs, who had refused to freeze on the big occasion, but it was the older hands of Scottish superstar Alex James, Arsenal's skipper, which were to lift the famous old trophy.

Drake had come back in the nick of time to save Arsenal's season.

1938

7 May

Arsenal 5 Bastin (2), Carr (2), Kirchen
Bolton Wanderers 0

Arsenal
Swindin, Male, Hapgood,
L Jones, Joy, Copping,
Kirchen, Bremner, Carr,
Drury, Bastin

Bolton Wanderers
Currier, Goslin, Grosvenor,
Hanson, Howe, Hubbick,
Hurst, Taylor, Tennant,
Westwood, Woodward

Attendance: **40,500**

Arsenal's history has shown they have a habit of making life difficult for themselves and the final weeks of a captivating 1937/38 season proved just that. They looked to have blown their title hopes over the Easter period, bogey team Brentford winning 2–0 at Highbury and then Birmingham claiming a point in a dreadfully poor goalless draw the following day.

A disappointing three-match spell ended with Arsenal making the return trip across west London, promising to exact revenge on Brentford. But instead the Bees completed an unlikely league double with a comprehensive 3–0 victory at Griffin Park, the swashbuckling Ted Drake having to be carried off semi-unconscious after a pummelling from the uncompromising home defenders.

Even the most biased Arsenal fan would have been forced to concede their hopes of winning the first division championship were fading fast. But Arsenal's response to their poor run was admirable. The Gunners won 3–1 at high-flying Preston, who were themselves an outside bet for the title. But they had their minds on the forthcoming FA Cup Final against Huddersfield and Arsenal took advantage with reserve centre-forward Eddie Carr scoring twice. It was Carr again who was to prove the match winner when he struck the only goal against Liverpool a week later.

It meant that Wolves went into the last Saturday of the season travelling to Sunderland a point clear of Arsenal but still needing a win to ensure the title was coming to the West Midlands. Arsenal hosted Bolton, knowing the destiny of the title was out of their hands if Wolves were to win, but if they won and Wolves only drew, a superior goal difference would ensure the championship was heading back south once again.

As the Arsenal matchday programme opined: 'It is a nicely balanced problem, and none will know the answer until around five o'clock this afternoon'. George Allison demanded a victory, so if his side were to miss out on the title it wouldn't be because of any last day slip-ups on the part of his side.

Flying winger Cliff Bastin, a stalwart of Chapman's first ever trophy-winning team in 1930 and an unerringly consistent performer throughout the decade, weighed in with two goals, his 14th and 15th of the season, while Carr hit a brace too, making it five in the last three games, a vital contribution. Alf Kirchen scored the other, but neither the crowd nor the players had any idea if the goals would be rendered meaningless by events on Wearside.

Highbury erupted when news filtered through that ten-man Sunderland had somehow managed to beat the Molineux side by the only goal of the game, so with the other Wanderers soundly beaten at Highbury, Arsenal had managed to somehow pull off yet another title, the fifth time they had managed to top the table at season's end in the last eight seasons, and certainly the most unexpected success of the lot. It would also prove to be the last major honour of the Club's golden era.

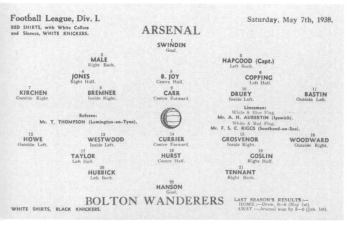

1943

1 May

Charlton Athletic 1 Green (pen)
Arsenal 7 Lewis (4), Drake (2), D Compton

Charlton Athletic
Hobbins, Cann, Shreeve,
Phipps, Oakes, Davies,
Green, Mason, Welsh,
Brown, Revell

Arsenal
Marks, Scott, L Compton,
Crayston, Joy, Male, Kirchen,
Drake, Lewis, Bastin,
D Compton

Attendance: **75,000**

For more than three years war had raged across the world, and by the time of this record-breaking win at a packed national stadium, the tide was slowly turning in the Allies' favour after decisive victories in the desert against Rommel's Afrika Korps in 1942. Arsenal, fittingly with their military foundations, had contributed much to the war effort.

All but two of the professional squad were serving on land, sea or air. Even Highbury, which was to be so badly bombed that Arsenal had to move temporarily to White Hart Lane, became an air raid warden centre manned by legendary winger Cliff Bastin. In 1941 the fascist press had amusingly claimed that Bastin – a household name in every football-conscious country – had been captured while serving in Italy. It was a bizarre claim as he had never left England, his increasing deafness precluding him from active service.

League football had been abandoned just three games into the 1939/40 season but football was to continue on a regional basis. Despite the ravages of conflict, Arsenal had continued their success of the 1930s in the various competitions and the team that took to the field for this record win at the Empire Stadium had a real pre-war feel. The likes of Ted Drake, Alf Kirchen, George Male and Cliff Bastin were all in the starting line-up while the south Londoners were without their world-famous goalkeeper Sam Bartram, otherwise engaged in his work as an army physical trainer.

But it was a star of the future, Reg Lewis, who was to be the hero in this one-sided affair, with a four-goal haul. He converted Kirchen's centre in the fifth minute to give the Gunners the lead and another five minutes had elapsed when Denis Compton's fierce drive made it 2–0.

Laurie Scott handled in the area shortly after and Green halved the deficit from the spot. But that was to be the only joy for the Addicks as rampant Arsenal had far too much firepower. Lewis hit his second from another Kirchen set-up and Drake, now in his ninth year with the Club, made it four with a splendid individual effort.

Laurie Scott (left) in RAF uniform. Like many of his contemporaries, he lost his peak years to the war.

Inside five minutes of the second half Drake headed his second and then Lewis weaved his way through for his hat-trick. Lewis was to hit a seventh with 20 minutes remaining to complete the scoring as Arsenal completed a 'double' after winning the Football League South.

For 90 minutes the horrors of war had been put to one side, Arsenal providing a top-class display for the crowd, heavily represented by servicemen on leave waiting to return to the theatre of war.

By the time hostilities ended in 1945, nine of the Gunners' 44 playing staff had been killed in action.

1948

17 January

Manchester United 1 Rowley
Arsenal 1 Lewis

Manchester United
Crompton, Carey, Aston,
Anderson, Chilton, Cockburn,
Delaney, Morris, Rowley,
Pearson, Mitten

Arsenal
Swindin, Scott, Barnes,
Macaulay, L Compton,
Mercer, Roper, Logie, Rooke,
Lewis, McPherson

Attendance: **83,260**

Arsenal and Manchester United were to play out a match of epic proportions in front of the largest ever crowd at an English league match. Leaders Arsenal were wobbling as they searched for a first championship in a decade and many outside North London believed this would be the game that would mark the beginning of the end of their title aspirations.

In the first few weeks of 1948 the Gunners had scraped unspectacular wins over Bolton Wanderers and Sheffield United but had then been rocked when unfancied Second Division Bradford City came away from Highbury with a shock 1–0 win in the FA Cup third round. With this alarming dip in form, the last side Arsenal needed to meet was Matt

League winning Team 1947–1948

Standing—W. Milne (*Trainer*), Leslie Compton, George Male, Joe Mercer, George Swindin, Walley Barnes, Reg. Lewis, Don Roper, H. Owen (*Ass't. Trainer*)
Seated—Bryn Jones, Jimmy Logie, Ronnie Rooke, Tom Whittaker (*Manager*), Alex Forbes, Ian McPherson, Archie Macaulay.
Inset—Laurie Scott   Inset—Denis Compton

A winners' medal from the 1947/48 title-winning campaign. A point at Maine Road was crucial to Arsenal's sixth championship.

Busby's freescoring Red Devils. Unbeaten in 14, last season's runners-up were imperiously moving up the league – they began this game in third spot – with some scintillating attacking football that had the neutrals purring and not giving Arsenal a hope in hell's chance of getting anything from a daunting trip to Manchester. Gunners' manager Tom Whittaker called for his squad to dig deep and avoid a potentially morale-sapping loss.

The morning papers all predicted a rough ride for the Londoners – but this was a day for big hearts and big performances in the Arsenal ranks.

Maine Road was the venue with United being forced to move in with their neighbours – for £5,000 a year rent – due to considerable wartime bomb damage to Old Trafford, but over 83,000 – still the biggest attendance for an English league game – made the trip to Moss Side, despite incessant rain, for the match of the season.

United responded to the mammoth crowd's urgings with a white-hot opening, Arsenal keeper George Swindin and the returning Walley Barnes excelling to repel their early attacks.

And once they began to emerge from the initial onslaught, Arsenal even found time to go forward and take an 18th minute lead. Ian McPherson swung over a corner and Ronnie Rooke rose, only to see his header cleared off the line. Don Roper retained possession for Arsenal and fed the loose ball through a crowd of players to Reg Lewis, who looked up and fired through a gap to score.

United were furious at going a goal behind after such a strong start and Jack Rowley immediately struck the Arsenal post and bar before he levelled with a lucky strike, the ball deflecting off an outstretched Arsenal leg to wrongfoot the inspirational Swindin. The keeper

Arsenal manager Tom Whittaker plots more success for his beloved Gunners in his office at Highbury.

– like his defence – was not phased and pulled off the save of the match on the stroke of half-time, fully stretching to push out Rowley's free-kick.

Laurie Scott was to clear from under the bar and then Jimmy Delaney struck the woodwork before Arsenal found a second wind. United's attacking – and title – aspirations flagged as the game wore on and with 16 minutes remaining Lewis could have sealed a perfect smash-and-grab but somehow shot against the post from just two yards.

Many United fans called Arsenal 'lucky' – sound familiar? – but in truth, on clear-cut chances, Arsenal should have won in one of the most intimidating atmospheres ever experienced in English football.

United had scored with a deflection while Arsenal's was a well-worked goal. And while the hosts tired dramatically late on, Arsenal's indomitable spirit saw them finish the far stronger side in demanding circumstances.

In the event, Arsenal's point was enough to set up a sixth Highbury-bound championship in 18 years.

1950
18 March

Chelsea 2 Bentley (2)
Arsenal 2 Cox, L Compton

Chelsea
Medhurst, Winter, Hughes,
Armstrong, Harris, Mitchell,
Gray, Goulden, Bentley,
Billington, Williams

Arsenal
Swindin, Scott, Barnes,
Forbes, L Compton, Mercer,
Cox, Logie, Goring, Lewis,
D Compton

Attendance: **67,752**

The legendary Compton brothers, Denis and Leslie, combined to send this rip-roaring tie to a replay in one of the most famous acts of footballing insubordination. On a sandpit of a pitch, Chelsea raced into a two-goal lead and seemed sure of reaching the first major Wembley final in their history. Arsenal pulled one back on the stroke of half-time.

But, with the clock ticking down, and Arsenal trailing 2–1, Leslie Compton trotted forward to make a nuisance of himself in the Chelsea area. Skipper Joe Mercer desperately called out to the big defender to get back to the halfway line. But he thought better of it – maybe he failed to hear Mercer's orders over the din of an excitable 68,000 crowd – and continued his run, and when brother Denis, who had come out of semi-retirement and managed to muscle his way back into the team, sent over his corner kick with pace, his brother steamed through to head in a dramatic leveller.

All this had seemed highly unlikely after a torrid first half for Arsenal.

The Gunners had not had to leave North London to progress to the last four. They had stumbled through Highbury ties with Sheffield Wednesday, Swansea, Burnley and Leeds on their way to a White Hart Lane battle with West London rivals Chelsea.

But with Arsenal on the verge of their first FA Cup Final since 1936, it was Chelsea who showed the greater desire in the first half and appeared to bury their Wembley dream with prolific striker Roy Bentley in tremendous form. The Stamford Bridge legend – one of the most natural goalscorers these islands have ever produced – hit a super opener when he sprang the Arsenal offside trap, allowed George Swindin to advance a little too far from his goal, and lobbed in a precision effort under the bar.

It was all Chelsea as they looked to kill the tie dead, their legs seemingly the sprightlier on a heavy surface. Just five minutes later he made it two with an altogether different kind of goal, leaping high to head past Swindin.

Arsenal were rocking at 2–0 down with only 25 minutes played, and it took all of Mercer's considerable experience to settle his rattled team-mates.

Compton brothers Denis (left) and Leslie during a training session at Highbury.

Chelsea goalkeeper Harry Medhurst (right) saves under pressure from Arsenal's Jimmy Logie (second right) as team-mates Billy Hughes (3) and Frank Mitchell (left) look on.

But with Arsenal's forward line virtually anonymous, it would need a moment of brilliant opportunism or a freak goal to pierce the Chelsea defence.

It is still debated in Highbury's marble halls whether it was the former or the latter. Freddie Cox hit a straight, high corner into the Chelsea box and – was it a gust of wind or precision bend? – the ball took a final sharp turn to the right and went in under the bar despite the best efforts of Chelsea keeper Harry Medhurst to keep it out.

It set up a thrilling second half with Arsenal camping in the Chelsea half for long periods, but the Blues going dangerously close to restoring their two-goal advantage with some lightning breaks, spearheaded by 37-year-old forward Len Goulden, whose shock recall to the side after half a year out of favour was leaked to the press on the eve of the game.

But it was the other 37-year-old on the pitch who was to make the following day's headlines with a late leap of brotherly faith – defying his captain's orders – to earn Arsenal a dramatic, brilliantly timed, equaliser.

The replay the following Wednesday was not so exciting, but far more satisfactory from an Arsenal point of view. Cox – back on a pitch he knew so well after moving to Arsenal from Spurs in 1949 – scored the only goal of the game to set up Arsenal's fourth FA Cup Final appearance.

Leslie Compton (far right) heads the second goal from brother Denis' corner to save Arsenal's season at White Hart Lane.

1950

29 April

Arsenal 2 Lewis (2)
Liverpool 0

Arsenal
Swindin, Scott, Barnes,
Forbes, L Compton, Mercer,
Cox, Logie, Goring, Lewis,
D Compton

Liverpool
Sidlow, Lambert, Spicer,
Taylor, Hughes, Jones,
Payne, Baron, Stubbins,
Fagan, Liddell

Attendance: **100,000**

Reg Lewis scored both goals as Arsenal won their third FA Cup, but this match was all about inspirational skipper Joe Mercer, the former Everton star who had joined the Gunners in the twilight of his career, and Denis Compton, whose troublesome knee injury forced his retirement from football at the end of the season.

Mercer, an affable Merseysider, still lived in the area – he had a grocery business in Wallasey – and even trained with the Anfield side in the week leading up to the final, as his southern team-mates enjoyed the fresh sea air of Brighton. Most neutrals wanted to see Arsenal win for the popular veteran – crowned Footballer of the Year by the Football Writers' Association the week before – but for Liverpool, this was the biggest game in their history.

Their first visit to Wembley had captured the imagination of the Liverpool public, more than 100,000 fans applying for just under 10,000 tickets made available to the club. And they were confident. They had already beaten the Gunners twice in the league and the bookies had even

made them slight favourites to take the cup north. Older Liverpool fans still claim the horrendous weather that wet April day put paid to their side's chances. But that is to do the Londoners a disservice.

Scottish wing-half Alex Forbes played the game of his life to nullify the threat of Liverpool star striker Billy Liddell as Arsenal won all the key battles. They dominated for much of the game and once Lewis had broken through to score the opener in the first half, they rarely looked like relinquishing that lead.

It was Jimmy Logie who had set up the 30-year-old forward, and he allowed Liverpool's Wales international goalkeeper Cyril Sidlow to advance before dinking the ball in the right-hand side of the goal. Lewis, in the eyes of some fans, was lucky to make the team. He was sometimes accused of being lethargic but, as this day proved, his goalscoring talents could never be doubted.

Both sides had to don alternative kits because of a clash of colours, Arsenal opting for a popular gold shirt and white shorts, Liverpool in white with black shorts. And although the white shirts pushed forward in search of an equaliser,

The Arsenal squad train at Brighton's ground prior to the FA Cup Final.

Arsenal captain Joe Mercer (centre) clings on to the FA Cup as he is carried shoulder high by his jubilant team-mates. The veteran had finally got his hands on an FA Cup winner's medal.

roared on by the travelling Kop, Arsenal always looked the side more likely to score. Denis Compton, whose tired legs were revived by a half-time brandy, played his part for the second when he and Freddie Cox combined to give Lewis his chance and he shot through Sidlow.

For 36-year-old Mercer, this achievement even surpassed league title wins with Everton in 1939 and Arsenal two years before. 'This is the greatest moment of my life – but I would like to say how wonderful the Liverpool boys have been,' he said on the pitch afterwards, not forgetting his friends at Anfield.

However, after climbing the famous old steps to pick up the trophy, King George VI inadvertently gave him a loser's medal. The error was spotted, the medal replaced, and Mercer lifted the cup to the delight of the massed Arsenal fans, many Liverpool followers staying behind to applaud, too.

More than 63,000 turned out to hail the cup holders – and in particular Mercer – for their final home game of the season, a 2–0 win over Portsmouth. For Denis Compton, it was to prove the last game of his soccer career, as he was to retire from the game within weeks.

Arsenal's Denis Compton (right) fires in a shot under pressure from Liverpool's Ray Lambert (left).

1951

19 September

Arsenal 6　Holton (3), Lewis (2), Milton
Hapoel Tel Aviv 1　Stodinsky

Arsenal
Swindin, Barnes, L Smith,
Forbes, Daniel, Bowen,
Milton, Logie, Holton,
Lishman (Lewis),
Cox (Roper)

Hapoel Tel Aviv
Hodorov, Schneor, Litvak,
Bluth, Weiss, Smuelevitch,
J Glaser, Czezik, Yalovsky,
Stodinsky, Raskin

Attendance: **44,385**

For many students of the national game, Wolverhampton Wanderers' exciting evening friendlies with sides such as Honved and Spartak Moscow in the mid-1950s – a precursor to European cup football – are seen as the arrival of floodlit football in England.

But several years earlier, it was the visit of the Hapoel club of Tel Aviv to London that was to officially kick-start this exciting new development which would change the face of football, with 44,000 curious souls – including a huge contingent from North London's Jewish community – making their way to Highbury for a night of innovation.

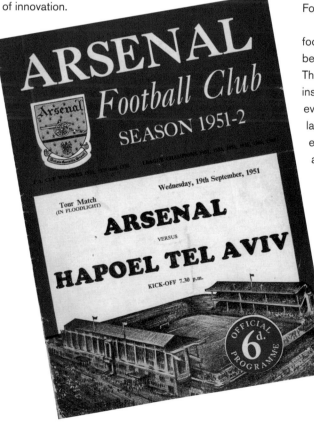

Once again, Arsenal were leading the way in revolutionising football and legendary manager Herbert Chapman would have been delighted, if a little exasperated, had he still been alive. The Yorkshireman had on more than one occasion called for a trial of floodlit football 20 years earlier, only to be knocked back by the Football Association.

There had been crude, unofficial trials of artificially lit football matches even in Victorian times and Chapman had been desperate to light up Highbury with official backing. The foundations for top quality lighting had already been installed at the stadium in the inter-war years to provide evening training sessions. But, finally, 84 1,500-watt lamps had been placed on the roofs of the imposing east and west stands, and the football world watched in anticipation, many now beginning to wake up to artificial light and its obvious benefits.

For years cup replays and hastily rearranged end-of-season fixtures had been played on Tuesday and Wednesday afternoons in front of severely depleted crowds with fans staying away due to work, a problem that had constantly hit clubs in the pocket.

This was to be the first of two trial games, with Glasgow Rangers also due to visit to Arsenal a few days later and, if they were a success, the possibilities were endless.

A few moments before kick off, manager Tom Whittaker sent out the order to switch on the lamps, with the large and curious crowd greeting the illumination show with one big 'oooooh!'

Hapoel Tel Aviv goalkeeper Yaacov Hodorov (right) saves at his near post, watched by Arsenal's Cliff Holton (second right).

The next day one enthusiastic journalist who had been at the game excitedly penned, 'I am sure this will attract many new visitors to Highbury… I'm glad there were so many officials of the Football Association and Football League to see this extraordinarily attractive spectacle. Perhaps floodlit league football is not so very far off.'

As for events on the pitch, Hapoel were the first Israeli team to ever play in England, following their visit to Highbury with trips to Manchester and Leeds. Their enthusiastic team of amateurs showed plenty of running, but were simply no match for Arsenal, who scored six goals and also hit the woodwork on another five occasions.

The Gunners put on a first-class display, Cliff Holton firing an excellent hat-trick, second-half substitute Reg Lewis a brace, and the other coming from Arthur Milton.

But the biggest cheer on a wonderful sporting night was reserved for Hapoel's deserved consolation five minutes from time, when Stodinsky fired past George Swindin in the Arsenal goal.

But this was one of those rare occasions, when the result was of little importance. The future of football was brighter than ever…

Doug Lishman in the gym. He was part of an historic Highbury evening.

1952
15 November

Liverpool 1 Payne
Arsenal 5 Holton (3), Marden (2)

Liverpool
Ashcroft, Jones, Spicer,
Heydon, Hughes, Paisley,
Payne, Baron, Smith,
Brierley, Liddell

Arsenal
Kelsey, Chenhall, Wade,
Forbes, Daniel, Mercer,
Milton, Logie, Holton,
Lishman, Marden

Attendance: **45,010**

Arsenal finally re-discovered the belief that they could earn their second post-war championship after crushing Liverpool at Anfield. Swashbuckling target man Cliff Holton enjoyed a prolific day with a hat-trick, Ben Marden hitting the other two in a colossal away win.

Cliff Holton proved the hero on Merseyside with an excellent hat-trick.

Tom Whittaker's team had already lost four times by mid-November, but they had shown some steel on the road with a clutch of fine away performances most notably at Villa Park and White Hart Lane.

More than two years on the scars of their 1950 FA Cup Final defeat to Arsenal were still raw for Liverpool and they started off at a feverish pace against Joe Mercer's side. Bob Paisley, who would later go on to manage Liverpool with unprecedented success, was at the heart of most of their attacking moves, alongside Kop hero Billy Liddell, a man still revered on Merseyside to this day.

The Reds should have taken an early lead when Liddell and winger Jimmy Payne combined to free Jack Smith whose shot smacked against Arsenal centre-half Ray Daniel's chest and away to safety. But goalkeeper Jack Kelsey was finally beaten shortly after when Payne gave him no chance with a hard right-foot shot.

Arsenal came out fighting as the contest got physical, wing-half Alex Forbes finding Jimmy Logie who showed great awareness to play in Marden with a clever angled ball and he made it 1–1. Veteran Logie, now 33, had won his one and only Scottish cap the week before against Austria. A wily, cunning inside-forward in the Alex James mould, it was recognition long overdue of his extensive talents. And he was to slowly exert his grip on the game as Liverpool faded.

But Arsenal had to wait until seven minutes into the second half to take the lead for the first time with Mercer, as ever relishing playing in his hometown, combining with Doug Lishman to release Holton, who cracked the ball into the roof of the net.

The Kop urged their team to find an equaliser, but Arsenal were now keeping them at arm's length, while themselves looking for a third to kill the game.

Holton scored it four minutes later when he adjusted his body well after slipping, to convert Marden's centre. Holton nearly claimed a hat-trick, only for Liverpool goalkeeper Charlie Ashcroft to save brilliantly, and Lishman then smashed an effort against the crossbar after Logie's outrageous back-heel gave him the chance.

Liverpool mounted a mini-comeback and Kelsey had to be at his brilliant best to somehow deny Liddell his first of the game, but Marden put the match beyond the hosts four minutes from the end when he headed in Arthur Milton's centre. And with both players desperate for the matchball Holton, who would score 88 times in an eight-year Highbury career, claimed it when he sent in a glorious drive which clipped an upright before settling in the far corner.

"TURF" CIGARETTES

D. LISHMAN
ARSENAL
50 FOOTBALLERS Nº 40

1952
25 December

Bolton Wanderers 4 Moir (2), Lofthouse (2)
Arsenal 6 Milton, Holton (2), Logie, Roper, Daniel (pen)

Bolton Wanderers
Hanson, Ball, Higgins,
Wheeler, Barrass, Neill,
Holden, Moir, Lofthouse,
Webster, Langton

Arsenal
Kelsey, Wade, Smith, Shaw,
Daniel, Mercer, Milton,
Logie, Holton, Lishman,
Roper

Attendance: **47,344**

J. LOGIE (Arsenal)

A crowd of over 47,000 – many with full bellies after their turkey dinners – gorged themselves on ten goals in a real Christmas cracker at Burnden Park. The home crowd revelled in Bolton's attacking qualities and this thriller was decided by a penalty save five minutes from time.

As strange as it may seem, one of the big talking points that season had been the effect the ever-growing number of televisions in English houses was having on attendances up and down the country. But Bolton's famous old ground was packed to the rafters as the locals clearly cared little for sitting in front of the box, rather braving the icy cold to catch a rare glimpse of glamorous Arsenal, still one of the biggest draws in football.

And it proved to be a wise decision even if the result would not be to the liking of the vast majority. Local hero Nat Lofthouse was a huge star of English football after his heroic hat-trick in a win against Austria the season before had seen him dubbed the 'Lion of Vienna'. And in September he hit the headlines when he scored six goals for the Football League against an Irish Select XI – but even his goalscoring prowess could not stop freescoring Arsenal from claiming all three points.

John Kelsey

Scottish international Willie Moir had given Wanderers the lead within the opening couple of minutes, giving the fans a taste of what was to come, but Gunner Arthur Milton restored parity within minutes as the game ebbed and flowed. Wanderers enjoyed most of the

possession, but it was the Londoners who were to go into the dressing room at the break leading when Don Roper crossed and Cliff Holton did the rest.

Arsenal seemed to have put the game beyond the Trotters' reach by the 50th minute when inside-forward Jimmy Logie made it 3–1 and Don Roper, with Bolton reeling, then hit a fourth. But the Lancastrians would not lie down and Moir, the First Division's leading scorer three years before, quickly scored his second of the game to make it 2–4.

It was Arsenal's turn next as big defender Ray Daniel scored their fifth of the game from the penalty spot. And when Holton added his second, and Arsenal's sixth, a stunning away win was all but sealed.

Only Bolton would not lie down. Lofthouse, the powerhouse striker with the never-say-die spirit, had other ideas and quickly stuck two past Arsenal's Wales international goalkeeper Jack Kelsey to make it 4–6, both goals coming in a five-minute spell of Bolton pressure. And things got very interesting with the game almost over when, with the skies darkening and no floodlights, the home team were awarded a penalty.

But Kelsey, a loveable individual whose association with the Club would continue to his retirement when he managed the Gunners shop at Highbury, chose the perfect moment to save his first ever penalty in league football when he denied winger Robert Langton. Arsenal, on their way to their first championship in five years, clung on to win a truly magnificent contest.

1953

1 May

Arsenal 3 Forbes, Lishman, Logie
Burnley 2 Mercer (o.g.), Elliott

Arsenal
Swindin, Wade, Smith,
Forbes, Daniel, Mercer,
Roper, Logie, Goring,
Lishman, Marden

Burnley
Thompson, Aird, Winton,
Adamson, Cummings, Brown,
Stephenson, McIlroy, Holden,
Shannon, Elliott

Attendance: **51, 586**

Arsenal sealed a record seventh title by the slimmest of margins on May Day 1953 – with the trophy's destiny uncertain right up to the referee's final whistle. The rain – and the goals – lashed in on a bog of a Highbury pitch in one of the tensest title finishes in league history. To make matters worse the match started badly when Joe Mercer scored an own goal in the third minute.

Preston North End had been battling it out with the Gunners for the past six weeks, both sides neck and neck as the season's conclusion neared. On the final Saturday of the campaign, with Arsenal two points clear, they had to travel to Deepdale and avoid defeat to all but seal their first Championship in five years. Nearly 40,000 packed into the famous old ground to see a Tom Finney-inspired North End dispose of their southern rivals 2–0.

The Lancastrians then wrapped up their league programme with a single goal victory at relegated Derby County, going top of the table for the first time in months and leaving Arsenal to sweat over the visit of Burnley two days later on the eve of the FA Cup Final between Bolton Wanderers and Blackpool.

Arsenal needed two points to draw level with Preston's final haul of 54 – and take the title by goal average. A draw or defeat for Arsenal, and the trophy was Preston's.

With nerves jangling the first meaningful action on a miserable, dank North London evening came very early. Only nine minutes had passed when Roy Stephenson gave fired-up Burnley the lead with a volley that flew past George Swindin, aided by a deflection from Joe Mercer, in the visitors' first attack.

The Clarets were seeking revenge for a 2–0 cup defeat earlier in the season – and to secure fourth place to end a fine season at Turf Moor. But the goal kick-started Arsenal who, by the 26th

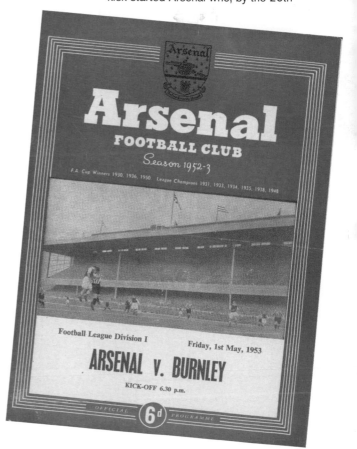

Arsenal's Jimmy Logie (second left) sneaks in at the back post to knock Arsenal's third goal past Burnley goalkeeper Des Thompson (right).

minute, had waded through the Highbury mudbath to score three of their own.

Within two minutes of the Burnley goal, defiant red-headed Alex Forbes smacked a 25-yard effort in to level matters. Forbes was playing the game of his life – showing almost freakish energy levels which Burnley struggled to contain all evening – and his team-mates responded to his wholehearted example.

In a breathless spell of attacking football, Jimmy Logie ducked out of the way of Don Roper's corner and Doug Lishman sprinted in behind him to lash home a super volley. Only 13 minutes had been played and Arsenal had already battled back from a goal down to take the lead. There was another just before the half-hour when Ben Marden flicked an overhead kick back into the area and Logie stroked home the third from close-range.

The excitement died down on the pitch with the crowd already planning their celebrations, but Burnley would slowly claw their way back and ensure a grandstand finish. With just 15 minutes remaining, England international Billy Elliott cut the deficit to set up a nervy ending for the hosts.

There were close shaves at both ends, a few missed heartbeats and gnawed fingernails, but the Gunners just held on to give an emotional Mercer his third title.

The calculators were brought out, but it was Arsenal's trophy by one-tenth of a goal, despite the fact that both they and Preston had recorded 21 wins, 12 draws and nine defeats – the Gunners' goal average of 1.51, compared to North End's 1.41, tipping the title balance south by 0.099 of a goal and the title celebrations began at Highbury for the seventh time in their history.

1958
1 February

Arsenal 4 Bloomfield (2), Herd, Tapscott
Manchester United 5 Edwards, Charlton, Taylor (2), Viollet

Arsenal
Kelsey, Charlton, Evans,
Ward, Fotheringham, Bowen,
Groves, Tapscott, Herd,
Bloomfield, Nutt

Manchester United
Gregg, Foulkes, Byrne, Colman,
Jones, Edwards, Morgans,
Charlton, Taylor, Viollet,
Scanlon

Attendance: **63,578**

It may seem odd to include a home defeat in a list of Arsenal's greatest games, but the events that took place on 1 February 1958 at Highbury, coupled with those a few days later on an icy Bavarian runway, ensure this game will live on for generations to come. By half time United's 'Busby Babes' were 3–0 up after an awe-inspiring 45 minutes.

This was to be the last game the Busby Babes were to play in England before the tragedy of the Munich disaster. That in itself puts it into the possibles list. But the fact that United and Arsenal produced a spectacular nine-goal feast of immense quality, still remembered nearly 50 years on, places it firmly in the final 100.

The visitors, striving for a third successive title, raced into a seemingly unassailable lead, and then somehow

David Herd sparks Arsenal's spirited fightback with this goal past Manchester United goalkeeper Harry Gregg to make it 1–3. Within minutes the sides were level.

Manchester United's Mark Jones (centre) and Duncan Edwards (right) playing in their last match before the Munich Disaster, in which they were tragically killed.

held off a feverish Arsenal side, hell-bent on making up for their poor first half display. A packed Highbury, with well in excess of 60,000 souls present, was to witness a true thriller. Take a deep breath…

Duncan Edwards – touted as a future England World-Cup winning skipper – shot United into an early lead. Vic Groves was denied an equaliser when Harry Gregg saved his header, and within minutes a youthful Bobby Charlton rattled in a second from Albert Scanlon's centre. Before the Gunners could recover Tommy Taylor gave United a seemingly invincible lead.

Gunners' manager Jack Crayston had his work cut out to lift his battered and beleaguered troops. United had given a masterclass and strolled on to the pitch for the second half in imperious mood.

Within three second-half minutes Arsenal had ripped United to shreds. In the 58th minute David Herd stole in at the far post to pull one back from six yards and shortly after the hour mark Arsenal, unbelievably, were level. First, Jimmy Bloomfield swept the ball home from Groves' unselfish set-up and two minutes later he stretched full-length to head past a despairing Gregg in the Manchester United goal.

The champions were all over the place. But, as is the hallmark of great sides, Matt Busby's men managed to pick themselves up and regain the initiative. Dennis Viollet restored their advantage minutes later and with Arsenal pressing forward again Taylor sneaked the ball past Jack Kelsey from the narrowest of angles to seal it.

But Arsenal would not lie down. Derek Tapscott hit Arsenal's fourth, 13 minutes from time, to set up a grandstand finish. And for the remainder of this topsy-turvy affair, Arsenal were camped in United's half, but Busby's side clung on to take both points. Arsenal, it should be said, played their part, winning the second-half 4–2, and coming within a whisker of avoiding defeat. As for United, what a fitting way for such a wonderful collection of talented young men to play their last ever game in their homeland.

Scorers that day Duncan Edwards and Tommy Taylor, captain Roger Byrne and Eddie Colman and a host of other players, staff and journalists were all dead within days, killed in an air crash while returning from a European Cup quarter-final in Belgrade, a tragic waste of young lives and brilliant talents.

What great moments were we never to see?

1958

6 September

Everton 1 Temple
Arsenal 6 Herd (4), Groves, Bloomfield

Everton
O'Neill, Sanders, Griffiths,
B Harris, Jones, Meagan,
J Harris, Temple, Hickson,
Fielding, O'Hare

Arsenal
Kelsey, Wills, Evans, Ward,
Dodgin, Docherty, Clapton,
Groves, Herd, Bloomfield,
Nutt

Attendance: **40,557**

Manager George Swindin's summer appointment had proved to be a masterstroke – and a resurgent Arsenal produced their best display for years at a shell-shocked Goodison Park. Swindin had served the Club with distinction as first choice goalkeeper from the glory years of the 1930s to the mid-1950s.

But, after two championships and an FA Cup medal, the emergence of Jack Kelsey saw his first team opportunities limited. His final game between the sticks was a devastating 7–1 defeat at Sunderland, an inglorious ending for one of the Club's longest-serving players.

But just five years later the directors had decided he was the man to revive the Club's ailing fortunes, and the early signs were promising, despite two wins and two defeats in Arsenal's first four games of the 1958/59 season. A new confidence was sweeping through Highbury, with the team adopting an all-out attacking game – and recalled David Herd was revelling in it, hitting four goals in this rout of Everton.

By the end of this Merseyside supershow even the diehard Evertonians among a 40,000 plus audience were applauding the Scottish striker off the pitch.

Arsenal could have hit double figures and saw two efforts disallowed, while popular striker Vic Groves hit the woodwork three times. The first goal came after just two minutes – and it was made in the East End. Stepney-born Danny Clapton, a hugely talented winger, set up Groves – also a Stepney boy – and he touched home to give the Gunners a lead they were to hold for the remainder of the game. But Derek Temple blew a gilt-edged opportunity to fire the Toffees level eight minutes later after he was set up by Dave Hickson, but shot wide with only Jack Kelsey to beat.

Herd then struck his first of the game 20 minutes in and Jimmy Bloomfield showed he could take as well as create goals when he rolled home Herd's pass a minute after the restart to kill off any lingering Everton hopes.

With the hosts reeling, Gordon Nutt thrust down the left to cross for Herd to guide home the Londoners' fourth. His hat-trick duly arrived when Tommy Jones – having a torrid time in defence – miskicked his clearance and Herd drove the ball into the back of the net. Jones slipped again with 20 minutes to go, allowing Herd to run on to Clapton's through ball to make it 6–0.

Temple finally got a consolation for Everton when he drilled Brian Harris' pass past Wales international Kelsey, who had made his name on the international stage during the summer's World Cup in Sweden, the last time the principality qualified for a major tournament.

David Herd justified his recall with a four-goal show at Goodison Park.

1962

3 November

Blackburn Rovers 5 Douglas (2), Pickering (2), Lawther
Arsenal 5 Skirton (2), Baker (2), Eastham

Blackburn Rovers
Jones, Bray, Newton,
Clayton, Woods, McGrath,
Ferguson, Lawther, Pickering,
Douglas, Harrison

Arsenal
McClelland, Magill, McCullough,
Snedden, Brown, Groves,
MacLeod, Strong, Baker,
Eastham, Skirton

Attendance: **15,545**

If any long-suffering Arsenal fans thought the appointment of England legend Billy Wright would bring a return to defensive excellence – a strength in past sides – they were sorely mistaken. The former national skipper was one of the finest defenders to have graced the game in a long and distinguished career with Wolverhapton Wanderers.

His appointment had raised eyebrows – but also expectations – when the board opted to hand him the responsibility of bringing the glory years back to Highbury in the summer of 1962.

He was the first post-war manager who had no previous association with the Club – except for supporting the great 1930s side as a wide eyed lad growing up in faraway Shropshire – and he had no previous management experience. Generally considered the quintessential English gentleman, Billy was married to loving wife Joy – a singer with the Beverley Sisters, the 1950s Spice Girls.

Shortly after his arrival in north London he had managed to bring some much-needed excitement to a rather sorry-looking Arsenal when he prised England striker Joe Baker from Italian side Torino, a major coup with a host of clubs vying for his signature.

Two wins in the opening two games gave Wright a good start, but his defence was doing him no favours, keeping just one clean sheet in the first 15 matches. But entertainment was almost a guarantee with a breathless 4–4 draw at Tottenham in October and, a week before visiting Ewood Park, Arsenal beat Wright's other love, Wolves, 5–4, in the most thrilling game Highbury had seen since Manchester United's last ever game on English soil, shortly before the Munich plane crash in February 1958.

And so the Arsenal goalscoring circus headed for Lancashire for a game that was to highlight all of Arsenal's strengths and weaknesses in 90 mad minutes. Three times Arsenal fought back to level the scores, at one stage trailing by three goals before restoring parity by the 49th minute of a see-saw battle.

George Eastham was magnificent for Arsenal as they staged a remarkable second-half comeback, but not before Rovers had raced into a 3–0 lead by the 27th minute, Bryan Douglas netting either side of a Fred Pickering goal, the fullback-turned-forward relishing his change of position earlier in the season.

Arsenal got into gear at last and made it 1–3 when Baker got on the scoresheet and Rovers' hearts began to flutter when the excellent Alan Skirton raced down the left flank to pull back another in the 40th minute. Nine minutes later Skirton, improving by the minute, levelled matters but Arsenal relaxed to allow Ian Lawther to give the home side the lead again. Baker made it 4–4 with 14 minutes remaining but Pickering hit his second in the 85th minute – Arsenal's defence again failing to clear the ball – to set up a thrilling victory for Blackburn.

However, Arsenal were to have the final word with 30 seconds on the clock when Eastham, the Gunners' best performer on the day, struck the tenth goal of the game to earn a hard-fought point.

GEORGE
EASTHAM
Inside Left
Arsenal & England

1963

25 September

Staevnet København 1 Jørgensen
Arsenal 7 Baker (3), Strong (3), MacLeod

Staevnet København
N Jensen, Fangel, K Hansen,
B Hansen, FW Sørensen, Nielsen,
Holten, Jørgensen, Petersen,
O Sørensen, F Jensen

Arsenal
McKechnie, Magill, McCullough,
Brown, Ure, Groves, MacLeod,
Strong, Baker, Eastham,
Armstrong

Attendance: **8,300** approx.

Arsenal's first ever European match went off with a bang as they rattled in seven goals in Copenhagen against the Danes with hat-tricks for centre-forward Joe Baker, signed the previous year from Italian giants Torino, and Geoff Strong.

It had been tough for Arsenal's players and fans alike watching the birth of European competition from the touchlines. In the mid-1950s European football had been frowned upon by many English sides, 1955 champions Chelsea even choosing not to take part in the competition, a clearly unimpressed Football Association leaning on them to give this new fangled idea a miss because of possible fixture congestion.

But the vision of the likes of Manchester United's Sir Matt Busby had seen a new attitude and Gunners' fans had to look on as rivals Spurs became the first English side to win a European trophy, a 5–1 hammering of Atletico Madrid earning them the Cup-Winners' Cup in May 1963.

However, just a few months later Arsenal finally got in on the act, kicking off their European challenge with a thumping victory in front of 8,300 fans in the Danish capital. It was big news in Denmark, where Arsenal's name was almost as famous as in England, the success of the legendary 1930s team proving a big draw. But many fans stayed away fearing another crushing victory for Arsenal, who had not lost to a Danish side in 27 friendlies since 1924. Coupled with the fact Arsenal had also just won their four previous First Division games, a big scoreline was on the cards.

And all the predictions were to be proved right.

Many of the crowd supported Arsenal and they were cheering after only ten minutes when Edinburgh-born forward Johnny MacLeod had the honour of scoring Arsenal's first ever goal in European competition. Joe Baker made it 2–0 by the 23rd minute when he went on a mazy solo run before side-footing home and Geoff Strong

got in on the goals – netting a hat-trick with five minutes of the half remaining. First England inside forward George Eastham played him in for his first goal three minutes after Baker's effort, and he added further strikes in the 35th and 40th minutes. The poor Danes, who were made up from the cream of the capital's clubs – 'staevnet' in fact is the Danish word for 'competition' – were being blown away and were now forced into a serious damage limitation exercise.

Baker hit his second ten minutes after the restart with a virtual carbon copy of his first, leaving a trail of Staevnet defenders in his wake before drilling the ball into the Danish net. Not to be outdone the England striker with the Scottish accent – he had been born in Liverpool but raised in Edinburgh by English parents – matched Strong's hat-trick with 15 minutes remaining to leave a fight for the match ball.

With nine minutes remaining, Staevnet finally got their reward for never giving up through Ole Jørgensen, but by now Arsenal were so far ahead it didn't matter.

The second leg at Highbury would surely be a formality. Not so, as the Danes showed courage to beat a below-par Gunners side 3–2 in north London, losing the tie 9–4 on aggregate but regaining some pride. Arsenal's first European adventure would come to an end in the following round with FC Liège beating them comfortably.

1970

8 April

Arsenal 3 George (2, 1pen), Sammels
Ajax 0

Arsenal
Wilson, Storey, McNab,
Kelly, McLintock, Simpson,
Marinello (Armstrong), Sammels,
Radford, George, Graham

Ajax
Bals, Vasovic, Suurbier,
Hulshoff, Krol, Reynders,
Muhren, Swart, Cruyff,
van Dijk, Keizer (Suurendonk)

Attendance: 46,271

If there were any doubts over Arsenal's desire to end 17 barren years without a trophy, this devastating show against the side that would rule Europe not long after showed Bertie Mee's new kids on the block meant business. Glentoran, Sporting Lisbon and Dinamo Bacau had all been beaten at fortress Highbury in the previous rounds. But Ajax were a step-up.

Few people expected the total football of the Dutch title holders – Rudi Krol, Johan Cruyff et al – who had only been denied the previous season's Champions' Cup by a more accomplished AC Milan side in the final, to be swatted aside so comprehensively in Arsenal's finest European hour to date.

The Highbury pitch resembled a muddy gluepot, but both sides overcame the limitations of the surface to produce a semi-final first leg of quality. Arsenal grabbed an early advantage on the quarter hour mark through teenager Charlie George. He had looked a threat from the off, with two efforts going close in the opening stages, and his third attempt of the game from the edge of the box was driven low and hard through a crowd of players and beyond Ajax keeper Gert Bals into the corner of the net.

Ajax threatened little as an aggressive Arsenal display, epitomised by teenager Eddie Kelly's stirring performance and Bob McNab flying up and down the pitch barely stopping for breath, kept them at arm's length for most of the game. But there was no denying the Dutchmen's quality, with Cruyff and Krol displaying some delightful touches in the centre of the midfield to reveal a little of the talents that would leave Europe spellbound in later years.

But while Ajax appeared to want to wait until the second leg in the Netherlands to go for the jugular, Arsenal were keen to finish the tie off in North London. John Radford played one of his finest games in the red and white as he proved a constant thorn in the side of the Ajax defence, but with the clock winding down, and the ineffectual Peter Marinello being replaced by George Armstrong, Arsenal looked as if they would only have one goal to take back across the North Sea.

But Armstrong's entrance proved a masterstroke as he first crossed for Jon Sammels to double the lead at the second attempt. And with Ajax now clearly rattled, the 46,000 crowd was sent into raptures with a third nearly on the whistle. Outside-right Sjaak Swart blatantly fouled George Graham, and Charlie George made the punishment fit the crime when he scored his second of the night from the penalty spot.

Arsenal had all but sealed their place in the final and completed the task the following Wednesday when they restricted the Dutch side to a 1–0 win. In the final they unexpectedly faced further competition from the Low Countries in the form of Anderlecht rather than AC Milan, who were beaten in the other semi-final by the Belgians.

Maybe Ajax had been punished for their sheer arrogance, but for Arsenal it was to prove a confidence-boosting performance that was to help shape the 'double'-winning side of the following season.

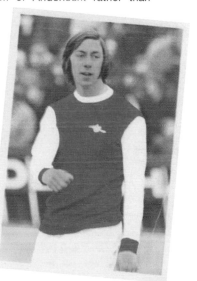

Charlie George's double strike stunned the aristocrats of Ajax.

1971

27 March

Stoke City 2 Smith, Ritchie
Arsenal 2 Storey (2, 1 pen)

Stoke City
Banks, Skeels, Pejic, Mahoney, Smith, Bloor, Bernard, Conroy, Ritchie, Greenhoff, Burrows

Arsenal
Wilson, Rice, McNab, Storey, McLintock, Simpson, Armstrong, Graham, Radford, Kennedy, George (Sammels)

Attendance: 53,436

At half-time in this gripping battle in the steel city, only the most biased Arsenal fan would have given their team any hope. Outplayed by a side that had already beaten them 5–0 that season, two down in this game, the 'double' dream lay in tatters. The only good news was that title rivals Leeds were on their way to a 3–1 defeat at Chelsea.

Fewer games – second halves, to be precise – have proved more important in Arsenal's history as Bertie Mee's battlers drew on all their reserves to snatch a draw and take this tie to a replay. In fact, it eerily echoed semi-finals in 1930 and 1950 when the Gunners had fought back from two goal deficits to live another day.

Arsenal had started the game in tentative fashion, keeping possession but making few inroads into the Stoke penalty area. They were forced to come out of their shell though when City took the lead with a freakish goal after 21 minutes of the game. Bob Wilson tipped over Jimmy Greenhoff's teasing cross, and from the resulting corner Peter Storey cleared the ball against Denis Smith and it flew straight back past Wilson, who was left with no chance.

Stoke grew in confidence, stretching a struggling Arsenal defence with the kind of bold enterprise they had shown in that devastating win back in September. And with Arsenal being swept away, the last thing they needed to do was to contribute again to their own downfall, Charlie George this time gift-wrapping them a second. His unnecessary back pass, which he played blindly, went directly to the prowling John Ritchie and he skipped over the advancing Wilson's challenge to place the ball into the empty net.

With half an hour gone the game appeared to be over – as did the 'double' bid.

They limped through the rest of the half and then trooped back to the sanctuary of the dressing

Peter Storey's deflected effort flies past Stoke's legendary goalkeeper Gordon Banks for Arsenal's first goal.

Arsenal's Peter Storey (left) wrongfoots Stoke City goalkeeper Gordon Banks (right) to score the equalising goal from the penalty spot, earning his team a replay.

room for inspiration from Bertie Mee and his assistant Don Howe. The duo clearly found the words needed to coax the real Arsenal out of their shells.

The team in yellow that took to the field for the second half fought back tigerishly and Storey in particular was to make a massive impact on Arsenal's season. First he gave his side hope when his 20-yard deflection flew past England goalkeeper Gordon Banks, who until that stage had enjoyed another impeccable game.

Desperate Arsenal piled forward, Bob McNab and Pat Rice bombarding cross after cross into the Stoke area, but the Potters looked to have held on until deep into injury time when the Gunners were awarded a penalty after Frank McLintock's goalbound header was stopped by the hand of Stoke defender John Mahoney. Storey only had to put the ball past the best goalkeeper in the world.

The pressure was incredible, but mindful that Banks had a habit of moving right at penalties, Storey coolly rolled the

spot-kick to his own right to cap a stirring comeback.

It had saved Arsenal's 'double' and they made no mistake four days later as a 62,356 Villa Park audience saw goals from George Graham and Ray Kennedy give Arsenal a 2–0 win and a place in the final.

George Graham (right) raises a glass alongside coach Don Howe after winning the replay at Villa Park.

1976

4 December

Arsenal 5 Macdonald (3), Ross, Stapleton
Newcastle United 3 Burns (2), Gowling

Arsenal
Rimmer, Rice (Matthews), Nelson, Ross, O'Leary, Howard, Ball, Brady, Macdonald, Stapleton, Armstrong

Newcastle United
Mahoney, Nattrass, Kennedy, Cassidy, McCaffery, Nulty, Barrowclough, Cannell, Burns, Gowling, Craig

Attendance: 34,053

Such is the legend of 'Supermac' that Arsenal fans have always found it difficult to accept that Malcolm Macdonald only thrilled Highbury for two full seasons. A rampaging, old-fashioned centre-forward of the old school, he cruelly had his career cut short in his prime due to an arthritic knee.

He had virtually achieved the same status as 'Wor' Jackie Milburn at Newcastle, before Arsenal manager Terry Neill was given the funds to bring the Londoner back south. It caused an outcry on Tyneside, but in north London there was real hope that his arrival, along with the emergence of talented Irish youngsters like David O'Leary, Liam Brady and Frank Stapleton, could see Arsenal once again challenging for major trophies.

Macdonald had scored in only his second game, a 3–1 win at Norwich in August, but on the whole it had been a joyless four months as Arsenal showed inconsistent form in the First Division, treading water in mid-table.

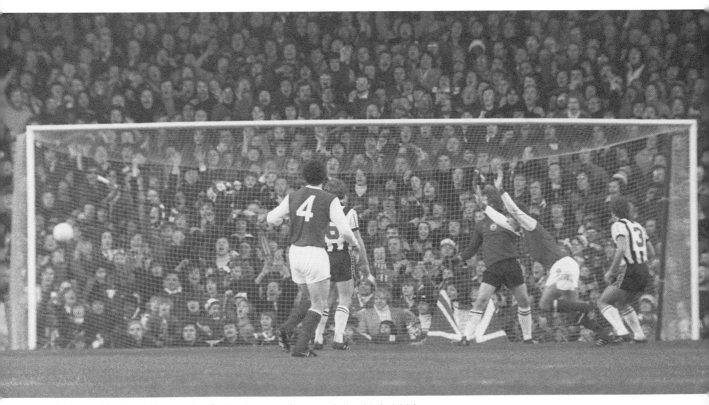

Malcolm Macdonald (arms raised) wheels away after completing his hat-trick.

He always had one eye on this fixture against his old team, and proved once again how he relished the big occasion with a hat-trick that sparked a prolific goalscoring streak that would see him end the season with 29 goals – just one short of his August target of 30.

On a freezing cold Highbury afternoon, with the undersoil heating working overtime to ensure the game was played, Supermac was back to his St James' Park best after the visitors took an early lead.

Mick Burns darted past Pat Rice to fire Newcastle ahead in the 14th minute, but first Trevor Ross levelled for Arsenal and then Macdonald got the first of his three 27 minutes into the game with a powerful header to give the Gunners a lead they never relinquished.

Alan Ball – who some were demanding Don Revie recall to the England squad – and Liam Brady began to stroke some exquisite passes around the frosty Highbury turf.

Frank Stapleton, getting better with every game, was also beginning to combine almost telepathically with his new star striking partner and it was he who slotted home a third in first-half injury time after retrieving the ball from a near hopeless position.

Fans on the North Bank now had 15 minutes to warm up with a half-time Bovril before Macdonald's second-half show. Jimmy Rimmer in the Arsenal goal, a talented and brave custodian unlucky to join Arsenal in barren times, twice denied Burns brilliantly before Macdonald made it 4–1 with his easiest goal of the match.

Desperate for the hat-trick he then hit post and bar but, before he knew it, it was 4–3 as Newcastle hit back, Tommy Cassidy setting up goals for Alan Gowling and Burns with his second.

The game hung in the balance as the Geordies searched for an equaliser that wouldn't come and Macdonald, as only he could, had the final say when he outjumped his marker at the far post to place a perfect downward header into the net.

It proved the catalyst for a change in fortune for the Fulham-born striker; a fortnight later he was to hit two in a 3–1 home win over Manchester United and, even better for Gunners' fans, scored a brace at White Hart Lane in a 2–2 draw.

The following month he and Trevor Francis both hit hat-tricks as Arsenal drew 3–3 with Birmingham in a memorable encounter at St Andrew's.

Supermac was – finally – off and running.

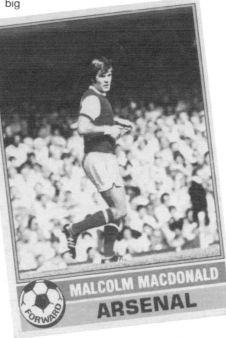

MALCOLM MACDONALD
ARSENAL

1980

23 April

Juventus 0
Arsenal 1 Vaessen

Juventus
Zoff, Cucceruddu, Cabrini,
Furino, Gentile, Scirea,
Causio, Prandelli, Bettega,
Tavola (Marocchina), Fanna

Arsenal
Jennings, Rice, Devine,
Talbot (Hollins), O'Leary, Young,
Brady, Sunderland, Stapleton,
Price (Vaessen), Rix

Attendance: **66,386**

This intoxicating night in north-west Italy will go down as one of the greatest – and unlikeliest – results in Arsenal's history. Nearly a year to the day since Alan Sunderland's late, late winner won the FA Cup, a 19-year-old from Bermondsey was to make himself an instant hero. For rookie striker Paul Vaessen it was to be the highlight of a career – tragically cut short far too soon.

The promising teenager, who came on as a substitute for David Price with a quarter of an hour remaining, scored the goal that put Arsenal into their second European final. The goal came in dramatic fashion, in the final throes of an absorbing contest, like Michael Thomas' title-winner at Anfield almost ten years later. It was the Old Lady's (as Juventus are known) first home defeat in European competition for ten years, and gave Arsenal the distinguished honour of becoming the first British side to ever win at the famous Turin club.

This all seemed a virtual impossibility just two weeks before after a first leg at Highbury which came during a demanding run of four games in seven days. Despite being down to ten men following Marco Tardelli's dismissal, Juve looked to be coasting to a 1–0 victory in a bad-tempered affair that could have seen two more Italians shown the red card, notably Roberto Bettega for a disgraceful foul on David O'Leary. But Bettega may have wished that he had been sent off with just four minutes remaining when, under pressure from Frank Stapleton, he headed into his own net to give Arsenal a lifeline.

The Turin public turned out in force for the second leg, more than 66,000 fans expecting an easy passage to the final in Brussels. All the hosts needed to do was keep a clean sheet, not normally a problem for the defensive-minded Italians who boasted the great Dino Zoff in goal.

After a nervy opening by the Gunners, with smoke from a multitude of firecrackers filling the evening air and young Irish defender John Devine – a replacement for his more experienced compatriot Sammy Nelson who had failed a late fitness test – needlessly conceding possession three

times in as many minutes, the realisation kicked in that Juventus, also, were more nervous than they let on. And with Juve showing little attacking intent, Arsenal sensed their chance. Liam Brady began to exert his grip on the game – clearly noted by the Italians who snapped him up a few months later – as he had been given the freedom of Piemonte to probe the Italian defence, without the suspended Tardelli snapping at his heels in the middle of the park.

The game wore on with no score and Arsenal manager Terry Neill decided to throw on Vaessen, who had ingratiated himself to the fans a fortnight before with the opening goal in a 2–1 win at White Hart Lane. John Hollins was also brought into the fray and Neill boldly ordered giant defender Willie Young to 'make a nuisance of himself' in the hosts' penalty area.

Young Vaessen put himself about but it looked to be a valiant, and ultimately failed, effort by the manager. But with one last push Graham Rix, in almost exactly the same position he was in a year before at Wembley for Alan Sunderland's FA Cup winner, raced to the touchline and swung over an excellent left-foot cross. Sunderland jumped with Zoff, the ball eluded them both, and Vaessen was all alone at the back post to nod it into the net. Juventus were devastated. 'That was one of the greatest results in Arsenal's history,' Brady said. They had booked their place at Heysel for the final against Valencia.

But for Vaessen, the man of the moment, a knee injury would end his career within a couple of years. It was a disappointment from which he never recovered and he died in tragic circumstances before he was 40.

1980
1 May

Liverpool 0
Arsenal 1 Talbot

Liverpool
Clemence, Neal, Cohen,
Thompson, Kennedy, Hansen,
Dalglish, Lee, Johnson (Fairclough),
McDermott, Souness

Arsenal
Jennings, Rice, Devine, Talbot,
O'Leary, Young, Brady,
Sunderland, Stapleton,
Price, Rix

Attendance: 35,335

This was the most protracted semi-final in FA Cup history. It all began on 12 April when the two sides saw out a 0–0 draw at Hillsborough. From Sheffield they moved to Birmingham, Alan Sunderland scoring in a 1–1 draw at Villa Park. He scored again after 13 seconds in the third match, also at Villa Park, but the Reds levelled to take the tie to Coventry.

Whoever was to finally win this tie had the relatively easy task of beating a waiting West Ham side, then in the old second division, in the final. In the end Brian Talbot, the scorer of many vital goals in his six-and-a-half highly productive years at Highbury, was the man for the job at Coventry – hosting its first ever semi-final – and in another battle royale, which gripped the country, he netted the fifth and final goal of an engrossing series to finally prise these two great sides apart.

With just 12 minutes on the clock Frank Stapleton lost the ball to former Gunner Ray Kennedy who was in an unfamiliar left-back position. The forward-turned-midfielder, facing his own deadball line, attempted to clear but instead swung at thin air as he lost his balance and fell into the row of photographers behind the goal. Stapleton instantly took advantage of his good fortune to cross into the danger area and Talbot flew in – Sunderland ducking as he heard the call from his charging team-mate – to head the ball emphatically past Liverpool goalkeeper Ray Clemence.

Liverpool, as expected, reacted in spirited fashion and it took a breathtaking double save from veteran Pat Jennings late on to book Arsenal's passage to Wembley. England left-back Phil Neal

galloped forward on to a clearance and held off the attentions of Arsenal defender David O'Leary. Neal teed up the supporting Kenny Dalglish, who turned one way before driving low and hard at Jennings, the big Irishman's right leg taking the sting out of the shot as it went under him. Graeme Souness raced in from the right to slot home the loose ball, but Jennings recovered magnificently to beat the ball out and preserve a valuable clean sheet.

Liverpool were beaten, and Arsenal had ten days to prepare for the final – with two league games still to play in between and a Cup-Winners' Cup Final to look forward to afterwards.

Brian Talbot prepares to celebrate after his 12th-minute strike gives Arsenal the lead at Highfield Road.

1983

29 October

Aston Villa 2 <small>Morley, Evans (pen)</small>
Arsenal 6 <small>Woodcock (5), McDermott</small>

Aston Villa

Spink, Jones, Williams,
Evans, Ormsby, Mortimer,
Bremner, Walters, Withe,
McMahon, Morley

Arsenal

Jennings, Robson (McDermott),
Sansom, Whyte, O'Leary,
Hill, Sunderland, Davis,
Woodcock, Nicholas, Rix

Attendance: 23,678

England striker Tony Woodcock rekindled memories of Arsenal's golden era in the 1930s with a one-man demolition job of Aston Villa on their own pitch. Woody hit five goals by the 48th minute – and seriously threatened Ted Drake's spectacular seven-goal haul on the same ground 48 years earlier. And Villa were no slouches.

It had only been 17 months since they been champions of the continent with a 1–0 victory over German giants Bayern Munich in the European Cup Final. And they had not been beaten at Villa Park for ten months before Arsenal – and Woodcock in particular – left that record in tatters.

He struck two past his former club Nottingham Forest the game before and took only four minutes to crack home a beauty for his opener in Birmingham. By the 14th minute Arsenal led 2–0 when Woodcock smartly headed Colin Hill's pass past Villa goalkeeper Nigel Spink. 'Wherever I went the ball seemed to follow me,' he said afterwards, still dazed by his own achievement. Ten minutes before the break he could claim the match ball when he fired past Spink from Charlie Nicholas' pass.

England winger Tony Morley pulled one back for the Villans two minutes later, but Woodcock hit his, and Arsenal's, fourth within 60 seconds when he reacted first after substitute Brian McDermott's header bounced back off the bar. Like Drake almost half a century before him, the claret and blue backline could not cope with Woodcock's movement and guile.

And their heads dropped furthermore just three minutes after the restart when he made it 5–1 – leaving a certain Mr Drake, of Wimbledon SW19, nervously watching events from afar. The Arsenal legend – now a director at Fulham – was at his south London home recovering from flu and realised his record was under serious threat.

But Whirlwind Woody's goalscoring show was over, McDermott adding the other Arsenal goal two minutes from time after Allan Evans had hit a second for Villa from the spot when Chris Whyte handled Peter Withe's drive.

The good natured Drake admitted he was preparing to drop Woody a line if he had matched or beaten his achievement. He admitted: 'I thought, "Good luck to him, he is going break my record after all these years." I was getting ready to send him my congratulations.'

Tony Woodcock put Ted Drake's 48-year-old record under serious threat at Villa Park.

1983

26 December

Tottenham Hotspur 2 Roberts, Archibald
Arsenal 4 Nicholas (2), Meade (2)

Tottenham Hotspur
Clemence, Hughton (Falco),
Cooke, Roberts, Stevens,
Perryman, Ardiles, Archibald,
Brazil, Hoddle, Dick

Arsenal
Jennings, Hill, Sansom,
Robson (Cork), O'Leary, Caton,
Meade, Davis, Woodcock,
Nicholas, Allinson

Attendance: 38,756

St Nicholas' Day came 24 hours late to north London in 1983, as North Bank darling Charlie glittered on a freezing cold afternoon at White Hart Lane to give Arsenal fans the best possible Christmas present. The fans had waited four agonising months for a goal from the record signing from Celtic, who had turned down Liverpool, Manchester United and Inter to come to Highbury.

But the move was turning sour with Terry Neill's side performing in fits and starts and the Scottish starlet struggling to find his form.

Neill was soon forced to step down after a defeat to Walsall in the Milk Cup – which followed a win at Spurs earlier in the competition – and Don Howe, not for the first time, found himself in the position of steadying the ship of his beloved club. And a win at the Lane on Boxing Day would be just the tonic.

What was not expected was Nicholas' virtuoso performance, scoring two and setting up the other two for another youngster, Raphael Meade. The big Islington-born striker had impressed in his previous outing, getting a hat-trick against Watford, and his determination and power in the box was proving the perfect foil for the more honed skills of Nicholas.

It was Howe who had spotted Meade's potential and promoted him to a starting role. 'Meade is a strong runner and determined in the box, the sort of qualities front players needed these days,' explained Howe, after seeing his young charge help destroy Tottenham alongside the Scottish star, who had cost the Club a large sum to seal his move south of the border. 'Nicholas and Woodcock were too similar in style. Both of them were dropping back and wanting the ball at their feet. We were becoming too predictable,' concluded Howe.

Gary Stevens hit the Arsenal bar within the first minute but the visitors shrugged off that early scare to take the lead as their new strike force combined with devastating results. Meade galloped down the right flank and found Nicholas 25 yards out. He hit a fierce right-foot drive

that was deflected back into his path and, like a double-barrelled shotgun, shot instantly with his left to score.

Graham Roberts bundled home for Spurs from Chris Hughton's free-kick but Arsenal merely dismissed it and Nicholas scored again in the 48th minute when he ran on to Ian Allinson's chip and lobbed a helpless Ray Clemence.

Spurs' strikeforce – which also had a misfiring Scottish forward in the shape of Alan Brazil – had got in on the goalscoring act with Steve Archibald cleanly blasting in Glenn Hoddle's free-kick, but two late goals from Meade were to put the game beyond them. Paul Davis played a clever one-two with Nicholas and crossed for the rookie striker to head in at the near post for his fourth in two games. And he made it four for Arsenal when Tony Woodcock sprang Nicholas, on a hat-trick, who saw Clemence beat out his effort only for Meade to follow up.

Nicholas' compatriot Brazil, with only one goal to his name since moving from Ipswich Town to Spurs, should have made a game of it but failed to convert twice with 'only' the mighty frame of Pat Jennings to beat.

But Arsenal were still more than worth the three points and would go on to complete a league double over Tottenham the following April with a thrilling 3–2 win at Highbury, Nicholas again on the scoresheet. Caretaker boss Howe admitted afterwards that 'had this happened a fortnight ago Terry would still be in charge'.

The doom and gloom that had enveloped Highbury for so long during that wretched first half of the season had upped sticks and moved further up the Seven Sisters Road. And now, at last, Bonnie Prince Charlie had really arrived in England.

1984

8 September

Arsenal 3 Talbot (2), Woodcock
Liverpool 1 Kennedy

Arsenal
Jennings, Anderson, Sansom,
Talbot, O'Leary, Caton,
Robson, Davis, Mariner,
Woodcock, Nicholas

Liverpool
Grobbelaar, Neal, Kennedy,
Lawrenson, Whelan, Hansen,
Dalglish, Lee, Walsh,
Molby, Wark

Attendance: **50,006**

The early 1980s was not a golden era for Arsenal Football Club. The odd semi-final appearance here, a false dawn there, crowds regularly dipping under the 20,000 mark and, of course, there was also the matter of Spurs a few short miles away, with their exotic foreign stars and cup glories, stealing all the north London glamour after the indignity of relegation back in the late 1970s.

So a fun-packed afternoon at Highbury – humiliating reigning European champions and division one title holders Liverpool – was just what was needed.

A brilliant spell of eight league wins in nine games gave Arsenal a new-found confidence sadly lacking since Liam Brady's twinkling toes – and peerless left foot – had disappeared to Turin four years before. And this mauling of Liverpool – in the middle of that run – was to propel the Gunners to the top of the league for the first time since February 1973, when, coincidentally, it was an Alan Ball-inspired victory over the Merseysiders at their Anfield lair which earned them their place at the summit. More than a decade later at Highbury, with 50,000 expectant fans shoehorned into Highbury, it was another England midfielder, Brian Talbot, in his final season with the Club, who proved the catalyst for the win, weighing in with two goals – including one majestic free-kick – which earned him the man-of-the-match champagne.

Liverpool were to lose their patience and their cool as Arsenal squeezed all three points out of them, although it came after the visitors controlled the early stages. Kenny Dalglish, in his absolute prime, forced a wonder save from Gunners' keeper Pat Jennings for the first real goalmouth action. The two sides sparred for most of the opening half before Arsenal took control – and the lead – courtesy of the popular 31-year-old number four. Just outside the area, with the bulk of the Liverpool team between ball and goal, Talbot chipped a delicious free-kick just inside the corner of crossbar and upright, Bruce Grobbelaar beaten by both its accuracy and pace. It was a virtual carbon copy of his strike in a 2–0 win over previous league leaders Newcastle

United in the previous home game. Talbot was certainly the man of the moment; and would finish the season with an impressive 12 goals in all competitions.

Liverpool were furious as it had come at the end of four minutes of first-half stoppage time given by referee Tommy Bune. Where those four minutes and 19 seconds had come from even the staunchest Arsenal fan would have been hard-pushed to have offered a reasonable explanation, but their side had stolen a precious advantage they would not relinquish. The break failed to placate the visitors and their cause was not helped when Tony Woodcock scored a second three minutes after the restart. Viv Anderson – Mr Consistency at right-back in his three years with the Club – made ground on the right and drilled in a low cross, Paul Davis teed up the incoming Woodcock who thumped the ball into the roof of the net. The Gunners' confidence was flowing and Talbot put the fans into dreamland with a third in the 73rd minute, producing a spectacular diving header from another Anderson centre.

England international Anderson was having an inspired start to his Highbury career and Don Howe, an integral part of national team manager Bobby Robson's coaching set-up, admitted afterwards that his would be the first name on the team sheet if he had it his way, eyeing one or two journalists who in previous weeks had suggested it was he and not Robson who was actually picking the English team. Even a super strike from Alan Kennedy – playing a lovely one-two with Dalglish before beating Jennings – failed to dampen the spirits, much of the vast crowd staying behind after the final whistle for confirmation over the public address system. Arsenal were top of the league.

1985
21 December

Manchester United 0
Arsenal 1   Nicholas

Manchester United
Bailey, Gidman, Gibson,
Whiteside, McGrath, Garton,
Blackmore, Strachan, Hughes,
Stapleton, Olsen

Arsenal
Lukic, Caesar, Sansom,
Davis, O'Leary, Keown,
Allinson, Robson, Nicholas,
Quinn, Rix

Attendance: **44,386**

Arsenal's Young Guns were finally emerging, laying the foundations for George Graham's successes in the late 1980s, and for one in particular it was a debut that provided the best moments of his Gunners' career. Gus Caesar was drafted in for his debut at right-back to replace injured Viv Anderson in what was a daunting prospect for the 19-year-old.

Manchester United had been the form side of the opening half of the 1985/86 season and, with Christmas approaching, led the table by five points from second-placed Liverpool. The freescoring FA Cup holders were looking odds-on to end their 18-year wait for the title, winning their opening ten league matches.

But Caesar was extremely impressive at Old Trafford, unphased by reputations and simply getting on with the job in hand. In fact, few players have started their first-team career in such an accomplished manner, the Haringey-born defender performing like a veteran to nullify the threat of United's hugely influential Danish winger Jesper Olsen and set up an unlikely victory.

It was to be United's first home defeat of the season, the second time in a week that Arsenal were to end a long unbeaten run, and it was another new boy who had made an immediate impact on that occasion. Irish striker Niall Quinn had scored on his league debut at Highbury against Liverpool seven days before to end their own 14-game run without defeat, and again found himself in the starting line-up for the trip to Manchester.

But it was to be the more experienced Charlie Nicholas – actually still only 23 for another nine days – who was to score the winner in this great victory that was to reignite Arsenal's own title ambitions. The goal came 15 minutes from time after Arsenal's miserly defence had sapped the life out of United's attack. Quinn hit a low shot that England goalkeeper Gary Bailey failed to gather and Nicholas converted the loose ball before the defence could react.

John Lukic had also played a big part, saving Norman Whiteside's first-half penalty after Paul Davis had tripped Olsen's dancing feet in the box. Whiteside admitted afterwards that 'it was more of a backpass really', but for Lukic it was the closest effort he had to deal with all game, as Ron Atkinson's side had no answer to the youngsters in yellow and rarely threatened as they were forced down cul-de-sac after cul-de-sac.

After Nicholas' goal United did finally find some urgency with former Gunner Frank Stapleton – barracked from the away end throughout – heading wide in the last minute and Mark Hughes seeing his goalbound effort cleared by the mighty Quinn in injury time.

For Caesar, he would never be so happy in an Arsenal shirt again.

Manchester United's Mark Hughes beats Arsenal's Gus Caesar to a header, watched by Keown and O'Leary.

1986
23 August

Arsenal 1 Nicholas
Manchester United 0

Arsenal
Lukic, Anderson, Sansom,
Robson, O'Leary, Adams,
Rocastle (Hayes), Davis,
Quinn, Nicholas, Rix

Manchester United
Turner, Duxbury, Albiston,
Whiteside, McGrath, Moran,
Strachan, Blackmore, Stapleton,
Davenport, Gibson (Olsen)

Attendance: **41,382**

The George Graham era, spawning a period of success that is still going 20 years later, kicked off amid unbridled enthusiasm with this victory over Ron Atkinson's title contenders on the first day of the 1986/87 season. Bargeddie-born Graham had unexpectedly arrived at his spiritual home from south Londoners Millwall in May.

There had been talk of Johan Cruyff – as there would be ten years later before Arsène Wenger's appointment – and Terry Venables both being in the frame for the Highbury hotseat, before the Board opted to stay with tradition and go with another former Arsenal player.

In his playing days he had earned the nickname 'Stroller', a reference to the casual manner that often betrayed a steeliness and determination which he would take into management. By the time he left the Club for the second time in February 1995, he had been renamed 'Gadaffi', his almost fanatical emphasis on hard work and the team ethic – so badly missing in the early 1980s – spawning six major honours.

In the summer of 1986, while Maradona's 'Hand of God' was breaking English hearts down Mexico way, Graham was getting to work quickly in north London, allowing several senior pros to depart along with young defenders Martin Keown and Tommy Caton, as Graham made the vital decision to hand rookie Tony Adams a regular first-team spot and learn from the invaluable guidance of David O'Leary.

Steve Williams, one of the few senior players who stayed, said Graham's idea was to get back to basics. 'The batch of youngsters coming through at the Club were phenomenal – all George did was assess the situation and realise there was so much talent there already, he should just stick them in the first team straight away,' he explained. 'He could see what had been staring others in the face for ages. But George had the guts, the determination and the desire to make big decisions. He was a shot in the arm for the Club.'

One seasoned old hand to escape the cull was Charlie Nicholas, instead being handed a new role as an out-and-out striker for the afternoon. Indeed his industry on a sweltering afternoon could – and should – have seen goals for both Stewart Robson and Niall Quinn long before his winner.

However, it was Nicholas who was to make the decisive contribution with just 11 minutes of the match remaining to give Graham a winning start. Robson nodded Graham Rix's cross into the path of Paul Davis whose shot was turned in by Nicholas with United goalkeeper Chris Turner all at sea. The goal aroused great optimism amongst the Highbury faithful.

Even at this early stage, Graham has clearly instilled a strong work ethic, but the man who caught the eye was young box-of-tricks David Rocastle, who allied a vast array of skills with strength and aggression – all the attributes needed by a modern footballer. He lit up a contest that at times laboured in the sun, sufficient fitness levels still to be reached, with the kind of raw passion and sublime talent maybe not seen at Highbury since Charlie George snarled on to the scene a decade-and-a-half before.

United had been beaten by desire, superior fitness levels and a rock solid defence – and how fitting Graham's first game should end in a 1–0 win, a result that would be come the norm over the next decade.

By the return game at Old Trafford in January, a certain Alex Ferguson would be in charge of United. English football was on the verge of a new rivalry – and little were the satisfied Arsenal fans heading home after the game to know, the wilderness years were finally over.

1987

1 March

Tottenham Hotspur 1 C Allen

Arsenal 2 Anderson, Quinn

**2–2 on
aggregate
(after extra time)**

Tottenham Hotspur

Clemence, D Thomas, M Thomas,
Ardiles, Gough, Mabbutt,
C Allen, P Allen, Waddle,
Hoddle, Claesen (Galvin)

Arsenal

Lukic, Anderson, Sansom,
Thomas, O'Leary, Adams,
Rocastle, Davis, Quinn,
Nicholas, Hayes (Allinson)

Attendance: **37,099**

George Graham's fearless young team completed a glorious comeback to send this gripping Littlewoods Cup semi-final to a third game. The goals were scrappy and the tackling at times wild, just staying the right side of legal, as these two old foes locked horns. But for sheer entertainment value, this was an absolute classic.

Spurs surely thought they had done enough to set up a Wembley date with Liverpool after Clive Allen's goal settled the first leg at Highbury. And when the striker further punished his former employers with an 11th minute opener in the second leg – driving a loose ball home after John Lukic had dropped Richard Gough's cross – his side looked certain to go through. Indeed, Arsenal had looked dead and buried after Allen's strike, his 38th of the season. But the Gunners responded in magnificent style, bouncing back to fight another day despite heading into the interval with a two goal deficit to overcome.

Within five minutes of the restart Anderson, a prolific scorer from fullback, threw them a lifeline with the scrappiest of scrappy goals, but who cared? The goal that mattered though, hauling Arsenal level after all had seemed lost, came in the 65th minute as David Rocastle found space to send a cross skidding along the length of the goal, eluding Clemence, and gangly Irish striker Quinn slid in the mud to divert the ball into the net.

Both sides went for a killer goal in the final stages with Arsenal missing two opportunities to seal their first Wembley appearance in seven years. First Nicholas fired over after Kenny Sansom put him clear and then Martin Hayes, enjoying his best ever season for the Club, wasted a free header in the final minute of normal time.

The 30 minutes of extra time failed to produce a goal, both sides exhausted with the aggregate score locked at 2–2. At the whistle Graham and Spurs manager David Pleat had to rely on the toss of a coin by referee Allan Gunn to decide the venue for the replay three days later. The first attempt landed on its side in the thick mud, but at the second attempt Pleat won and opted to play it again at the Lane. Both managers pointed down at the ground to their respective fans, and the Arsenal masses roared their approval.

They had already won here twice already this season – now for the hat-trick.

Tottenham's goalkeeper Ray Clemence punches clear from (left to right) Arsenal's Niall Quinn, Viv Anderson and David Rocastle.

1987

Tottenham Hotspur 1 C Allen
Arsenal 2 Allinson, Rocastle

4 March

Tottenham Hotspur
Clemence, D Thomas,
M Thomas, Ardiles (Stevens),
Gough, Mabbutt, C Allen,
P Allen, Waddle, Hoddle,
Claesen (Galvin)

Arsenal
Lukic, Anderson, Sansom,
Thomas, O'Leary, Adams,
Rocastle, Davis, Quinn,
Nicholas (Allinson), Hayes

Attendance: 41,005

Arsenal were the team who refused to die after another epic battle at White Hart Lane ended with David Rocastle's dramatic injury-time winner. A roller-coaster finale saw Arsenal turn around a 1–0 deficit, with just eight minutes left to score twice in front of 10,000 ecstatic travelling fans.

For sheer drama it matched even that historic night 16 years before when Ray Kennedy's last-gasp goal gave Arsenal the title.

A first trip to Wembley in seven years had seemed impossible when Clive Allen – the most lethal striker in England in a season that would see him finish with an

Gunners Kenny Sansom, Viv Anderson and Tony Adams finally get to grips with goalscoring nemesis Clive Allen (second right) while on England duty together.

The clock reads 9:44 as Gary Mabbut dives in vain at the feet of David Rocastle, who has just scored Arsenal's incredible last-minute winner.

incredible 49 goals – had put his side ahead for the third time in as many games. But Ian Allinson, on for the injured Charlie Nicholas, drilled in an equaliser from a tight angle in the 82nd minute and then Rocky – enjoying a terrific first full season – somehow squeezed the ball over the line in injury time to leave Spurs devastated.

Even manager George Graham admitted afterwards he did not expect his side to bounce back again, but as happened three days before they visibly grew in stature once they had gone a goal down. The raucous scenes at the end with the entire squad celebrating in front of the Arsenal fans in the Park Lane stand showed just what it meant to the Club and was just reward for the spirited way they battled back from the dead.

The game was played at a 100 mph throughout with individual battles raging all over the pitch. The one man Arsenal couldn't stop was Allen and when he scored a minute after the hour mark even the most die-hard Arsenal fans must have felt the dream was finally over. Richard Gough rose to nod down Osvaldo Ardiles' free-kick and Allen pounced in typical predatory manner with a low left foot drive. It was goal number 39 for the striker – all achieved in just 38 games – and it set a new competition record of 12 goals in one season.

And it got worse for Arsenal when Charlie Nicholas, who had wasted a great opportunity to kill Sunday's tie, was carried off to be replaced by Allinson. But it proved to be a turning point for the visitors and it was Allinson who was to level the scores. Paul Davis diverted Kenny Sansom's pass through to the Hitchin-born striker on the left and he just managed to squeeze the ball through Richard Gough's legs and under Ray Clemence.

Arsenal pounded Spurs – roared on by some magnificent support in the away end behind Clemence's goal – and Michael Thomas nearly clinched it a few minutes later but shot just a yard wide. Tottenham's legs had gone and with extra time looming one final Gunners burst saw Allinson's cross-cum-shot deflect into Rocastle's path. Rocky's touch put the ball through Clemence's legs with no time for the shattered hosts to hit back.

It was the first time in 300 minutes of exhilarating cup football that Arsenal had been in the lead. And they had timed it to perfection.

1987
Arsenal 2 Nicholas (2)
Liverpool 1 Rush

5 April

Arsenal
Lukic, Anderson, Sansom,
Williams, O'Leary, Adams,
Rocastle, Davis, Quinn (Groves),
Nicholas, Hayes (Thomas)

Liverpool
Grobbelaar, Gillespie, Venison,
Spackman, Whelan, Hansen,
Walsh (Dalglish), Johnston,
Rush, Molby, McMahon (Wark)

Attendance: **96,000**

Just 11 months after arriving from Millwall, George Graham had revived Arsenal's fortunes with an unexpected challenge for the title and a passage through to the final of the Littlewoods Cup. Arsenal's Wembley opponents, Liverpool, were installed as overwhelming favourites, but the Londoners had a 100 per cent record against the Reds in cup finals.

They just had to make sure Ian Rush didn't score because when he did Liverpool never lost, a run that extended six years and to almost 150 games. So when the Welsh striker, poised for a summer move to Serie A giants Juventus, dispatched Steve McMahon's pull-back past a helpless John Lukic in the 23rd minute, that, as they say, seemed to be that.

Liverpool had won the League Cup four years on the trot earlier in the decade and with the league destined for rivals Everton, a trophyless season at Anfield was unthinkable. Arsenal, in short, now had to do the impossible.

But Graham's young side had shown little fear against a far more experienced Tottenham side in the epic semi-final battles, and with Charlie Nicholas in the side, revitalised under the Scottish manager, the Gunners always had a chance. And anyway, records are there to be broken.

After conceding the Londoners settled back into their stride and knuckled down to pin back Liverpool. And it was Nicholas who was to cancel out Rush's strike before the interval. Kenny Sansom drifted a ball wide to Viv Anderson, Tony Adams shot against a defender and the ball fell to Nicholas whose effort skimmed off the post and back out.

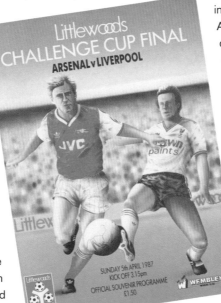

With a mass of bodies entrenched in the six-yard box, Anderson crossed low and hard again and Nicholas, who had strayed in front of Liverpool keeper Bruce Grobbelaar, flicked the ball into the net.

While Liverpool, packed with internationals, had the pedigree, Arsenal's fearless approach was proving dividends and from the moment the equaliser went in, they dominated much of the remaining game.

With the clock ticking down, and both sides beginning to flag in the hot weather, Graham decided on one last throw of the dice to avert extra time when he threw on rookie winger Perry Groves, his first signing for the Club from Colchester United. Groves, never the most technically gifted, had pace to burn and immediately set about the tiring Kop defence.

Only seven minutes remained when Groves, hugging the left touchline, picked up the ball and ran full pelt at defender Gary Gillespie. The Scotsman dived in and Groves beautifully slipped the ball under him and raced into the area where he spotted Nicholas pulling back on the edge of the six-yard box. He slid a pass to him and Nicholas shot first time past Grobbelaar, the ball squeezing in via a wicked deflection off the heel of Ronnie Whelan.

Charlie Nicholas levels the scores from close range. It was to be his proudest hour – or rather, 90 minutes – in an Arsenal jersey ...

Whether the ball would have gone in had Whelan not diverted it past his own keeper, we'll never know, but all that mattered was that Bonnie Prince Charlie, signed back in the summer of 1983, finally had that elusive winner's medal he had so longed for.

A trophy had seemed a long way off after Graham's appointment in May 1986, his remit simply to steady the ship after an extended period of failure for the Club. His bravery in promoting a batch of talented youngsters from the reserves had paid off. 'We have often played better but the prize at the end made it one of Arsenal's more memorable performances ... and this is just the start!' he roared afterwards.

Arsenal were back!

... And he finally gets his hands on a trophy south of the border.

1987

14 November

Norwich City 2 Drinkell (2)
Arsenal 4 Rocastle (2), Thomas, Groves

Norwich City
Gunn, Brown, Elliott,
Bruce, Phelan, Butterworth,
Crook (Biggins), Drinkell,
Rosario, Goss, Gordon

Arsenal
Lukic, Thomas, Sansom,
Williams, O'Leary, Adams (Caesar),
Rocastle, Davis, Smith,
Groves, Richardson

Attendance: 20,558

Optimism had been sky high in August after George Graham's first season had seen Arsenal end their eight-year trophy drought. His young Gunners were expected to kick on and make a real fight of the title race, with favourites Liverpool arriving at Highbury on a sweltering hot opening day of the season in front of nearly 55,000.

But a late, late 20-yard header by Steve Nicol earned the Merseysiders – giving debuts to England duo Peter Beardsley and John Barnes – a fortuitous 2–1 win, and following a goalless midweek draw at Old Trafford, the Gunners were then soundly beaten 2–0 at QPR, a game that would turn out to be Charlie Nicholas' last for the Club before moving back north of the border to Aberdeen.

With the title dream seemingly over by the second Saturday of the 1987/88 season, Graham's players had to dig deep, but they responded in outstanding fashion, astonishing even their manager with a breathtaking run of results that would lead to a new Club record. A 6–0 defeat of Portsmouth – striker Alan Smith hitting a hat-trick to get off the mark for his new club – sparked a run of 11 wins in 12 Division One games, with this result in Norfolk setting a new club record of ten successive league wins and 13 in all competitions.

Arsenal had dazzled and swept aside all before them with scintillating football and a rock solid defence, youngsters David Rocastle, Tony Adams and Martin Hayes along with the older heads of Steve Williams, Kenny Sansom and David O'Leary, proving an irresistible blend.

Crowds were gradually creeping up as the expectation levels grew with each victory, more than 40,000 seeing Kevin Richardson – a title winner with Everton in 1985 who was snapped up from Watford for a bargain fee in August – scoring twice in a 3–1 derby win over Chelsea in the previous home game, that following Alan Smith's winner up at Newcastle.

At Carrow Road there was no stopping the league leaders, plundering three quick goals in just five second-half minutes, after Norwich – no wins in five games and with a caretaker manager in Dave Stringer – had briefly threatened an upset when Kevin Drinkell fired home after John Lukic spilled Ian Crook's shot.

But, with a confidence that can only come after such a brilliant three months of football, rising England star Rocastle struck twice and Michael Thomas hit another with Perry Groves, fast maturing into an effective winger, also getting on the scoresheet in a killer spell.

It was an explosive passage of football that shocked the Canaries, while delighted Gunners boss George Graham gave a rare public display of emotion from the sidelines as he proudly watched his maturing Young Guns ruthlessly move up a couple of gears to ensure the result.

Despite weary limbs for many of the Gunners' players, who were now forcing their way into the England squad and Bobby Robson's plans for Euro 88, they then returned to a more defensive formation to see the game out and ensure the result.

Smith could have twice added to his six league goals and Adams went close with a header before Drinkell added his second of the game late on, but by then Arsenal had won the points and kept their record-breaking run going.

The win also meant Arsenal held on to top spot, two points clear of their nearest rivals and, in the bookies eyes, the only team capable of wrestling the title from reigning champions Liverpool.

In midweek Arsenal would take their winning streak to 14 at home to Stoke City in the Littlewoods Cup, before Southampton would finally end that proud run with a shock 1–0 win at Highbury the following Saturday.

1988

20 February

Arsenal 2 Smith, Duxbury (o.g.)
Manchester United 1 McClair

Arsenal
Lukic, Winterburn, Sansom,
Thomas, O'Leary (Rix), Adams,
Rocastle, Hayes, Smith, Groves,
Richardson

Manchester United
Turner, Anderson, Gibson,
Bruce, Hogg (O'Brien), Duxbury,
Strachan, McClair, Whiteside,
Davenport, Olsen (Blackmore)

Attendance: **54,161**

Arsenal kept alive their two-pronged Wembley assault – and ended Alex Ferguson's last realistic hope of a trophy – at a cacophonous Highbury as for the second time that season, more than 54,000 supporters filtered through the turnstiles, swelled by a large travelling Mancunian support.

They were to see a game that was everything the world's oldest and most famous cup competition is all about; frenzied, high-tempo football played with 100 per cent commitment – topped off with a moment of late drama! Significantly for Arsenal, Scottish striker Brian McClair skied his 86th-minute penalty into a baying North Bank, but they deserved their fair share of luck to progress to the last eight after a wonderful first-half performance.

An aggressive opening produced a 2–0 lead that United tried to overturn with a monumental effort after the break, but Arsenal just held on. George Graham's youngsters gave the older United heads the runaround with a 45-minute spell of almost total domination.

New signing Nigel Winterburn – playing in an unfamiliar right-back role following his move from Wimbledon – was the creator of the first goal after 21 minutes to reward a sustained spell of Gunners pressure. He exchanged passes with David Rocastle before floating over a fine cross to the far post. Alan Smith had spun off his marker and made a late run to meet it perfectly and send a powerful header into the roof of the net.

Arsenal, inspired by the intoxicating Highbury atmosphere, were on top and searched for a second goal to stamp their authority on the game. It duly arrived when another new boy, midfielder Kevin Richardson, sent in a dangerous cross under the bar and Groves just managed to pressure United's Mike Duxbury to head into his own net. Groves was credited with the goal, but TV replays confirmed it was the defender's touch that was decisive.

United, who had won in the league at Highbury a month earlier, played their part in a classic game of two halves,

improving immeasurably after the hairdryer treatment from Alex Ferguson at half-time. McClair gave them hope with a 51st minute volley to reduce Arsenal's advantage to a single goal and set up an absorbing second half. Viv Anderson, returning to his former club, and McClair both went close to equalising, and the pressure intensified when David O'Leary departed due to an Achilles injury, forcing Arsenal to reorganise at the back.

But, with United hammering at the door, Michael Thomas should have settled the game in the home side's favour with a breakaway in the 75th minute, but after a powerful 40-yard burst he slipped as he looked to pull the trigger with only Turner to beat.

And things got worse for him when he upended Norman Whiteside in the box with four minutes remaining to give McClair his chance. But facing the ear splitting shrills of the North Bank, he fired over Lukic's crossbar – and Arsenal were in the last eight.

New signing, Nigel Winterburn, played in an unfamiliar right-back role.

1988 Arsenal 3 Thomas, Rocastle, Smith

24 February

Everton 1 Heath

Arsenal
Lukic, Winterburn, Sansom,
Thomas, O'Leary (Davis),
Adams, Rocastle, Hayes,
Smith, Groves, Richardson

Everton
Southall, Stevens, Pointon,
Van Den Hauwe (Harper),
Watson, Bracewell, Steven,
Clarke, Sharp, Snodin (Heath),
Power

Attendance: **51,148**

The league legs were beginning to run out after another spirited title tilt by George Graham's inexperienced, paper-thin squad. But in the early months of 1988 the cups were a very different story. By the end of February Arsenal were dismissing all before them in the two domestic competitions, with the north London public converging on Highbury in their droves.

The fans were responding to some magnificent performances. Before Christmas progress in the Littlewoods Cup had been swift with victories over Doncaster Rovers, Bournemouth, Stoke City and Sheffield Wednesday. Since January the FA Cup had seen a 2–0 win over Millwall and a 2–1 victory over Brighton on the south coast. An action-packed FA Cup fifth round clash with Manchester United had ended in a 2–1 win on the Saturday, 54,000 turning out for a thriller. And with Arsenal also sweeping through to the last four of the Littlewoods Cup against league champions Everton, a double Wembley date was more than a distinct possibility.

Arsenal's Michael Thomas (left) lashes home his team's first goal, watched by Everton's Dave Watson (right).

Michael Thomas (right) grabs David Rocastle after the latter scores Arsenal's second at a packed Highbury.

Perry Groves had upset the formbook to score the only goal in the first leg at Goodison Park and put Arsenal within 90 minutes of a second successive final. Another bumper audience in excess of 51,000 was present for the return to see them book their place with a performance of genuine maturity and stature, Everton having no answer to Arsenal's enthusiastic pressing game.

The Toffees were looking for their ninth Wembley appearance – reflecting their mid-1980s dominance which had yielded two titles and a European trophy – but Arsenal were determined to defend a trophy they had won the previous April against Liverpool, and went for the jugular from the first minute.

David O'Leary had given Arsenal a boost before kick off when he was declared fit after an Achilles injury. At the other end Alan Smith, a scorer against United, was causing Everton's defence – without talisman Kevin Ratcliffe – huge discomfort with his aerial dominance, while the raw speed of Perry Groves posed a different kind of threat with his lively running. Everton should have been two down at the end of the opening 45 minutes, first Rocastle rolling the ball wide of the goal after rounding Neville Southall,

and then Martin Hayes slicing his penalty wide after he was brought down by the Wales goalkeeper.

Despite those setbacks, the red river continued to pour towards Everton's goal and Michael Thomas was to finally crack open the visitors' defence three minutes after the restart. Pat van den Hauwe and David Rocastle only had eyes for the ball when they crunched into each other, and it rebounded nicely into the path of Thomas who guided it into the net.

Adrian Heath instantly replied for Everton with a header, the first goal John Lukic had conceded in the competition, but with the Merseysiders searching for a second, Rocastle took advantage of huge gaps in their defence to race clear and collect Groves' inviting pass before finishing the job off with a neat finish past Southall.

The crowd was buzzing and for any remaining pessimists in the massed audience, Smith reinforced Arsenal's superiority – and their place in the Littlewoods Cup final against Luton Town – with a fine drive for the killer third as the famous old clock neared the 90-minute mark. With 15 goals scored and only one conceded en route to Wembley Arsenal had the wind in their cup sails.

1989

1 May

Arsenal 5 Winterburn, Smith (2), Thomas, Rocastle
Norwich City 0

Arsenal
Lukic, Dixon, Winterburn, Thomas, O'Leary, Adams, Rocastle, Richardson, Smith (Quinn), Bould, Merson (Hayes)

Norwich City
Gunn, Culverhouse, Bowen, Butterworth, Linighan, Gordon, Fleck, Phelan, Putney, Townsend, Coney

Attendance: 28,449

The football world had been left shattered after the awful events at Hillsborough a fortnight before. On that fateful day, 15 April 1989, 95 Liverpool fans were crushed to death at the antiquated Leppings Lane end of the stadium during a crush before the FA Cup semi-final between Liverpool and Nottingham Forest.

As a result of the tragedy the league programme had been suspended, and there were even calls to cancel the 1989 FA Cup competition with the beautiful game reeling from those needless deaths, a number that would rise later.

Slowly it was recognised that the show must go on, with Arsenal's next scheduled match on May Day at home to Norwich City. It had also been chosen by ITV to be screened as the live game that weekend. And with the nation's eyes on Arsenal, they did not disappoint as they

Arsenal's Alan Smith (right) celebrates one of his two goals with team-mate Lee Dixon.

finally got football back under way with a five-star showing against the Canaries, who had lasted until the final month of the season as outside title contenders. Sadly, the match was watched by Arsenal's lowest league attendance of the season.

Nigel Winterburn, who had joined the year before and ingratiated himself to fans with his wholehearted style – and a goal in a win at Spurs at the beginning of the season – started the rout when he latched on to Ian Butterworth's interception and fired the ball under Bryan Gunn. Arsenal looked hungrier than they had done for weeks and Alan Smith controlled John Lukic's mighty clearance and swivelled to hammer home a brilliant first-time volley. The Gunners were flying and David Rocastle, magnificent for Arsenal throughout the season, jinked through, drew Gunn, and then squared for Michael Thomas to tap in a third.

Norwich, who had built their game on a solid defence, were shell-shocked when Arsenal added two more in a crazy minute. First Paul Merson's low drive kicked up at the last minute, hit Gunn on the chest, and Smith pounced to score and confirm his status as the first division's leading scorer. Highbury was now in carnival mood, and football was slowly smiling again, when Rocastle raced through virtually from the kick-off to slot past Gunn, the yellow inflatable bananas – essential terrace equipment in 1989 – in the Clock End bouncing up and down in delight.

Arsenal had ended one of their two closest challenger's hopes. Norwich's dream of emulating their bitter East Anglian rivals Ipswich Town's championship success of 1962 was over. Now it was a straight fight between Arsenal and Liverpool for top spot.

1989
4 November

Arsenal 4 Quinn, Dixon (2, 1 pen), O'Leary
Norwich City 3 Allen, Phillips, Sherwood

Arsenal
Lukic, Dixon, Winterburn,
Thomas, O'Leary, Adams,
Rocastle, Richardson, Smith,
Quinn, Merson (Groves)

Norwich City
Gunn, Culverhouse, Bowen,
Butterworth, Linighan, Gordon,
Phillips, Sherwood, Rosario,
Allen, Goss

Attendance: **35,338**

It began with both sets of players massed in the centre circle applauding Arsenal stalwart David O'Leary as he made his 622nd appearance, overtaking George Armstrong's 12-year-old Club record. It ended with the smiles and sporting gestures long forgotten as the players were massed in the North Bank goal wantonly fighting at the end of a particular bad-tempered contest.

In between, Highbury had witnessed a thriller with seven goals, an astonishing comeback from the home side and a rare goal from the man-of-the-moment.

The Canaries had taken the lead in the 20th minute when fiery striker Malcolm Allen, the smallest man on the pitch, ghosted in at the far post to head past John Lukic. O'Leary and Allen were having a bitter battle, Allen clearly elbowing the Irishman and O'Leary retaliating with a crude foul on the edge of the box, earning himself a booking and Norwich a free-kick. Wales international Dave Phillips punished O'Leary fully when his curling drive flew over the wall and past Lukic's outstretched hand to make it 2–0 at the half-time break.

Niall Quinn, in one of his final games for the Club, halved the deficit ten minutes into the second half when he pounced after Gunn could only parry Kevin Richardson's free-kick. The equaliser came just after the hour when Lee Dixon – taking his first ever penalty in the league – scored after Norwich City defender Andy Linighan had handled in the box. Arsenal now looked for the expected winner, but moments later Lukic spilled Linighan's downward header and Tim Sherwood roofed the rebound.

O'Leary, 14 years after his debut and six years since his last league goal, wrote the next chapter of a remarkable game when his header from Nigel Winterburn's free-kick flew inside Gunn's near post as the Norwich defence went to sleep. A 3–3 draw would have been fair, but there was a sting in the tail in a pulsating match when referee George Tyson harshly penalised Ian Butterworth for hauling down Michael Thomas, and Dixon was back up again for his second penalty. With nerves jangling, Dixon shot to his

left, Gunn had guessed correctly and parried the ball back into the centre but the full-back just had the presence of mind to scuff the ball over the line before tumbling to the ground.

Arsenal were leading for the first time and Norwich, who had contributed so much to the game, were not happy, taking out their frustrations on Alan Smith as he went to retrieve the ball. The scenes that followed cannot be condoned as yellow and red shirts piled into each other – Arsenal and Norwich were later fined for their part in the brawling – but when the dust had settled those present could reflect on an extraordinary 90 minutes of football and the loyal service of a world-class defender.

David O'Leary remains Arsenal's longest-serving player.

1990
20 October

Manchester United 0
Arsenal 1 Limpar

Manchester United
Sealey, Irwin (Martin),
Blackmore, Bruce, Phelan,
Pallister, Webb, Ince, McClair,
Hughes, Sharpe (Robins)

Arsenal
Seaman, Dixon, Winterburn,
Thomas, Bould, Adams,
Rocastle (Groves), Davis, Smith,
Merson, Limpar

Attendance: **47,232**

Though this game is often remembered for the so-called mass brawl, in which all but one of the 22 players on the pitch were pushing and shoving each other in an petulant display of bravado, for the other 89 minutes the 47,000 in Old Trafford – with a large representation from north London – were treated to an absolute thriller, the kind of game that makes the English league unique.

The players barely had time to stop for a breather as United ceaselessly poured forward in a barnstorming first half, and Arsenal's legendary defence, a yellow wall reinforced with the magnificent David Seaman captured in the summer, soaked up each attack in masterful fashion.

Tony Adams, in particular, relished the challenge, the backs-against-the-wall siege mentality, which had been fostered under George Graham's stewardship, flourishing in the late autumn Mancunian sun. In the same fixture two seasons previously, Graham had controversially introduced

New signing David Seaman was proving a steal after his summer transfer from Queens Park Rangers.

The handbags are out as Manchester United and Arsenal's players get acquainted.

a third centre-back into the line-up as Arsenal drew 1–1, a vital point in that 1989 title run-in. Again, the Gunners adopted a cautious approach in the early exchanges as Brian McClair, Mark Hughes and Steve Bruce were all denied the opener for the hosts in a busy opening, as they started the game at a feverish pace.

But slowly the visitors found the confidence to break out and put pressure on Les Sealey's goal. And with 43 minutes gone of a gripping contest, they nosed ahead with the only goal of the game, and how right it was that it arrived from the boot of the delightful Anders Limpar, whose refined skills allowed him to rise above such a rumbustious encounter. The Swedish winger, a slight figure who from day one took to the rough and tumble of the first division like a duck to water, had skirted around some overzealous challenges to gradually find space as the game opened up.

In keeping with a contest that would dominate the headlines for all the wrong reasons over the coming weeks, his winning effort was a controversial one. He scurried over to collect a short corner and, shaping to cross, he instead curled a cheeky attempt inside the near-post. Sealey was wrong-footed but managed valiantly to beat the ball out, but not before it had crossed the line. The massed Arsenal fans behind Sealey were in no doubt it was a goal,

and despite the United players' heated protestations, significantly so was referee Keith Hackett.

TV replays would prove he was right, as he was minutes into the second half when he booked Limpar for a late challenge on Denis Irwin, which sparked the brawl. While players who should know better temporarily lost their heads, Seaman sensibly stayed ensconced in his six-yard box, shaking his head. Once the game restarted, Arsenal's concentration was impeccable, despite further questions being asked by an increasingly desperate home attack.

United lay siege to Seaman's goal in the dying stages but a succession of high balls into Arsenal's area were easily repelled by Seaman and centre-backs Adams and Steve Bould, before Hackett put blew for time – sparking wild celebrations among the 3,000 travelling fans at the Scoreboard End.

Within weeks Arsenal had been docked two points, United one, and both sides were handed hefty fines by the FA. Despite the loss of points, it was to set up Arsenal's second title in three years, the players responding by showing immense character, to lose just one league game all season.

The foundations of Arsenal's tenth title had been built at the ill-tempered Battle of Old Trafford.

1990

2 December

Arsenal 3 Merson, Dixon (pen), Smith
Liverpool 0

Arsenal
Seaman, Dixon, Winterburn,
Thomas, Bould, Adams,
O'Leary, Davis, Smith,
Merson, Limpar

Liverpool
Grobbelaar, Hysen, Burrows,
Nicol, Whelan, Molby (Rosenthal),
Gillespie, Rush, Barnes,
Venison (Houghton), Ablett

Attendance: 40,419

It is hard to think of fewer more satisfying, or indeed comprehensive, Highbury victories as this as league leaders Liverpool were dominated from first whistle to last in front of the watching TV cameras. Arsenal had been desperate to stay in touch with the Reds who had started the season in astonishing fashion, winning 12 of their opening 14 fixtures to remain unbeaten.

But Arsenal had also yet to taste defeat, winning ten and drawing the other four of their matches to date, new signings Anders Limpar and David Seaman key components of their impressive start.

Something had to give, but the bookies made Liverpool slight favourites after Arsenal had lost in the Rumbelows Cup five days before in spectacular fashion. A hat-trick from young winger Lee Sharpe had laid the foundations for an astonishing 6–2 win for Manchester United at Highbury, just a month after the Gunners' bad-tempered 1–0 win at Old Trafford in the league. It was all the more bizarre as Arsenal's miserly defence had only conceded two goals at Highbury since May and only six in total all season.

The question on everyone's lips was how would Arsenal react? Paul Merson, enjoying his most consistent season for the Club, dispelled any fears when he headed a controversial first after Liverpool had failed to clear Paul Davis' corner. Glenn Hysen only partially headed clear, Michael Thomas booted it straight back at goal and Bruce Grobbelaar did well to get a hand to it, before Merson bravely headed the loose ball over the line despite the attentions of Steve Nicol. Barry Venison hooked the ball clear but the referee immediately gave the goal, Merson not even looking behind him as he spun away to celebrate.

The goal settled Arsenal while Kenny Dalglish's side seemed to become more anxious and found it hard to retain possession. Arsenal's attacking was stretching Liverpool's defence and when Anders Limpar's pace saw him pull away from veteran defender Gary Gillespie, the Scotsman stuck out a leg and the Swede needed no further invitation to go down.

Ronnie Whelan berated an almost apologetic Limpar, but a penalty was given and Lee Dixon – now the Club's regular penalty taker – duly blasted the ball home.

Confidence flooded through the team and Liverpool, now on a damage limitation exercise, dropped deep to deny the home side – and Limpar in particular – any space in the final third. But the goal of the afternoon arrived with the game nearly over when Merson's invention put in Alan Smith with a wonderful back-heel and the lanky striker fired through Grobbelaar in front of the adoring North Bank.

It was Arsenal's third successive league win and demonstrated that when the pressure was on, George Graham's side had character in abundance.

Lee Dixon strokes home Arsenal's second from the spot after Gary Gillespie upended Anders Limpar.

1991

3 March

Liverpool 0
Arsenal 1 Merson

Liverpool
Grobbelaar, Hysen, Burrows,
Nicol, Molby, Gillespie (Speedie),
Houghton, Rush, Barnes,
Beardsley, Ablett

Arsenal
Seaman, Dixon, Winterburn,
Thomas, Bould, Adams (Davis),
O'Leary, Hillier, Smith,
Merson, Campbell (Rocastle)

Attendance: **37,221**

Arsenal survived a first-half Liverpool onslaught to snatch the points at Anfield and hand themselves a massive psychological advantage for the title run-in. Liverpool were still reeling from the shock departure of Kenny Dalglish, an Anfield legend, who had conceded the huge pressures of management were getting too much for him as he made a swift exit from Anfield.

But it was business as usual for his former charges as they peppered the Arsenal goal with David Seaman producing his best performance in a Gunners' jersey to date.

When he signed Seaman in the summer from Queens Park Rangers George Graham had claimed that he was the best in the league in his position. And he proved it at Anfield, repelling everything thrown, kicked and headed at him with a masterful exhibition of goalkeeping, drawing comparisons with the legendary Peter Shilton.

What a game, what a stage and what an atmosphere for Seaman's skipper and defensive cohort Tony Adams to make his long-awaited return to Division One action. The Gunners captain – no stranger to ridicule from rival fans for his ungainly style – had to run the gauntlet and endure the catcalls of the Kop as he slotted back into the Arsenal rearguard after nearly three months absence following a custodial sentence for drink-driving. His first game back – for the second string against Reading reserves – drew a crowd of 7,000 to Highbury before his first team return in a 1–0 FA Cup win at Shrewsbury the week before.

But Anfield was a different kettle of fish – and Adams responded in his usual courageous manner, after the ignominy of his private problems becoming public property, with a typical wholehearted display.

The winner of this encounter would go three points clear at the top of the league, and Liverpool started at a feverish pace. Seaman's first action was a world-class save to deny John Barnes at his near post after a sweeping Liverpool move. The Reds played some breathtaking football and Seaman again had to be alert to paw away Jan Molby's 20-yard snapshot.

On the stroke of half-time he produced another brilliant save after Adams had handled on the edge of the area. Barnes' curling free-kick cleared the wall and looked destined for the top corner, only for Seaman to not only save the situation, but cling on to the ball at full stretch.

The big Yorkshireman's heroics inspired his counterpart at the other end, Bruce Grobbelaar producing a top drawer stop to deny Michael Thomas. David Hillier swung over a deep cross from the left and Thomas connected first time to send the ball at the same goal in which he had scored that famous title decider two years before. But Grobbelaar raced across his line and somehow managed to deflect the ball clear with Thomas set to celebrate the opener.

Arsenal were without the hugely influential Anders Limpar so it was left to Paul Merson to take the game by the scruff of the neck. He was beginning to find more and more joy on the left and it was his invention that finally broke the deadlock with 66 minutes gone. Collecting the ball in midfield he pushed the ball to Alan Smith before accelerating away and collecting a perfectly weighted return ball. With Glenn Hysen struggling to keep up with him, Merson homed in on goal and allowed Grobbelaar to narrow the angle, side-footing the ball exquisitely past the Zimbabwean and into the far corner.

Liverpool, who had been in tremendous form all season, looked spent and Merson again nearly doubled Arsenal's advantage with the packed Arsenal fans in the Anfield Road end in celebratory mood. This victory completed a league double over Liverpool and now that they were in the driving seat for the title the talk around north London was slowly turning towards another possible 'double'.

1991

6 May

Arsenal 3 Smith (3, 1 pen)
Manchester United 1 Bruce (pen)

Arsenal
Seaman, Dixon, Winterburn,
Hillier (Thomas), Adams,
Bould, Campbell, Davis, Smith,
Merson, Limpar (O'Leary)

Manchester United
Walsh, Donaghy, Bruce,
Phelan, Webb, Ince, McClair,
Hughes (Beardsmore), Blackmore,
Robins, Robson (Ferguson)

Attendance: **40,229**

Arsenal became champions for the tenth time in their history less than an hour before a ball was even kicked at Highbury. But now faced with a meaningless fixture against a team fast becoming their most bitter rivals, it was to George Graham and his players' credit that they were utterly professional to the end, chalking up an exceptional victory on a celebratory night in north London.

At 5 p.m. Liverpool were four points behind Arsenal with two games left to play, necessitating an away win at Nottingham Forest. But they relinquished their title when Ian Woan – ironically a Scouser brought up on the traditions of the Kop – hit a second-half winner for Brian Clough's side at the City Ground.

Their form on the road since Kenny Dalglish departed as team manager in February had been impressive, with a dizzying 5–4 win at Leeds and a 7–1 tonking of Derby County at the Baseball Ground among their successes. But Woan's shock goal made it mathematically impossible for Liverpool to catch the Gunners, and the champagne corks were popping across Islington as jubilant fans raced to the ground for the evening game with United.

'I was surprised as I thought Liverpool would win their last two games,' admitted manager George Graham. But he typically would not allow any let-up from his title-winners, his team comfortably beating an ever-improving United side, gearing up for the forthcoming Cup-Winners' Cup Final against Barcelona in Rotterdam. It was one of the most comprehensive performances during Graham's tenure – and striker Alan Smith celebrated with a hat-trick.

But it was never going to be an easy ride with United being the only team to beat Arsenal at Highbury since Aston Villa's 1–0 win back in April 1990. The first goal came within minutes when Smith showed a true striker's instinct – another of his qualities barely recognised outside Leicester and north London – to expertly direct Lee Dixon's wild, low cross into the net. Desperate to up his tally with the Golden Boot on the horizon, he slotted home a second

before the half was over after controlling Kevin Campbell's delightful bending pass which just eluded Steve Bruce.

United, 6–2 winners at Highbury in November in the Rumbelows Cup, were being outplayed, but they were a touch unfortunate to concede a second-half penalty after Tony Adams smashed the ball against Bruce's arm. Dixon was the usual penalty taker but he passed over his responsibilities to Smith, mindful of an imminent hat-trick, and the striker did the rest, putting the ball in the top corner.

There was still time for Bruce to get a late consolation for the visitors, ruining Seaman's hopes of a 30th clean sheet of the campaign and emulating Liverpool's record of conceding just 16 goals in a league season. But even he could afford to be philosophical after a dream first season with his new club had ended with a title medal.

The watching television audience – and the 40,229 partygoers present – had been treated to another fine victory. Skipper Tony Adams, who had been missing for ten weeks of the season after a spell at Her Majesty's service for a driving offence, collected the coveted championship trophy for the second time in three years.

The mastermind of Arsenal's success – manager George Graham – had now been involved in the Club's last three title triumphs, two as boss, one as a player. But when he should have been out on the pitch with his players, he chose instead to watch their cavorting from the sanctuary of the players' tunnel. 'I didn't think it was important for me to join in,' he said afterwards, a picture of modesty. 'The fans pay their money every week to watch them play football, not to watch me sit in the dugout. The players are the ones who have done it.'

1991

11 May

Arsenal 6 Peake (o.g.), Limpar (3), Smith, Groves
Coventry City 1 Gallacher

Arsenal
Seaman, Dixon, Winterburn, Hillier, Bould, Adams, Campbell (Groves), Davis, Smith, Merson (Linighan), Limpar

Coventry City
Ogrizovic, Burrows, Sansom (Edwards), Emerson, Pearce, Peake, Woods, Gynn, Regis, Gallacher, Smith

Attendance: **41,039**

Highbury was in a celebratory mood after Liverpool's midweek defeat at Nottingham Forest had assured Arsenal of their second title in three seasons. The Gunners' 3–1 win over Manchester United later that same evening, courtesy of an Alan Smith hat-trick, had put Arsenal fans in a celebratory mood for what turned out to be a party in front of over 40,000 revellers.

The difficulties of a troubled season were all just fading memories. Now was the time to rejoice, and the fun and games were to continue for the final game of an unforgettable season in which they had lost just once in the league.

The previous November, Arsenal had struggled to break down the Midlanders at Highfield Road before Swede Anders Limpar, who had been a revelation from day one at Highbury, took the game by the scruff of the neck with a late match-winning double. And it was he again who was to put on another super solo showing.

It took only 14 minutes for Arsenal to make the breakthrough, City's veteran centre-back Trevor Peake diving full length to divert Paul Merson's cross past his own goalkeeper. Limpar, pulling all the strings for Arsenal, raced through to thump in a second just after the half-hour mark, but Scottish striker Kevin Gallacher, who enjoyed a decent scoring record against Arsenal over the years, turned the ball past David Seaman minutes later to bring the visitors back into contention.

However, 13 minutes from time the floodgates opened, Golden Boot winner Alan Smith running on to David Hillier's pass to fire into the roof of the net. Limpar then added a fourth when he converted Kevin Campbell's pull-back and then completed a deserved hat-trick when his quick feet took him around goalkeeper Steve Ogrizovic to score.

Perry Groves, who only came on as a substitute minutes before for Campbell, was to wrap things up with a controlled volley from Nigel Winterburn's cross.

Coventry had still avoided relegation by seven points, but more importantly Arsenal had won the title by seven, ending a remarkable campaign with this fitting victory. They had enjoyed their best ever start to a season and overcome that two-point deduction – the North Bank producing a defiant little 'ditty' regarding those confiscated points – to outscore every other team, concede only 18 goals in 38 games and lose just one league game all season, both new Club records. And they had also booked their passage into the European Cup for the first time in 20 years to ensure a summer of feverish anticipation.

The Arsenal squad pose after their second league title in three seasons.

1991

18 September

Arsenal 6 Linighan, Smith (4), Limpar
Austria Memphis 1 Ogris

Arsenal
Seaman, Dixon, Winterburn, Campbell, Linighan, Adams, Rocastle, Davis, Smith, Merson, Limpar (Groves)

Austria Memphis
Valov, Sekerlioglu, Pfeffer, Frind, Zsak, Flogel (Schneider), Ogris, Narbekovas, Prosenik, Stoger, Ivanauskas (Hasenhuttl)

Attendance: 24,124

The last time Arsenal had entered Europe's premier club competition, George Graham had ended the Gunners' hopes when he headed past his own goalkeeper, Bob Wilson, as Dutch masters Ajax sneaked out of north London with a 1–0 win, taking the tie 3–1 on aggregate. Nearly 20 years later Graham was convinced that Arsenal would be a real force in Europe.

The bookies agreed, installing the Gunners as one of the early favourites, while the fans, starved of European action since Spartak Moscow dismantled Arsenal nine years before, also held high hopes.

In the days before saturation Champions League coverage, the mysterious purple-clad Austrians from Vienna were an unknown quantity to a disappointing 24,000 crowd, many fans opting for the luxury of watching a rare televised terrestrial game at home.

Alan Smith, who was to enjoy an excellent European record for Arsenal culminating in glory in Copenhagen against Parma in 1994, was inspired with a four-goal show for one of the greatest European debuts from any player, in any era. However, it was the unlikely figure of defender Andy Linighan who was to make the breakthrough, thumping low and hard in typically no-nonsense fashion to give Arsenal the advantage seven minutes before the break.

But the second half belonged to Smudger. First Paul Merson, in one of those wonderfully creative moods few English players have matched since, unleashed a spectacular volley, the Austrian keeper parried and Smith reacted first to convert the rebound. Arsenal were sparkling and Kevin Campbell collected Linighan's flick on and used his considerable muscle to tee the ball up for Smith who belted the ball into the corner for his second.

Austrian international midfielder Andreas Ogris pulled one back when he took advantage of Linighan's hesitancy to fire past David Seaman, but Smith almost immediately scored the goal of the game, and again Merson was the instigator, skipping past a powderpuff challenge on the left, he delivered a magnificent centre with the outside of

The best of the six: Alan Smith dives full length to score his hat-trick and make it 4–1 to the Gunners.

his right boot, and the normally laconic Smith showboated with a full-length dive to bury the ball in the top corner. The industrious Campbell then powered his way through and saw his shot beaten out, but Smith made it a dream come true with his fourth, and Arsenal's fifth, when he forced the loose ball over the line.

Anders Limpar, so effective on the Arsenal left all evening, capped another excellent display when he made it six minutes from the end, capitalising on some tired Austrian defending before firing home, the ball clipping the inside of the near post as it darted in.

Arsenal had announced their return to Europe in the best possible fashion.

1991
28 September

Southampton 0
Arsenal 4   Wright (3), Rocastle

Southampton
Flowers, Dodd, Gray,
Horne, Hall, Ruddock, Le Tissier,
Cockerill, Shearer, Lee,
Dowie (Gittens)

Arsenal
Seaman, Dixon, Winterburn,
Thomas, Linighan, Adams,
Rocastle, Wright, Smith,
Merson (Campbell), Limpar

Attendance: **18,050**

It had seemed a strange decision by George Graham when he decided to buy Crystal Palace's livewire forward Ian Wright. In the previous two league outings, Sheffield United had conceded five at Highbury while Wright's own Palace had been crushed 4–1 in south London. It would turn out, in time, to be his most important signing – a true Arsenal legend was born.

'I just felt,' explained Graham, justifying the outlay, 'that we had badly missed Kevin Campbell when he was injured and needed more firepower.' In truth, the confident forward was always destined to play for the Gunners. He, like Arsenal, was born in Woolwich, south-east London. Neither was to regret their respective moves north of the river.

The hard-working forward's goals for Palace had shot him to prominence during the 1989/90 season when he made a miraculous recovery from a broken leg to come on as a substitute in the FA Cup final and score twice against Manchester United in a thrilling 3–3 draw. Liverpool and United were rumoured to be interested, Aston Villa's name was bandied around, as was Chelsea, but he remained at Selhurst Park for the following season – Palace's most successful league campaign as he and strike partner Mark Bright fired them to third place in the league.

But it was finally Arsenal who put their money where their mouth was and hand Wright the big move he had craved – with a reputed Club record offer, which was reluctantly accepted by the Eagles. For the traditionally frugal Gunners, back in 1991 this was a big investment. In time it would prove to be the best piece of business conducted by the Club to date as he went on to shatter Cliff Bastin's all-time Arsenal goalscoring record.

Wright's debut came in the Rumbelows Cup at Filbert Street in midweek, and naturally he scored, albeit with a fortuitous bobbler, to give Arsenal an early lead that they would eventually relinquish thanks to a last-minute equaliser from the Foxes. However, it was at a soaked and saturated Dell, where it had rained incessantly since the early hours,

that Wright was to prove that his was a purchase Arsenal could not have afforded to pass by.

Playing alongside boyhood pal David Rocastle he had already fulfilled one dream, but his day was to just get better and better. Rocky seemed inspired, too, with the arrival of his best friend, and gave Arsenal a first-half lead to reward a period of domination by the visitors. And Wright, naturally, was involved.

Rocky made a penetrative 60-yard run, fed Wright, whose shot was parried by Tim Flowers in the Saints goal, but his pal had kept his run going to react first to belt the rebound home. However, it was Wright who was the star of the show, his super-sharp movement and willingness to chase lost causes leaving the Saints' backline in knots.

He finally opened his league account for the Gunners early in the second half when Anders Limpar, provider of so many of his goals in that first season, played a delightful ball through and Wright latched on to it like a whippet to drill home the second. Alan Smith's cute touch again released Wright, who waited for Flowers to go down and then simply side-footed into the far corner. And he completed a golden treble when Flowers could only deflect Smith's shot into his path and, racing in on goal like an express train, he thumped the ball low and hard into the net.

He raced to the adoring hordes behind the goal, singing in the rain, and immediately endeared himself to fans, players and management.

'I still can't believe it,' Wright, flashing that toothy grin, said of his debut days later. But as Arsenal fans would discover over the next seven years, here was a man who, time and time again, would produce the unbelieveable.

1991
21 December

Arsenal 4 Wright (4)
Everton 2 Warzycha, Johnston

Arsenal
Seaman, Dixon, Winterburn,
Hillier, Bould, Adams,
Rocastle (O'Leary), Wright, Smith,
Merson (Campbell), Limpar

Everton
Southall, Atteveld, Harper,
Ebbrell, Watson, Jackson,
Warzycha, Beardsley, Johnston,
Sheedy, Beagrie

Attendance: **29,684**

The defence of the title won so convincingly the season before was not going well; just two wins in six league matches represented an alarming slump in form. But while George Graham's side were already falling too far behind the two Uniteds – Manchester and Leeds – one positive had been the scintillating displays of new striker Ian Wright and Sweden winger Anders Limpar.

The unlikely duo – Wright, all streetwise south Londoner and Limpar, the thoughtful Swede – had developed a seemingly telepathic understanding of each other's game from the moment Wright joined the Club in September. And while it was the Englishman who netted all four against Everton, the Highbury crowd – many managing to

Ian Wright – fast becoming a crowd favourite after his arrival from Crystal Palace – eludes Dave Watson to net his first of the match.

get out of the last-minute shopping on the final Saturday before Christmas – acknowledged the real star of the show was the mercurial winger, plucked from Italian outfit Cremonese in the summer of 1990.

The Swede had become a real crowd favourite, diligently scuttling around and making openings for his team-mates, while punctuating his consistent performances with some of his own moments of brilliance in front of goal. He laid on all four for Wright, a man never slow to praise the former Cremonese winger's contributions, who was already enjoying a hot-streak in front of goal that barely stuttered in his seven years at Highbury.

The Woolwich-born striker had made a sensational start to his Arsenal career – a goal on his debut at Leicester followed by a hat-trick on his league bow at Southampton. The fee George Graham paid Crystal Palace for his services had been sniffed at by some cynics, but by the time the Toffees had left north London, he had scored 13 in just 12 games for his new club.

He and Limpar seemed to be playing on their own at times, nurturing an almost telepathic understanding. Wright's first came after just three minutes when he showed all his predatory instincts to ram home Limpar's pinpoint corner, which was helped on with a neat near-post flick by big defender Steve Bould.

The goal had levelled the scores after Everton had taken a shock lead just 60 seconds earlier. Maurice Johnston launched the Merseysiders' first attack with a drilled cross that eluded Peter Beardsley but not Polish midfielder Robert Warzycha and he duly slid the ball past David Seaman.

By 13 minutes Limpar's intelligent play had given Arsenal the lead – and Wright his second goal of the afternoon. Watching the Toffees' backline, he easily beat a ponderous attempt at offside, drew goalkeeper Neville Southall, and fed the ball inside to Wright for one of the easiest goals he would ever score.

Limpar was laying on chances at will, and he would need to as Arsenal's defence fell asleep to let Everton back into the game two minutes later. This time Beardsley made the opening, Kevin Sheedy helped the ball on, and former Scotland striker Johnston finished well into the far corner, Seaman furious at the ease of the goal.

By the 26th minute the sparse crowd were treated to a fifth goal – Wright completing a quick-fire hat-trick – and Limpar again did all the work. Once again he eluded Everton's attempts to play offside with embarrassing ease and Wright was the only player who managed to keep up with him, accepting another easy finish for a carbon copy of his second.

Steve Bould nearly put Arsenal out of reach while young midfielder David Hillier should have with only Southall to beat, before Wright finished Everton off with 20 minutes to go, bravely sliding the ball in from close range. This was after the little Swedish wizard had again made the opening with more magic to bamboozle the visitors' thoroughly dispirited defenders.

The hat-trick hero flashes that famous grin.

1992

15 February

Arsenal 7 Smith, Campbell (2), Limpar (2), Merson, Wright
Sheffield Wednesday 1 Worthington

Arsenal
Seaman, Dixon, Winterburn,
Hillier, Bould, Adams,
Rocastle, Wright, Smith (Campbell),
Merson, Limpar

Sheffield Wednesday
Woods, Nilsson, King,
Palmer (Williams), Warhurst,
Wilson, Hirst, Worthington,
Anderson, Hyde (Harkes),
Johnson

Attendance: **26,805**

It had been a torrid few months for Arsenal manager George Graham. He had already seen his side come crashing down to earth in the European Cup, when an ordinary Benfica side taught them a valuable lesson at Highbury in November. The league had not been much better, with a string of disjointed performances allowing Leeds and Manchester United to seize the initiative.

And matters hit a new low in January in the third round of the FA Cup when Arsenal met Wrexham, languishing at the bottom of the Fourth Division. Steve Watkin's late winner saw the Gunners humiliated at the Racecourse, the nation rejoicing at Arsenal's North Wales nightmare.

So with Sheffield Wednesday – a surprise challenger for the title under Ron Atkinson – comfortably holding out for a draw, Graham threw on Kevin Campbell to try and muscle some good fortune Arsenal's way. It was a decision that was to see a frankly ordinary match end in sensational fashion. And it sparked a run of games that saw Arsenal playing football that no side in the land could live with.

Arsenal had led in the first half through Alan Smith's goal, but on the stroke of half-time Nigel Worthington

slid in an equaliser and, even at this stage, a 1–1 draw looked the most likely outcome of a tired contest. So when Smith, last season's Golden Boot winner, was replaced by Campbell it looked like a desperate gamble rather than an astute match-winning decision.

But Campbell sparkled from the off and fired Arsenal ahead when he juggled the ball with his back to goal and hit a screamer into the roof of the net. His team-mates responded spectacularly, Anders Limpar collecting Paul Warhurst's weak defensive header and his volley veering away from Woods and into the top corner.

The Owls were still reeling when Ian Wright twisted and turned at the corner flag and found enough space to cross for Campbell to nod in a fourth. Paul Merson was next up with Wednesday in full retreat, scoring the goal of the game with an arrogant lob with the outside of his boot that floated majestically into the far corner. Wright finally got a deserved goal when Woods parried Campbell's angled shot and he scooped in the loose ball. And Limpar tied up the scoring with a seventh when he found space on the right and curled the ball in off the far post.

It was Arsenal's biggest home win since a 7–0 thumping of Leeds in the League Cup in 1979 and the first time they had scored seven since Hereford's 7–2 FA Cup defeat in January 1985. It also proved the catalyst for a 17-match unbeaten end-of-season run which saw Arsenal just lose out on a place in the UEFA Cup... to Sheffield Wednesday!

Arsenal's Paul Merson (left) congratulates team-mate Kevin Campbell (right) on scoring their second goal.

1992

20 April

Arsenal 4 Hillier, Wright (2), Limpar
Liverpool 0

Arsenal
Seaman, Lydersen (O'Leary),
Winterburn, Hillier, Bould,
Adams, Rocastle, Wright,
Campbell, Merson, Limpar

Liverpool
Hooper, R Jones (Walters),
Tanner, Nicol, Molby,
Venison, Saunders (Hutchison),
Houghton, Rush, Barnes,
Marsh

Attendance: **38,517**

Anders Limpar scored maybe the most outrageous goal ever seen at Highbury as Arsenal imperiously swept Liverpool aside. As the first half drew to a close, the 'Super Swede' lit up an already captivating team performance with a moment of preposterous vision that those who were present among a 38,000 strong crowd will never forget.

With Arsenal two up and cruising, yet another meek Liverpool attack had broken down in the centre circle and the ball once again was attracted to the lively Limpar. Darting into the Liverpool half, and with the visiting defence playing high up the field, Limpar surveyed the situation and realised there were no options open to him… except one.

Two defenders jockeyed him, but with his head down he unleashed a perfectly executed 60-yard lob which Liverpool goalkeeper Mike Hooper could only admire as he watched it sail over his head and into the net. The technique was world-class, as was the vision. Even the visiting Liverpool fans, downhearted as they watched their club's slow decline from their 1980s heights, were forced to applaud. Limpar sunk to his knees, clasped his hands and looked to the skies, thanking God for the assist.

But it had been that type of day, when almost everything Arsenal did came off. Even David Hillier, a consistent midfielder who had come through the youth ranks, scored his first goal for the Club six minutes in, seizing on Mike Marsh's lame clearance and drilling the ball into the bottom corner. Liverpool seemed to suffer in the hot weather but Arsenal were thirsty for more and Ian Wright raced on to Limpar's swirling crossfield pass to score with consummate ease in one swift movement. Then came Limpar's moment of magic with Liverpool desperate to hold out until half-time.

When Wright made it four, just two minutes after the break, Kop manager Graeme Souness sunk his head in his hands. Merson played an intelligent ball over the top of the defence and Wright sped on, took the ball past Hooper, and rolled it into an empty net with Nicky Tanner

tantalisingly close to stopping its progress. Liverpool, in unfamiliar green, were being overrun with Arsenal winning battles all over the pitch.

In George Graham's nine year tenure at the Club, few, if any, performances matched this for sheer class and power. The opposition were simply swatted aside, steamrollered by exquisite one-touch play and lightning quick counter-attacking moves from a side brimming with confidence. It was a 90-minute window into the future football Arsène Wenger would bring to Highbury later in the decade. Credit must go to those players who, after the ignominy of the Racecourse Ground at the turn of the year, managed to pick themselves up to produce such a magnificent display, just the latest in a sensational sequence of performances.

Arsenal had been the in-form team in England since February, although they had left it a month too late to catch eventual champions Leeds United. But they were still desperate to end the season on a high, stringing together a 15-game unbeaten league run following a 2–0 defeat at Anfield in January.

But this was perfect revenge, and it could have been much worse for Liverpool had Hooper not brilliantly denied Wright a hat-trick and Limpar not seen his thumping 20-yard drive hit the underside of the bar and bounce away to safety. However, four was more than enough to beat the fading Merseysiders, and the impish Limpar, an absolute steal from Italian side Cremonese two years previously, had reinforced his cult status among the North Bank faithful with a goal that even the great Edson Arantes do Nascimento – better known as Pele – had famously tried and failed to execute.

1992
2 May

Arsenal 5 Wright (3, 1 pen), Smith, Campbell
Southampton 1 Cockerill

Arsenal
Seaman, Dixon, Winterburn,
Hillier, Bould, Adams,
Rocastle, Wright, Campbell,
Merson (Parlour), Limpar (Smith)

Southampton
Flowers, Horne, Hall,
Le Tissier, Cockerill, Shearer,
Adams, Benali, Hurlock,
Wood (Moore), Kenna (Dowie)

Attendance: **37,702**

An indifferent start coupled by a three-month dip from November, which saw Arsenal taught a European lesson by Benfica at Highbury and then humbled in North Wales by Wrexham, had left the season with a distinctly flat look.

But an astonishing turnaround from February onwards reignited the Gunners' hopes of European football as they ended the campaign with a scintillating 17-game unbeaten run. That elusive UEFA Cup place failed to materialise, but it is no exaggeration to say that some of the exciting football produced in those final few months surpassed even that of the previous season's title-winners.

With the bulldozers preparing to demolish the old North Bank – and Arsenal producing a special commemorative ticket for the occasion – at least one Arsenal player was still hopeful of a trophy. Ian Wright, signed the previous September, had enjoyed a profitable first season in the red and white, and had been neck-and-neck with Spurs' striker Gary Lineker for the Golden Boot. Wright's first league opponents in an Arsenal jersey had been Saints on a memorable day at the Dell when he had dispatched a stunning hat-trick past Tim Flowers. Could he do it again and beat England legend Lineker's total?

At half-time the game had failed to explode, but it all changed dramatically after the interval. Kevin Campbell's neat flick header finally gave Arsenal an advantage but Glenn Cockerill – never a popular figure at Highbury after an altercation with Paul Davis three years previously – levelled with a neat finish moments later.

Arsenal fought back and when Francis Benali tripped Paul Merson in the area, regular penalty taker Lee Dixon allowed Wright to score his 29th goal in all competitions. But still he needed more to beat Lineker. Alan Smith's glancing header made it three as the game looked to peter out to another comfortable Arsenal win, the North Bank satisfied with three more points.

But deep into injury time Wright, socks rolled down, summoned a huge burst of energy picking up David Seaman's throw and darting down the left wing on a mazy 70-yard run, before cutting inside, escaping the attentions of the muscular Terry Hurlock, and firing hard and low past an exposed Flowers.

But was it enough for the Golden Boot?

It needn't matter. With one final attack, Smith wrestled free to find Wright all alone 12 yards out. Exhausted, he managed to instinctively stick out a leg and the ball ricocheted off his shin and into the bottom corner in dramatic fashion.

The 79-year-old terrace withstood one more riotous celebration as news filtered through that Lineker's solitary strike at Old Trafford was not enough to snatch the gong back from Wright, who had registered 29 league goals – and 31 in total. When it came the celebration was a fitting finale to the famous old North Bank.

ARSENAL FOOTBALL
CLUB PLC
BARCLAYS LEAGUE DIVISION ONE
ARSENAL
V
SOUTHAMPTON
SATURDAY 2nd MAY 1992
KICK-OFF 3.00p.m.
YOU ARE ADVISED TO BE IN POSITION BY 2.15p.m.
STANDING TICKET   C   0393
NORTH BANK GILLESPIE ROAD
(See Map on Reverse)
£8
INC VAT
THIS PORTION TO BE RETAINED

A special commemorative ticket was made for the 79-year-old North Bank terrace, which was to make way for an impressive £16.5million 12,000-seater stand.

1993

3 February

Leeds United 2   Shutt, McAllister

Arsenal 3   Smith, Wright (2)

(after extra time)

Leeds United
Lukic, Fairclough (Rod Wallace),
Dorigo, Batty, Wetherall,
Whyte, Strachan (Rocastle),
Shutt, Chapman, McAllister,
Speed

Arsenal
Seaman, Dixon,
Winterburn (O'Leary), Adams,
Linighan, Selley, Morrow,
Parlour (Campbell), Merson
Wright, Smith

Attendance: **26,449**

Ian Wright's thirst for goals proved the difference as he brought a cup-tie of epic proportions to a thrilling climax at league champions Leeds United. The Yorkshire side had turned their Elland Road home into a fortress, so when Arsenal travelled the length of the M1 on a February night, they were given little chance of pulling off a rare away win and progressing to the fifth round of the FA Cup.

In the first game at Highbury, Leeds had raced into a 2–0 lead before Arsenal produced a spirited comeback to send this fourth round tie to a replay. Firstly Ray Parlour pulled a goal back, and then Paul Merson – playing some of the best football of his career despite personal demons that he would bravely reveal to the world the following year – deservedly hauled his side level with a spectacular 25-yard strike.

Arsenal had fast been developing a reputation as a team to avoid at all costs in cup competitions. But Howard Wilkinson's well-drilled Leeds fancied their chances of completing the job, despite blowing that lead in north London a week earlier. It was all set up for a cup thriller.

David Seaman was called into action early on when he had to stretch fully to deny former Arsenal forward Lee Chapman, who was enjoying a new lease of life up north. The England goalkeeper had to stretch again to deny Carl Shutt when Nigel Winterburn conceded possession after slipping on the boggy Elland Road surface. But with Leeds dominating, Arsenal were to score against the run of play through Alan Smith's brilliantly executed near-post volley from Ian Wright's cross. The joy was short-lived as Leeds roared back, Shutt taking full advantage of uncharacteristic dithering in the heart of the Arsenal defence to poke home Gary McAllister's header.

Elland Road was buzzing and the graceful McAllister, who had been a transfer target for Arsenal, gave the home side the lead with the goal of the game. Andy Linighan was adjudged to have fouled Shutt 30 yards out, and the Scotland midfielder did the rest with a sweetly struck rising free-kick into the far corner, Seaman beaten all ends up.

Leeds thought they were through but Wright, who had been strangely out-of-sorts up to this stage, took the game into extra time when he swung a foot at Kevin Campbell's knockdown and the ball just crept inside Lukic's post.

It was all-square again with the tie in the balance. But Arsenal seemed to find fresh legs on the allotment-like surface and Paul Merson was desperately unlucky to see his shot from an acute angle hit the post. Merson raced through again minutes later but Lukic denied him with a fine save to his left.

But Wright was to finally book the Gunners' passage into the next round in the 117th minute when Chris Fairclough swung wildly at Merson's poked ball and Wright latched on to it and fired a fierce effort which just managed to bounce over the line after Lukic got both hands to it. Even George Graham could not hide his emotion, punching the air at the final whistle with an exhausting cup-tie finally won.

Few Arsenal players have matched the precocious talents of the irrepressible Ian Wright who struck twice at Elland Road.

1993

4 April

Arsenal 1 Adams
Tottenham Hotspur 0

Arsenal
Seaman, Dixon, Winterburn,
Hillier, Linighan, Adams,
Parlour, Wright (Morrow),
Campbell (Smith),
Merson, Selley

Tottenham Hotspur
Thorsvedt, Austin, Edinburgh,
Samways (Barmby), Mabbutt,
Ruddock, Sedgley (Bergsson),
Nayim, Anderton,
Sheringham, Allen

Attendance: **76,263**

Revenge, finally, came almost two years to the day after a Paul Gascoigne-inspired Tottenham had ripped Arsenal apart to end their 'double' dream. That 3–1 win for the old enemy in 1991 – the first ever cup semi-final to be played at Wembley – had seen Arsenal dominate large chunks of a thrilling match, but it was Spurs who had showed the cutting edge up front.

The result had played on the minds of Arsenal fans ever since, so when the sides were paired together again, their desperation to see a red-and-white victory reached fever pitch in the run-up to the game.

The day before Sheffield Wednesday had just edged their bitter rivals United by the odd goal in three in the first semi-final, but the Steel City derby was a mere aperitif. A flowing game of expansive, attacking football was not on the menu for this Sunday clash. What followed was a bitter, bad-tempered local affair with both sides clearly too scared to lose a game of such magnitude. But despite the lack of quality on show, few of Arsenal's many victories over Tottenham have ever tasted as sweet. This was one of those days when the result was everything.

Spurs had started that semi-final two seasons ago with a two-goal salvo in the opening quarter of an hour to ensure Arsenal were always chasing the game. This encounter saw a more cautious approach, although Spurs felt they had earned a penalty – or at least a free-kick on the edge of the box – just before the half hour mark when Andy Linighan halted Darren Anderton's progress from behind, only for referee Phillip Don to award a corner, a mystifying decision even to the most hardened Arsenal follower. David Seaman then saved skipper Tony Adams' blushes when Vinny Samways seized on

Ian Wright tussles with Spurs'
uncompromising defender Neil Ruddock.

his miscued backpass, only for the big goalkeeper to deny him with a brave stop.

Bookings were coming thick and fast; Paul Allen for fouling Linighan, who in turn was shown a yellow for a foul on Teddy Sheringham. Nayim and Lee Dixon then squared up to each other, both going in Mr Don's book, as the game degenerated into niggly foul after niggly foul.

But Spurs became frustrated as Arsenal slowly began to exert their grip on the game, the Gunners' physical approach beginning to pay off. Erik Thorsvedt in the Tottenham goal became the busier keeper, smartly saving from Ian Selley and then repelling Ian Wright's follow-up effort.

Wright, who by now was confusing Spurs' centre-back Neil Ruddock with his smart running, twice went close again before the decisive moment 11 minutes from the end. However, in a game of such passion and commitment, the goal finally came thanks to a rare moment of quality rather than brute strength. Paul Merson, whose skills had little chance to shine, was the architect when he floated a delectable free-kick to the far post and Adams leaped to head down past Thorsvedt for a textbook strike. 'That has to be the most important goal of my career,' said Adams after the match.

Now Arsenal just needed to hold on and let their defence soak up the inevitable Spurs response. Their cause wasn't helped when Dixon's second yellow saw the team reduced to ten men. But try as they might, Tottenham could not break through and Arsenal held on to reach a second final against Sheffield Wednesday, to follow their League Cup clash a fortnight later.

The donkey wins the derby: Tottenham goalkeeper Erik Thorsvedt is left exposed as Arsenal skipper Tony Adams heads the only goal at Wembley. Revenge was sweet.

1993

18 April

Arsenal 2 Merson, Morrow
Sheffield Wednesday 1 Harkes

Arsenal	**Sheffield Wednesday**	Attendance: **74,007**
Seaman, O'Leary, Linighan, Adams, Winterburn, Parlour, Davis, Morrow, Merson, Campbell, Wright	Woods, Nilsson, Anderson, Palmer, King (Hyde), Waddle, Sheridan, Wilson (Hirst), Harkes, Warhurst, Bright	

Paul Merson was the architect of this win, scoring one goal, and having a hand in almost all of Arsenal's attacking moves, but all the attention went on 22-year-old Ulsterman Steve Morrow – in the end for the most unfortunate reason – as Arsenal deservedly won their first League Cup since 1987.

Morrow was the unlikely hero when he fired home the winner – his first goal for the Club – but he was to spend the night in hospital after a freak accident in the post-match celebrations.

Arsenal were missing Lee Dixon through suspension, injured striker Alan Smith and the cup-tied Martin Keown, who had recently returned to Highbury after stints at Aston Villa and Everton. Veteran David O'Leary, in the twilight of a magnificent Highbury career, was drafted into the right-back slot to join an elite group who have appeared in major cup finals in three separate decades. And another relative old-timer, Paul Davis, was also recalled to the starting line-up after injury, a move that pleasantly surprised fans.

But Wednesday, inspired by Chris Waddle, were a tough proposition, as the two sides laid on one of the more entertaining Wembley finals in recent years.

The same clubs were to compete in the following month's FA Cup Final and a win today would be a major psychological boost as well as securing the first major trophy of the season and European football into the bargain.

But Arsenal had to battle back from a goal down, as Wednesday's slick passing had George Graham's side chasing shadows early on. Centre-half-turned-striker Paul Warhurst had fired a warning in the fourth minute when his athletic volley hit the foot of David Seaman's post. But just seven minutes later they took the lead when John Harkes became the first American to score in a major Wembley

Steve Morrow cracks home the winner – he'd end the day in hospital.

The delighted Ulsterman salutes the crowd after his second-half strike.

Campbell nearly put Arsenal ahead minutes later but his shot bounced back off the inside of the post and into the grateful arms of Woods.

The game ebbed and flowed with Waddle and Merson the prime instigators of their respective teams' attacks. So it was predictable that one or the other would have a hand in the winner. Fortunately for Arsenal it was Merson. Danny Wilson, a scorer for Luton Town against Arsenal in the 1988 Littlewoods Cup Final, conceded possession and Merson dribbled with purpose down the left, cut inside and drove the ball hard into the area. England midfielder Carlton Palmer, not enjoying the best of games as emergency centre-back, tried to control the cross, but a poor first touch sent it straight to the feet of the incoming Morrow who duly whacked it straight back past him and into the net for the winner.

final, drilling in a well-struck shot after O'Leary failed to adequately clear Phil King's cross.

Arsenal responded strongly with Merson involved in all their attacking play. And he was to level shortly after with a stunning 25-yard effort, hitting across the ball to send it swerving past Owls keeper Chris Woods at speed. Kevin

However, his day would soon turn sour when Adams hoisted him up during the on-pitch celebrations after the final whistle and dropped him on to the lush Wembley turf. Unfortunately for Morrow he snapped his humerus in the process and had to be stretchered off as medics administered oxygen.

It was a sad end to the greatest day of his footballing career.

The Coca-Cola Cup Winners 1992/93

Arsenal complete the first stage of a unique domestic cup double. That also meant European football was guaranteed the following season.

1993

20 May

Arsenal 2 Wright, Linighan
Sheffield Wednesday 1 Waddle

(after extra time)

Arsenal
Seaman, Dixon, Winterburn, Adams, Linighan, Davis, Jensen, Merson, Campbell, Smith, Wright (O'Leary)

Sheffield Wednesday
Woods, Nilsson (Bart-Williams), Worthington, Harkes, Palmer, Warhurst, Wilson (Hyde), Waddle, Hirst, Bright, Sheridan

Attendance: **62,267**

Arsenal's league season, the first of the FA's new Premier League competition, had been no great shakes, finishing in a seriously disappointing 10th place, but the cups, on the other hand, had proved more than a welcome distraction. And with the League Cup already in the bag, Arsenal had the chance of winning another 'double' in the FA Cup Final.

Indeed, Arsenal's tiresome 'boring' label rang a little too true for comfort for the North Bank faithful who had had to endure some quite pitiful displays in the Premier League. George Graham's side had merely gone through the motions in achieving mid-table mediocrity, saving the excitement for knockout football.

They had already won the Cola-Cola Cup the previous month against the same opponents and in the FA Cup they had achieved some notable victories en route to the final; overcoming Leeds 3–2 in a replay at Elland Road, producing an extraordinary display of character to beat Ipswich 4–2 at Portman Road, and most notably that 1–0 win over Spurs in the semi at an emotion-charged Wembley.

In the final the previous Saturday, Wednesday could count themselves unlucky not to have taken the pot back up the M1. Ian Wright's smart header gave Arsenal the lead but American John Harkes, enjoying a fine season for the Owls, levelled emphatically with Wednesday in the ascendancy.

The replay, at a sopping wet national stadium, was never going to be a classic, but would produce one of the most dramatic finales in Wembley history. A crowd of only 62,000 – Wembley's lowest post-war cup final attendance – were there to see it, Arsenal fans outnumbering the Owls faithful two to one.

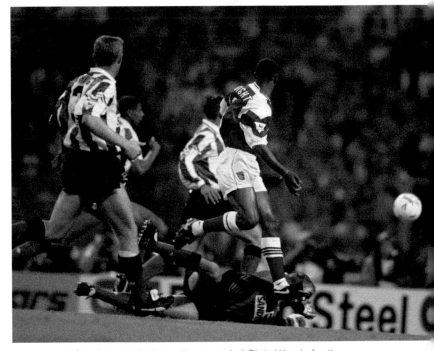

Ian Wright deftly chips the ball over the grounded Chris Woods for the opening goal at a rain-soaked Wembley.

And they celebrated first blood as Wright, again, nudged Arsenal forward when he ran through a static rearguard and chipped exquisitely over the advancing Chris Woods midway through the first half. But, as in the weekend's tussle, Wednesday slowly exerted a grip on proceedings and Chris Waddle, back from forging his reputation on the European stage after an excellent spell in French football with Marseille, equalised

Andy Linighan seals his place in Arsenal history with a dramatic 120th-minute winner. Wednesday, who had played their part in this absorbing replay, were finally buried.

with a fierce effort which deflected off Lee Dixon's outstretched leg and past David Seaman to make it 1–1 again and send the game into extra time.

But this time it was Arsenal who had the final say.

With the unpleasant prospect of penalties just seconds away, Arsenal won a corner. Paul Merson swung it in, and Andy Linighan – who had been a target for the Highbury boo boys earlier in the season – rose to meet it powerfully with his head and send the ball goalwards. Woods got good contact, but only managed to push the ball into the roof of the net to leave the Wednesday players devastated.

Linighan had sealed his position in Highbury folklore in a season of unlikely Wembley cup-winning goal heroes, and Arsenal celebrated a hitherto unique 'double' domestic cup-winning season, long-serving David O'Leary – sub for the evening – winning another cup medal on his last appearance for the Club, 18 years after his debut.

Ian Wright 'quietly' bonds with the old trophy.

1993
3 November

Standard Liège 0
Arsenal 7 Smith, Selley, Adams, Campbell (2), Merson, McGoldrick

Standard Liege
Munaron, Hellers, Cruz,
Leonard, Pister, Genaux,
Wilmots, van Rooy, Bisconti,
Goossens, Asselman

Arsenal
Seaman, Dixon, Adams,
Keown (Bould), Winterburn,
Campbell, Selley, Jensen, Davis,
Merson, Smith (McGoldrick)

Attendance: **15,000** approx.

It seems amazing, with the benefit of hindsight, that even defending a 3–0 first-leg lead, some Arsenal fans were concerned that the Belgians could mount an unlikely comeback in the second leg. They felt that George Graham's decision to drop leading scorer Ian Wright to protect him from picking up another booking – and therefore a suspension – could backfire spectacularly.

Seven goals later the huge travelling support rocking in a creaking wooden stand had witnessed Arsenal's biggest ever away win in Europe – beating a 7–1 victory at Danish outfit Staevnet in the Club's first ever competitive European tie 30 years before. It was also Arsenal's biggest aggregate win on the continent and the largest victory in any competition during George Graham's tenure. It also stretched Arsenal's unbeaten run in all cup competitions to an impressive 23 ties. Not a bad night's work.

Arsenal have rarely performed with such panache and authority either at home or abroad, although once Alan Smith had increased the aggregate lead to 4–0 with the Gunners' first attack, Les Rouches visibly wilted to such an extent, even their vociferous fans turned on them.

It was all the more amazing as Standard enjoyed a reputation in their homeland for their miserly defence, boasting the best goals against record in their league. Not that it impressed the enterprising Paul Merson, magnificent on the night, who swapped passes with Ian Selley and lofted the ball over to Smith who volleyed in only his second goal of the season with just two minutes played at the Sclession Stadium.

Selley made it two with his first senior goal, Merson making a hash of his attempted half-volley only for the youngster to blast into the unprotected goal. Skipper Tony Adams flung himself

on to the end of Kevin Campbell's flick-on before the burly striker got on the scoresheet himself by running on to David Seaman's huge clearance, powering his way through the flaky Liège defence, and drilling in the fourth, just four minutes from the interval.

Arsenal played keepball before another attacking burst produced three more goals. Eddie McGoldrick, coming on as a half-time substitute for Smith, set up Merson for a fifth and then Campbell for his second, before completing the scoring – with his first goal for the Club – when he roofed a seventh with stunning power past Standard's demoralised veteran international goalkeeper Jacques Munaron.

Tony Adams expertly tucks away the third on a magical night in Liège.

1995

23 September

Arsenal 4 Bergkamp (2), Wright, Adams
Southampton 2 Watson, Monkou

Arsenal
Seaman, Dixon, Winterburn, Keown, Bould, Adams, Parlour, Wright, Merson, Bergkamp, Helder

Southampton
Beasant, Dodd, Benali (Heaney), Magilton, Hall, Monkou, Le Tissier, Watson, Shipperley (Warren), Maddison, Widdrington

Attendance: **38,136**

It seems remarkable now that Dennis Bergkamp, for many the finest player to have worn an Arsenal jersey, was an object of ridicule among opposition fans and so-called media experts in the opening weeks of the 1995/96 season. Bought by Bruce Rioch in the summer, his capture from Internazionale had propelled the fans' expectations into the stratosphere.

Bergkamp had been joined at Highbury by another Serie A star, England international David Platt. But it was not to be an easy start for the team or the Amsterdam-born forward. He had endured a wretched season at Inter, despite UEFA Cup success, after moving to Italy from Ajax with compatriot Wim Jonk. Played out of position at the perennially transitional Inter, he yearned for the footballing freedom he had enjoyed at De Meer.

The Gunners had promised him that, but the notoriously fickle English press were not impressed as he struggled to adapt to the physical side of English football. In midweek, against ten-man Hartlepool in the Coca-Cola Cup, he had again failed to make an impact and some journalists, even one or two fans, were beginning to ask serious questions.

One rival club chairman – who shall remain nameless – even famously questioned Arsenal's wisdom in buying the Dutchman, a move which Barcelona, with its long history of Oranje connections, reportedly tried to thwart with a late bid for his services.

In truth, Bergkamp had improved with every game, but his price tag had weighed heavy on his shoulders. So when Southampton came to visit Highbury, the rumour was he was due to be dropped from the starting line-up. But he started, and his response was sensational.

This match will be remembered for years to come as the moment Dennis Bergkamp finally arrived on these shores. When the Iceman opened his Arsenal account at around quarter past three, it is difficult to remember a goal that has been met with such fervour by the Highbury crowd. Fittingly, it was another Dutchman – the altogether more erratic figure of Glenn Helder – who was to play a

significant part in that first goal. This was a day when he decided he wanted to play – and in this mood his pace was devastating. Tearing away from the left, his pinpoint cross found Bergkamp, 12 yards out and all on his own, to clinically volley past Dave Beasant with the minimum of fuss. Bergkamp tore off in celebration and the crowd let out an almost primal roar. You could taste the relief. The autumnal sun even seemed to shine that bit brighter for a second or two.

But the No. 10's brilliance shone through even more. With his confidence visibly lifted, the trademark touches, vision, accuracy and incisiveness that have treated Highbury crowds for a decade, were activated.

Adams headed a second before Gordon Watson and Ken Monkou levelled for Saints. But it was Bergkamp's day and he nosed the Gunners in front again with a storming third in the 68th minute before Wright hit a late fourth. Picking up the ball just inside his own half, the Dutch master probed forward, glided past a couple of lesser mortals, and unleashed a swirling, venomous effort that flashed past Beasant in an instant.

Well, astonishingly, there were *still* those among the press corp who remained unconvinced. One tabloid hack later wrote: 'He has good technique but lacks passion and commitment to make him an outstanding success.' Ten years on and Bergkamp – who arrived in England to bring 'joy' back into his game – still thrills the Premiership like few others, with his rare talents and unerring consistency, and remains in an elite group of maybe five players of the past 25 years who can lay claim to the crown of greatest ever foreign player.

1996

5 May

Arsenal 2 Platt, Bergkamp
Bolton Wanderers 1 Todd

Arsenal
Seaman, Dixon, Winterburn, Marshall (Shaw), Linighan, Keown, Platt, Wright (Hartson), Merson, Bergkamp, Parlour

Bolton Wanderers
Branagan, McAnespie, Small, Curcic (Thompson), Bergsson, Coleman (Blake), Sellars, Stubbs, Paatelainen, McGinlay, Todd

Attendance: **38,104**

Bruce Rioch's first season at Highbury ended in glory with his two big-name signings combining to fire the Gunners into Europe. His side turned around a 1–0 deficit with just eight minutes remaining to earn them fifth place in the Premiership – and the final UEFA Cup spot. The match also brought the curtain down on a campaign of transition, excitement and controversy.

Rioch's former club Bolton had arrived already relegated, but with the pressure now off they played some excellent football with the weight of expectation appearing to prove too much to the home side, who played in fits and starts for the opening hour. The usually reliable Wright – who had dyed his hair blonde – was not having a great deal of fun in front of goal, missing several opportunities as he huffed and puffed in the May sunshine. When he was replaced by John Hartson, the home fans showed their displeasure, but it proved to be an astute move by Rioch.

Not before Bolton had taken the lead though. Scott Sellars found Andy Todd, the burly son of new Bolton boss Colin, and he battered his way through the centre of Arsenal's defence via a deflection or two to dispatch the ball past David Seaman.

Arsenal could see their European aspirations

David Platt: the England star capped a fine first season with an important leveller.

slipping away. But the Gunners producing a thrilling final 20 minutes, the much-maligned Highbury crowd proving on their day they are a match for any fans in the country, with fanatical encouragement.

First David Platt scrambled an 82nd minute equaliser when he shot home from close-range, through the legs of former Spurs defender Gudni Bergsson on the line after Dennis Bergkamp brilliantly tamed Hartson's flick-on. And it was the Dutchman who was to seal a European place with yet another majestic strike. Only two minutes later he collected Platt's pass with his back to the Bolton goal, swivelled and smashed an absolute beauty into the top corner with goalkeeper Keith Branagan given no chance.

European football, the minimum requirement at Arsenal, was confirmed. It was enough to persuade Wright of his future at the Club after a fractious start with Rioch, but neither was to know Arsène Wenger would be in the hot-seat within a few short months.

Rioch's role in Arsenal's development is sometimes forgotten, but this was the man who brought Bergkamp to Highbury. Afterwards he was delighted with Bergkamp's contribution. 'It was a good script. The two players I brought to the Club got us into Europe,' he said. 'It was a great goal from Dennis, a wonderful strike. He's come to Arsenal from Inter Milan and you always wonder how players from abroad will cope with the Premier League... Dennis has lasted the pace magnificently. He's stamped his class on games and worked for the team. It was so important to get into Europe.'

It was to be Rioch's last game in charge – but what a way to leave his mark on Highbury.

1997
13 September

Arsenal 4 Wright (3), Parlour
Bolton Wanderers 1 Thompson

Arsenal
Seaman, Dixon, Grimandi,
Bould, Winterburn,
Parlour (Platt), Vieira, Petit,
Overmars (Boa Morte),
Bergkamp, Wright (Anelka)

Bolton Wanderers
Branagan, McAnespie (Todd),
Bergsson, Taggart, Phillips,
Pollock, Frandsen, Sellars,
Thompson, Beardsley (Gunnlaugsson),
Blake

Attendance: 38,138

Ian Wright became the highest scorer in Arsenal's history after his hat-trick saw him break Cliff Bastin's long-standing record of 178 goals. The south Londoner, maybe the most charismatic player to have worn the Club's red and white, had been left hanging on 177 since his two goals beat Coventry City in the first home game of the season.

Supporters had even been expecting the record – now a talking point among fans nationally, not just in north London – to tumble by the end of August. But an unexpected three-game barren spell, during which time strike partner Dennis Bergkamp had scored five times, had seen the pressure slowly build by the time Bolton visited Highbury.

The Trotters had even had the audacity to take an early lead through Alan Thompson's thumping header, but Wright equalled Bastin's record seven minutes later with a cross shot from the right side of the area. All hell broke loose with Wright ripping off his shirt to reveal a vest with the message '179 Just Done It' courtesy of kit manufacturers Nike. Only he hadn't… he had only equalled the record of 178, he needed another for the record.

Dennis Bergkamp, despite being restricted by an ankle injury picked up on international duty for Holland, was running the game in a way few players can. He had already fed Wright the first and he had an assist in his second – and the record-breaking 179th – when the striker tapped in possibly the simplest of all his Arsenal goals from little more than a yard.

Now Highbury could really celebrate with the entire team converging on Wright as he flashed that famous smile before being buried under his colleagues. The shirt came off again and this time it showed the right number, the player achieving his incredible tally almost six years to the day after he arrived at Highbury from Crystal Palace.

But while it was no doubt Wright's day, even Bolton appearing to concede they were there to make up the numbers, Bergkamp was the prime performer on the field. He set up a third goal before the break when he found

Ray Parlour whose deflected shot beat Bolton goalkeeper Keith Branagan.

Wright finished off Bolton with his hat-trick – was there any other way to end his record-breaking day? – when he raced on to substitute David Platt's pass nine minutes from time to nonchalantly score his 180th Arsenal goal. He left the field moments later, making way for Nicolas Anelka, to a standing ovation from both sets of fans.

What was so remarkable about Wright's record was that he was nearly 28 when he joined Arsenal, while Bastin spent virtually his entire career at Highbury after joining as a teenager. Wright's rate was just under two goals every three games, a record as good as any in Europe.

Lee Dixon and Dennis Bergkamp congratulate Ian Wright after he equalled Cliff Bastin's 178-goal record.

2000

2 March

Arsenal 5 Dixon, Henry (2), Kanu, Bergkamp
Deportivo La Coruña 1 Djalminha (pen)

Arsenal
Seaman, Dixon, Silvinho,
Keown, Luzhny, Petit,
Grimandi, Ljungberg, Overmars
(Kanu), Bergkamp (Parlour),
Henry (Suker)

Deportivo La Coruña
Songo'o, Pablo, Donato,
Naybet, Romero, Jokanovic (Victor),
Mauro Silva, Conceição,
Flores (Fernando), Djalminha,
Makaay (Pauleta)

Attendance: **37,831**

They say there's no place like home, and that was certainly the case for Arsenal in the early months of 2000. The Gunners' Board had ambitiously decided to move their home Champions League games to Wembley as cosy-but-cramped Highbury proved woefully inadequate to cope with demand.

All six games played at the national stadium, three this season and three the year before, had seen crowds in excess of 70,000, convincing the Club of the need for many more seats, whether it be at Highbury or elsewhere. But results on the pitch were not so impressive, with only two wins – against moderate opposition in Panathinaikos and AIK Solna – contributing to early exits from the competition.

However, this year Arsenal were offered another chance of European glory with entry into the less lucrative UEFA Cup – and a move back to Highbury. In N5's first

New French signing Thierry Henry finishes with confidence for his first – and Arsenal's second.

Dutch master Dennis Bergkamp fires the fifth with the aid of a deflection off the Deportivo wall.

home European game for two and a half years, Nantes had been comfortably defeated 3–0, Arsenal progressing 6–3 on aggregate. The Galicians were next up and on paper were the hardest opposition left in the competition, six points clear at the top of La Liga on their way to the title and firing on all cylinders.

But they could not even get close to a rampant Arsenal who led from the fifth minute and thoroughly deserved this thumping victory in one of their best-ever European displays. Veteran fullback Lee Dixon, captaining the side for the evening with Tony Adams and Patrick Vieira both out of action, opened the scoring with a rare header after Thierry Henry's cross eluded Dennis Bergkamp.

Young striker Henry, a scorer in their only Champions League home win that season against Swedes AIK, then doubled the lead 20 minutes later and just seconds after Djalminha had nearly levelled for La Coruña with a 35-yard free-kick saved by David Seaman. Dennis Bergkamp delayed his pass forward long enough for Dutch colleague Marc Overmars to arrive, and he pulled the ball back for Henry to side-foot inside Jacques Songo'o's near post.

La Coruña enjoyed their best passage of play after the break, Djalminha netting from the spot after Flavio Conceição crumpled to the ground under Freddie Ljungberg's challenge. The Brazilian then saw red when he shoved Gilles Grimandi to the ground and from then on Arsenal toyed with the ten men, hitting three more to finish them off with some terrific attacking play.

First Henry netted his second of the night with a perfect header from Manu Petit's free-kick before the pick of the goals came from Nwankwo Kanu. The big Nigerian weaved his way through on goal, sold Songo'o a quite preposterous dummy – the keeper landing on his backside in a daze as Kanu shaped to shoot – and then casually walk the ball around the prostrate custodian and into the net in his usual languid fashion, the North Bank roaring its approval. He had been docked a fortnight's wages only a week before after arriving back late from African Nations Cup duty, but more than made up for it with a mesmerising display. Afterwards he purred, 'Goals like that don't come along very often, but when they do it makes me feel happy that people have seen me produce a bit of magic.'

Everything was going Arsenal's way and when substitute Ray Parlour, preparing to come on for Bergkamp, failed to put on his shirt in time, the Dutchman made one last contribution before departing the field of play when his deflected free-kick arrowed into the net for a fifth.

It was that kind of night.

2000

23 March

Werder Bremen 2 Bode, Bogdanovic
Arsenal 4 Parlour (3), Henry

Werder Bremen
Rost, Frings, Barten,
Baumann, Eilts (Maximov),
Trares (Bogdanovic),
Herzog, Wiedener, Ailton,
Pizarro, Bode

Arsenal
Manninger, Dixon, Luzhny,
Adams (Petit), Silvinho,
Parlour, Vieira (Winterburn),
Grimandi, Ljungberg, Henry,
Kanu (Overmars)

Attendance: **33,875**

Arsenal's record in Europe under Arsène Wenger – especially on foreign shores – often comes in for criticism. But when his team does turn it on across the Channel, it is normally with devastating results. Just ask Werder Bremen, who were blown away at the Weserstadion by an unlikely hat-trick from Ray Parlour.

However, it could be argued his team-mate from Romford, Tony Adams, was equally important, giving a commanding defensive display to snuff out the 1992 UEFA Cup winners' normally potent attack and setting the foundations for this brilliant win. Adams later hobbled off with a groin strain, but by that time Arsenal were so far in front – with the added bonus of a 2–0 lead from the first-leg – they could afford to rest easy.

It had been a disappointing Champions League campaign for Arsenal who had been eliminated from the competition, winning only once at their adopted Wembley home in three games. They were given another chance in the UEFA Cup and once they returned to the more familiar confines of N5, results picked up with French side Nantes and Spanish league leaders Deportivo La Coruña both beaten well.

As were Bremen, who trailed to first-leg goals from Thierry Henry and Freddie Ljungberg but clearly fancied their chances of overhauling their Highbury deficit. However, Parlour all but extinguished German hopes eight minutes into the second leg when he curled a stunning effort in off the far post to make it 3–0 overall. With Bremen stunned, Parlour hit his second of the night in the 25th minute, wriggling through the green defence and poking the ball past goalkeeper Frank Rost despite the close attentions of two defenders.

Adams was giving little change to Peruvian striker Claudio Pizarro, returning from injury, but the Bundesliga side were given the smallest scrap of hope just minutes before the half-time whistle when Marco Bode rose unchallenged to send a thumping header past Alex Manninger, who was deputising for David Seaman.

Bremen, now 'only' needing four more, made a game of it after the break but it was Arsenal who were to score again, silencing the reinvigorated home crowd when Parlour ran through and unselfishly squared for Thierry Henry to tap home. Things took a turn for the worse though with Adams having to come off and Wenger reshuffling to make an odd centre-back pairing of Manu Petit and Oleg Luzhny. With Arsenal reorganising, Rade Bogdanovic hit Bremen's second of the night and when referee Kim Milton Nielsen harshly sent Thierry Henry off for a silly trip on Bremen defender Mike Barten, the hosts perked up even more.

Thomas Schaaf's side laid siege to the Arsenal goal but it was the visitors who were to score the sixth and final goal of a remarkable night 20 minutes from the end, when Parlour latched on to Freddie Ljungberg's pass and placed the ball confidently past Rost to make it 4–2 much to the delight of the 2,500 travelling Arsenal fans.

Left: The Bremen defence can only watch as Ray Parlour hits an excellent opening goal.

Right: The 'Romford Pele' salutes the travelling Arsenal fans at the Weserstadion.

2001

8 April

Arsenal 2 Vieira, Pires
Tottenham Hotspur 1 Doherty

Arsenal
Seaman, Dixon, Keown,
Adams, Silvinho, Lauren,
Vieira, Parlour, Pires (Ljungberg),
Henry, Wiltord (Cole)

Tottenham Hotspur
Sullivan, Perry, Campbell (King),
Doherty, Carr, Sherwood,
Clemence (Thelwell), Young,
Rebrov, Iversen,
Ferdinand (Leonhardsen)

Attendance: 63,541

Forget the scoreline, this was as one-sided a north London derby as you are ever likely to see. In fact, it was virtually a carbon copy of the league match at Highbury between the two sides the previous month, a slender advantage at the end masking another masterful Arsenal performance. The Gunners' passage to Old Trafford had been relatively comfortable.

A hard-fought 1–0 win at Carlisle in the third round was followed with a 6–0 demolition of QPR at a partisan Loftus Road. Chelsea proved sterner opposition in the fifth round, but a 3–1 win at Highbury put Arsenal through to the sixth round, another home draw this time seeing Blackburn Rovers dispatched 3–0. Spurs, welcoming back their hero Glenn Hoddle in charge for his first game as manager, wanted desperately to end another turbulent season with a cup final appearance. After all, the year did end in 'one'!

With Old Trafford packed out, north London had temporarily moved to Manchester for the day to create a magnificent atmosphere, and it was the white hordes who were soon celebrating when Tottenham took a shock lead. Steffen Iversen's wild strike was going well wide of the Arsenal goal but Republic of Ireland international Gary Doherty instinctively stuck out his head and the ball deflected past David Seaman.

Arsenal were behind after only 13 minutes but refused to panic, proceeding to exert maximum pressure on the Tottenham backline, Silvinho and Lauren in particular proving dangerous from deep with some spirited bursts. The equaliser, which had an air of inevitability about it, finally came in the 33rd minute when Patrick Vieira rose to head Robert Pires' free-kick past Neil Sullivan.

Spurs' skipper Sol Campbell had been off the field receiving treatment when the equaliser went in, and just five minutes later was forced off permanently. Little were any of the 63,000 present to know it would be his last appearance in a Tottenham shirt and that he would still be plying his trade in north London the following season.

Scotland international goalkeeper Sullivan was playing the game of his life as Arsenal looked for a second, saving brilliantly from Henry, Parlour and Wiltord. When Parlour sent a free header from Henry's cross straight into the arms of Sullivan again, there was real concern that Spurs may just be able to hold on for extra time.

With time running out Arsenal continued to probe for the opening as their rivals tired badly, and the winner finally came 16 minutes from the end of a pulsating clash. Vieira once again got the better of a hopelessly outclassed Tim Sherwood in the middle of the pitch and found Wiltord who broke down the right to cross for Robert Pires to tap in to an unguarded net.

Rarely had Arsenal dominated a north London derby in such a fashion. Meanwhile, for the first time in 60 years Spurs would be trophyless in a year ending in a 'one'.

Robert Pires finally breaks Spurs' resistance with a late winner at Old Trafford.

2001

4 December

Arsenal 3 Ljungberg (2), Henry

Juventus 1 Taylor (o.g.)

Arsenal
Taylor, Lauren, Campbell, Upson, Cole (Keown), Ljungberg, Parlour, Vieira, Pires, Kanu (Bergkamp), Henry (Grimandi)

Juventus
Buffon, Birindelli, Pessotto (Paranatti), Tachinardi, Montero, Thuram, Zambrotta, Tudor (Davids), Del Piero, Trezeguet, Nedved (Amoruso)

Attendance: **35,421**

Arsenal made it two wins and one draw in their last three competitive games against the 'Old Lady' of Turin with a brilliant display in this Champions League Group D clash. The tie rekindled memories of that famous 1–0 away win in the semi-final of the 1980 Cup-Winners' Cup when Paul Vaessen headed his way into Arsenal folklore with a last-gasp winner.

And this comprehensive victory – Arsenal could easily have scored five as they extended their unbeaten home run in Europe to 16 games – was just as impressive as that night at the old Stadio Communale.

Young Romford-born stopper Stuart Taylor was starting in place of the injured David Seaman in the Arsenal goal while Matthew Upson was also drafted in, taking Tony Adams' place alongside Sol Campbell in the heart of the defence. And the inexperienced backline was tested by Juventus' top-quality forwards from the first whistle, Alessandro Del Piero and David Trezeguet's movement causing all kinds of problems. Taylor twice denied skipper Del Piero, plunging to his left to deflect his swirling drive and then getting down quick to stop a close-range effort.

Pavel Nedved also went close, but all the time Arsenal were slowly building attack after attack as the game edged closer to the Italians' goal. Emerging fullback Ashley Cole had already seen his smart strike repelled by Gianluigi Buffon, the world's most expensive goalkeeper, but even he was powerless to stop Arsenal breaking the deadlock after 21 minutes. Lauren made ground down the right and found Patrick Vieira who cracked a fierce drive at the Juve goal. Buffon failed to hold on to the ball and Freddie Ljungberg followed up to slot home from eight yards.

Arsenal searched for a second, with the Italians struggling to cope with the pace of the hosts' attacks, and Ray Parlour nearly made it two only to see Buffon tip over his 20-yard piledriver. But minutes later the lead was doubled as the Azzuri No. 1 could do nothing to stop Thierry Henry curl a wonderful 25-yard free-kick into the net after Robert Pires had been upended.

It must have been a particularly sweet goal for the Frenchman who had endured a torrid time at the Stadio delle Alpi before Arsène Wenger rescued him in the autumn of 1999.

Henry nearly scored a third although he just failed to hit the target with a stunning volley. But Juve pulled one back against the run of play six minutes after the break when Trezeguet's shot was cleared by Campbell, only for the ball to cannon off Taylor's back and into the net. It was rotten luck for Taylor who had enjoyed an impeccable game, but Arsenal would not let it affect them and Ljungberg finally restored the two-goal advantage just two minutes from time with the best goal of the game.

Dennis Bergkamp, another who failed to shine in Serie A with Internazionale, showed brilliant feet on the edge of the area to feed the ball through the black and white wall, and the Sweden international dinked it over the advancing Buffon to seal three points and Arsenal's fifth successive win in all competitions. The Old Lady had no answer.

But Arsène Wenger *did* have an answer for the Arsenal board, which had been anxiously waiting for his decision on whether to sign a new deal to stay with the Club. The next morning the Frenchman extended his contract by a further three years. Gunners vice-chairman David Dein could not his his delight – and relief – at the manager's decision. 'We never want to lose a person of his talents. He is a miracle-worker.'

The following Monday, Islington Council's planning committee gave the green light for a new 60,000 seater stadium at nearby Ashburton Grove – 'the most important decision in the Club's recent history.' said Dein.

2002
2 March

Newcastle United 0
Arsenal 2 Bergkamp, Campbell

Newcastle United
Given, Hughes (Cort), Distin, Dabizas, O'Brien, Solano, Jenas, Speed, Shearer, Ameobi (Lua-Lua), Robert

Arsenal
Seaman, Dixon, Campbell, Stepanovs, Luzhny, Lauren, Vieira, Grimandi, Pires, Bergkamp (Kanu), Wiltord (Edu)

Attendance: **52,067**

Only 11 minutes had elapsed at St James' Park when Dennis Bergkamp produced a moment of such breathtaking quality, such utter brilliance, that for a split second one of the most boisterous sets of fans in world football were stunned into total silence. Ironically, the Dutchman would not have been in the starting line-up but for a freak injury to Thierry Henry the day before at training.

The Frenchman had limped out of the Gunners' final training session late on Friday afternoon before heading north with a groin strain, promoting Bergkamp to the starting eleven. If Henry had been fit, we would never have seen possibly the greatest goal in Premiership history.

The stunning victory – one of the most impressive of the season with Manchester United breathing down their necks – extended Arsenal's unbeaten run to 16 matches and ended Newcastle's own nine-match run without a loss, and along with it their faltering Premiership challenge.

Poor old Nikos Dabizas (left) can only sit and admire Dennis Bergkamp's outrageous moment of magic.

The pressure had been on Arsenal, with this tricky trip to Tyneside seen as one of the most likely stumbling blocks in the title run-in. After all, the last time the Gunners had failed to score in domestic competition was at St James' Park the previous season.

But with less than a quarter of an hour played the Iceman's rare genius would ensure the scoring run was to continue – and would leave one of the real cathedrals of football, with all its Geordie bias, speechless. Patrick Vieira's telescopic legs managed to free the ball from Laurent Robert and Bergkamp, on the halfway line, pushed the ball to Robert Pires on the left-wing. The former Holland forward, who had scored a sublime chip against Bayer Leverkusen in the Champions League the week before, sped towards the edge of the box in support and when the return ball came, with back to goal, he immediately flicked the ball with his right foot past his marker Nikos Dabizas and spun to his left.

With Dabizas completely perplexed, Bergkamp was now behind him and steadied the ball with one exquisite touch, before placing it in the back of the net with an impossibly cool finish, before goalkeeper Shay Given could react. It was the latest in a long line of Bergkamp wondergoals, and who's to say it wasn't his best ever?

Newcastle gave themselves a minute or two to recover from a genius moment, before using more orthodox methods to try and pull level. But it was Bergkamp who was to kill the game, and Newcastle's Premiership dream, when his perfectly executed deadball was headed in by Sol Campbell, his second goal since moving from Spurs.

Newcastle refused to lie down and twice David Seaman was forced to save smartly, including one exceptional point-blank stop from Alan Shearer's header. But Oleg Luzhny almost made it three and Pires was unlucky to see his deflected effort dribble wide of the open goal, as Arsenal put on a display which would prove to be a defining 90 minutes of their Premiership season.

Newcastle manager Bobby Robson, a footballing veteran of half a century, was in no doubt of the genius the Amsterdam-born striker had displayed for his goal. 'You can't blame anyone for that', said the former England manager, throwing his hands up in the air in disbelief, 'You just have to accept that Bergkamp did a beautiful thing'.

An airborne Sol Campbell punches the air after his vital second.

2002
4 May

Arsenal 2 Parlour, Ljungberg
Chelsea 0

Arsenal
Seaman, Lauren, Campbell,
Adams, Cole, Wiltord (Keown),
Parlour, Vieira, Ljungberg,
Bergkamp (Edu),
Henry (Kanu)

Chelsea
Cudicini, Melchiot (Zenden),
Gallas, Desailly, Babayaro (Terry),
Gronkjaer, Lampard, Petit,
Le Saux, Gudjohnsen,
Hasselbaink (Zola)

Attendance: **76,963**

Two moments of stunning quality sealed the first part of Arsenal's third domestic 'double' on a glorious afternoon in the Welsh capital. The result also helped ease the pain of the previous year when two late Michael Owen goals cruelly snatched defeat from the jaws of victory for the unlucky Gunners.

Ray Parlour and Freddie Ljungberg – Arsenal's scorer 12 months before against Liverpool – both hit spectacular goals in the final 21 minutes against their London rivals, as Arsenal ensured no repeat this time around. And it left Arsène Wenger's team just one tantalising point away from matching the success of his class of '98.

The Gunners had missed the inspirational Robert Pires due to injury for the last two months of the season, but they barely noticed his absence as Arsenal always had a little too much quality for the Blues. The first half was more a game of cat and mouse as the hot sun and the respect the two teams clearly held for each other combined to make it a slow-paced 45 minutes. But the game finally sprang to life after the interval.

First Thierry Henry went desperately close for Arsenal but his close-range shot was brilliantly saved by Chelsea goalkeeper Carlo Cudicini, who had been in tremendous form all season for the Blues. David Seaman then went one better when he extended himself to keep out Eidur Gudjohnsen's inventive angled drive.

The FA had drawn criticism for taking the final outside England, ironically to the only non-English city to have snatched the cup, Cardiff beating Arsenal 1–0 in the 1927 final. But the magnificent Welsh national stadium had won over the doubters with its unrivalled setting and atmosphere, much better than the building site left behind in the London borough of Brent.

And when Parlour finally gave Arsenal the lead, it was a goal worthy of such an impressive new stage. Adams and Wiltord combined to force the ball to the man dubbed the 'Romford Pele'. The former England midfielder – still with

Ray Parlour's curling effort nestles into the corner of the net.

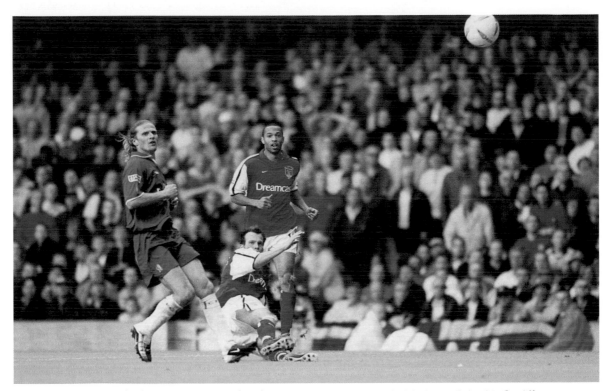

Ex-Gunner Manu Petit (left) and Thierry Henry (right) watch Freddie Ljungberg double Arsenal's lead in Cardiff.

much to do – cut inside and unleashed a fabulous right foot drive just inside Carlo Cudicini's top corner from more than 25 yards.

The massed Arsenal fans behind the goal went into ecstasy and before they knew it, Freddie Ljungberg sealed the cup with a goal that was arguably even better. The Swede found a burst of energy just inside the Arsenal half to ride two challenges, then like Parlour he cut inside and scooped an absolute beauty past the helpless Italian in the Chelsea goal. In doing so Ljungberg had become the first player since Spurs' Bobby Smith 40 years ago to score in successive FA Cup Finals.

Arsenal did not rest on their laurels as they had done the year before, seeing the game out to record a richly deserved win, their eighth cup final win

since 1930. Retiring skipper Tony Adams and the man who was to take over his armband, Patrick Vieira, jointly raised the famous old trophy to make it a job well done. Now all that was left was to avoid defeat at, of all places, Manchester United the following Wednesday and another 'double' would be in the bag.

Skipper Tony Adams and his successor Patrick Vieira lift the FA Cup.

2002
25 September

PSV 0
Arsenal 4 Gilberto, Ljungberg, Henry (2)

PSV
Waterreus, Bogelund, Ooijer,
Hofland (Vennegoor of Hesselink),
Heintze (Lucius), Vogel (de Bomfim),
van Bommel, Rommedahl, Bouma,
Bruggink, Kezman

Arsenal
Seaman, Lauren, Keown (Cygan),
Campbell, Cole,
Ljungberg (Toure), Gilberto,
Vieira, Wiltord, Bergkamp (Kanu),
Henry

Attendance: **29,500**

Gilberto scored the fastest goal in Champions League history as Arsenal finally showed they could win away in Europe – and win well – at the Philips Stadion. The Eredivisie leaders were crushed, with Arsenal recording their biggest away win on the continent since Standard Liège had seven put past them without reply in November 1993.

Arsenal – who had won their opening game at home to Borussia Dortmund – showed their intentions from the off, taking the lead with their first attack of the game. PSV goalkeeper Ronald Waterreus' first action was to pick the ball out of the back of the net after a sweeping move saw Freddie Ljungberg find Thierry Henry who accelerated down the left after easily skipping past Dutch international Andre Ooijer. The Frenchman looked up and quickly pulled the ball back, and with the keeper hopelessly exposed, Gilberto raced from deep to bury it in the back of the net – 20.07 seconds after the first whistle. It was also the fastest goal ever scored by an Arsenal player and even the Brazilian couldn't believe it.

But PSV nearly went straight up the other end and equalised when Mateja Kezman nodded Wilfred Bouma's cross down and Arnold Bruggink netted. Fortunately for Arsenal, eagle-eyed Slovakian referee Lubos Michel noticed the Dutchman had used his hand to put the ball in.

It sparked more PSV attacks though and Arsenal were on the back foot for much of the first half. But with no luck in front of goal PSV grew increasingly disheartened with substitute Pascal Cygan, who had replaced the injured Martin Keown, playing a blinder at centre-back. Arsenal ended the half in dominant mood.

And after the break it was all Arsenal with Wiltord being denied bravely by Waterreus and then Henry going close with a fierce drive at the near post. But the second finally came on 66 minutes when Ljungberg just got the outside of his right boot to Lauren's chip over the defence to divert the ball past the goalkeeper and over the line.

Arsenal were flying and Gilberto spurned a great chance to score his second while Henry also went close with PSV reeling. But it was the Frenchman who was to have the final say when he hit a late double to finally put the game beyond the Dutch. First he played a neat one-two with substitute Kanu before sliding the ball home and then, with only seconds remaining, Arsenal ended the game as they started it with the Gallic goal machine again in the thick of things, exchanging passes with Sylvain Wiltord before another accomplished finish made it four.

The victory consolidated Arsenal's position at the top of Champions League Group A with maximum points from their opening two games.

Ljungberg drills the ball past PSV goalkeeper Ronald Waterreus.

2002

28 September

Leeds United 1 Kewell
Arsenal 4 Kanu (2), Toure, Henry

Leeds United
Robinson, Kelly, Radebe (Duberry), Matteo, Mills, Bakke, Bowyer, Dacourt (McPhail), Kewell, Smith, Viduka

Arsenal
Seaman, Lauren, Cygan, Campbell, Cole, Wiltord (Pennant), Gilberto, Vieira, Toure (Luzhny), Kanu (Jeffers), Henry

Attendance: **40,199**

Arsenal took just nine minutes to set a new English league record. Kanu's goal meant the Gunners had scored in an incredible 47 consecutive league matches to overhaul Chesterfield's 72-year record. But records aside, this was still a contender for best performance to date in Arsène Wenger's six-year reign.

His rampant side, bristling with creativity and pace, commanded the game from start to finish against Terry Venables' Leeds, a team some considered a genuine contender for the Premiership title. Arsenal showed no weaknesses, from solid foundations at the back, an industrious midfield dictating play and a forward line seemingly scoring at will. It was just a shame that the Gunners switched off late in the game to allow Leeds a consolation goal through the trusty left foot of Harry Kewell, who continued to enjoy a fine scoring record against Arsenal.

Leeds though, were undone by the Londoners' razor sharp play from early on, Kanu finishing a majestic, sweeping move involving Ashley Cole and new Ivorian signing Kolo Toure. With a new scoring record Arsenal laid into Leeds' defence, dismantling it at regular intervals with the type of invention normally reserved, at the risk of getting carried away, for World Cup-winning sides.

Arsenal really were that good, making a very strong Leeds outfit look rather ordinary, and they scored a second in the 20th minute when Sylvain Wiltord, cutting inside and leaving Danny Mills and Olivier Dacourt in his wake, planted a delicious cross on to the head of rising star Toure.

Leeds' normally partisan Elland Road crowd were shocked into silence and it got worse for the beleaguered Yorkshiremen as they conceded another within two minutes of the restart when Thierry Henry was played in by Kanu and he shrugged off Lucas Radebe to slide the ball under Paul Robinson with ease for his customary goal.

Kanu, the Nigerian striker who was in irresistible form at Elland Road, scores his second of the game.

Leeds finally showed some steel and England striker Alan Smith thumped a header against the bar from Lee Bowyer's free-kick before Kewell drilled home from ten yards after David Seaman had twice denied Bowyer.

It was a goal that was barely deserved but, fittingly, Arsenal had the final word as they all but extinguished Leeds' title hopes just one month into the season, when substitute Jermaine Pennant threaded an exquisite crossfield ball – the best pass of the day – through to Kanu and the big Nigerian made no mistake from 12 yards.

Skipper Vieira said afterwards the performance was perfection; Venables conceded: 'All we can be is dignified in defeat.'

2002
16 November

Arsenal 3 Henry, Ljungberg, Wiltord
Tottenham Hotspur 0

Arsenal
Shaaban, Luzhny, Campbell, Cygan, Cole, Wiltord, Gilberto, Vieira (Van Bronckhorst), Ljungberg, Bergkamp (Pires), Henry (Jeffers)

Tottenham Hotspur
Keller, Carr, King, Richards, Bunjevcevic, Davies, Freund, Redknapp (Anderton), Etherington (Poyet), Sheringham (Iversen), Keane

Attendance: **38,152**

Thierry Henry scored a contender for greatest ever north London derby goal in this one-sided show at Highbury. In fact, Tottenham were ruthlessly swatted aside in all areas of the pitch, although their cause wasn't helped when they lost Wales international Simon Davies inside the opening half-hour with a harsh second yellow card.

Spurs had not won at Highbury since the last week of the 1992/93 season when Arsenal, fielding a virtual reserve side due to their forthcoming FA Cup Final appearance, slipped to a 1–3 reverse. Rami Shaaban was making his league debut for Arsenal but one or two minor excursions aside, the visitors barely made him sweat.

Sylvain Wiltord had already seen one effort disallowed and another cleared off the line by the impressive Ledley King, when Arsenal took a 13th minute lead. The Gunners had already swept forward with wave after wave of attack from the off, but Henry's opener was an absolute revelation.

Collecting Patrick Vieira's clearance deep inside his own half, Henry accelerated away from his own area. With no support, he skipped past Matthew Etherington and then Steven Carr as he raced 70 yards from box to box, cleverly made some space with a neat flick of the boot to rid himself of the attentions of King, before burying a decisive low shot past Kasey Keller.

After such exertions he should have collapsed in a heap, but got carried away with the emotions only a north London derby can stir and ran another 70 yards along the West Stand before sinking to his knees to lap up the adoration.

It was a truly memorable derby moment, and Arsenal still had plenty left. After Davies' dismissal Arsenal went for the jugular and Henry saw another effort disallowed with Spurs on the back foot. Freddie Ljungberg was to finally add a deserved second ten minutes into the second half when he finished off a neat passage of play by Wiltord and Henry from eight yards.

And Arsenal, who had won their past two league games following a Wayne Rooney-inspired defeat to Everton and a home slip up to Blackburn, made sure of the points, with Spurs close to humiliation, when Wiltord made it three. The French winger, in excellent form all game,

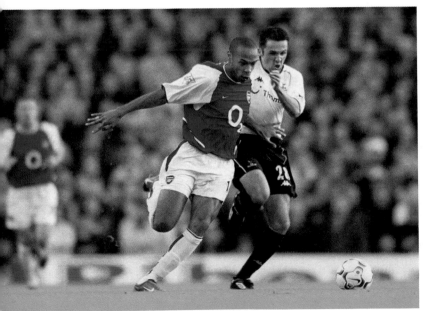

Thierry Henry accelerates away from Tottenham's Matthew Etherington on his way to scoring the Goal of the Season.

Tottenham's American goalkeeper Kasey Keller dives in vain as Freddie Ljungberg makes it two in one of the most one-sided north London derbies in years.

smashed the ball into the roof of the net after Keller only parried Henry's effort into the path of Robert Pires, and his compatriot played a neat diagonal to him.

If Arsenal had scored five, six or even seven, Spurs really could have had no complaint, although they did nearly come close to snatching an undeserved consolation when Shaaban had to be alert at the end to fist away former England midfielder Darren Anderton's well-struck free-kick. But by then, the battered and beleaguered visitors – hopelessly outclassed for long periods – just wanted to hear referee Mike Riley's full-time whistle.

Henry, to be crowned both Professional Footballers' Association (PFA) and Football Writers' Association (FWA) Footballer of the Year at season's end, also saw his first-half strike named Premiership Goal of the Season.

Sylvain Wiltord settles matters with a third while Steven Carr is powerless on the goal-line.

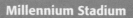
2003 Arsenal 1 Pires
Southampton 0

17 May

Arsenal
Seaman, Lauren, Keown, Luzhny, Cole, Pires, Parlour, Gilberto, Ljungberg, Henry, Bergkamp (Wiltord)

Southampton
Niemi (Jones), Baird (Fernandes), Lundekvam, M Svensson, Bridge, Telfer, Oakley, A Svensson (Tessem), Marsden, Ormerod, Beattie

Attendance: **73,726**

Robert Pires eased some of the agony of missing out on a second successive Premiership crown with the FA Cup winner in Cardiff's magnificent Millennium Stadium. His goal finally brought Arsenal a deserved trophy for a season of football that, at times, had reached heights that the domestic game has rarely ever seen.

The France international had missed the 2002 win over Chelsea because of injury, and had been eager to make his mark on English football's showpiece event.

Arsenal had reached the final thanks largely to veteran goalkeeper David Seaman – who was to make his final appearance for the Club in Cardiff. At Old Trafford in the semi-final he produced maybe his best ever save against a resilient Sheffield United, somehow twisting and contorting his body to pluck out Paul Peschisolido's close-range header and preserve his clean sheet on his 1,000th

league appearance. Coupled with Freddie Ljungberg's early goal, it helped Arsenal progress to a third final on the trot. Ljungberg, in fact, just needed a goal in Cardiff to become the first player ever to net in three successive FA Cup Finals.

Saints were lucky not to lose Claus Lundekvam in the opening minutes, when he hauled down Thierry Henry as he bore in on goal. Henry still managed to get his shot in, Antti Niemi saving, and that may have made referee Graham Barber's mind up not to take any action against

The FA Cup heads to Highbury for a ninth time courtesy of this strike by Robert Pires.

Thierry Henry shows some neat control.

continued to dominate, and when Niemi pulled up injured and was replaced by Paul Jones, Arsenal eased up. It could have proved fatal as first Lauren only just managed to intercept as Saints' sub Jo Tessem nearly levelled with his first touch and then Seaman, virtually a spectator for most of the game, showed his class. With just eight minutes remaining Brett Ormerod hit a belter but the big Yorkshireman flung up a strong arm and deflected the ball away for a corner.

Saints took heart and five minutes into injury time Ashley Cole proved the hero when he cleared James Beattie's header off the line for the last significant action of a final that had really come to life in the second half.

For Seaman the curtain had finally come down on a fantastic Arsenal career 13 years – and 405 appearances – after his move across London from Queens Park Rangers in 1990. With Jens Lehmann arriving, the big Yorkshireman moved back north to Manchester City, before being forced to retire midway through the following season as one injury too many took its toll on his weary body.

'Safe Hands' though, had fittingly left Highbury on a high, clutching the famous old trophy for a fourth time.

the defender, Niemi then fumbled another Henry effort – youngster Chris Baird clearing as Dennis Bergkamp looked to pounce – before Arsenal's superiority finally told seven minutes from the interval. Henry played in the Dutchman, and when Ljungberg's shot was kept out, Pires swept the rebound home from eight yards.

Ljungberg should have made it two shortly after the restart but shot tamely into the side-netting as Arsenal

The 2003 FA Cup winners line up for the after-match photos while (right) David Seaman lifts his last trophy for Arsenal.

2004
6 March

Portsmouth 1 Sheringham
Arsenal 5 Henry (2), Ljungberg (2), Toure

Portsmouth
Hislop, Primus, Pasanen,
De Zeeuw, Smertin,
Quashie (Hughes), Faye,
Berkovic (Stone), Taylor,
Yakubu, Mornar (Sheringham)

Arsenal
Lehmann, Lauren, Toure,
Campbell, Cole, Ljungberg (Bentley),
Vieira (Clichy), Edu, Silva,
Reyes, Henry (Kanu)

Attendance: **20,137**

Arsenal reinforced their position as English football's unrivalled entertainers with a devastating exhibition of attacking football that left even the Pompey faithful drooling. In a season of football that had reached new heights – some fans had even dubbed it 'Wengerball' – this was quite possibly the finest, most accomplished display seen by Arsène Wenger's side.

Thierry Henry scores his first goal on a memorable evening at Fratton Park.

1970s, with a very good Pompey side chasing shadows for long periods.

Playing with such a swagger, a goal was inevitable and the opener finally came 25 minutes into the game, Henry taking one touch before producing an assured finish past Shaka Hislop. Edu almost made it two but was denied by a smart save from Hislop after a period of play which had seen Arsenal string together more than two-dozen passes.

The hosts were clinging on to the yellow-clad visitors' shirt-tails but were dealt a body blow when they conceded two more goals just before the break. First Sweden international Ljungberg latched on to Edu's curling pass to place the ball into the corner, and with referee Jeff Winter set to blow for

All the components were there: defensive strength, attacking imagination, skills in abundance, intelligence and top drawer finishing, with every Arsenal player playing their part. Thierry Henry and Freddie Ljungberg had fired Arsenal 2–0 up and Kolo Toure hit a third on the stroke of half-time. Henry and Ljungberg made it five by the 57th minute before sub Teddy Sheringham, so often Arsenal's nemesis, hit a consolation in injury time.

New Spanish signing José Antonio Reyes had shown Arsenal's intentions in the first minute of the game when his snapshot struck the bar. Arsenal's ability to string 15 to 20 pass moves together with the minimum of fuss was reminiscent of the great Dutch sides of the

Henry points the way after firing home his second of the game.

half-time, Toure fired low and hard into the net after the Pompey defence had failed to clear a corner. It led to the wonderful gesture from the normally vociferous home fans when they gave the Arsenal team a standing ovation as they jogged back to the changing rooms for their half-time cuppa.

Arsenal had now found their range, sweeping forward imperiously, and just four minutes into the second half they dashed any slim hopes Harry Redknapp's team may have had of a dramatic comeback.

Reyes and Ljungberg combined to free Henry who sprinted down on Hislop's goal. Ljungberg had scuttled forward, hopeful for a return pass, but the French striker had other ideas and curled an inch-perfect shot just around Ljungberg into the far corner, taking the goalkeeper completely by surprise for the best goal of the game. Just seven minutes later Arsenal wrapped up their scoring with Ljungberg – full of running throughout – squirming a shot past Hislop with the aid of a decisive deflection off Pompey defender Linvoy Primus.

By now Arsenal were dominating completely, playing long periods of keepball and turning the final half-hour into a practice session. But Pompey must take credit for fighting back enough to see Matthew Taylor and Ayegbeni Yakubu both hit the woodwork before Sheringham's defiant effort, much too little, much too late.

José Antonio Reyes and Thierry Henry rush to greet Freddie Ljungberg after the Swede wrapped up the scoring for the Gunners.

Again, the Pompey fans stayed to the end to enthusiastically applaud the visitors' efforts. And they reserved a special cheer for Henry as he departed the scene, wearing a vanquished opponent's shirt.

Reyes, a recent arrival from Seville, holds off Portsmouth's Petri Pasanen.

2004

9 April

Arsenal 4 Pires, Henry (3)
Liverpool 2 Hyypia, Owen

Arsenal
Lehmann, Lauren, Toure,
Campbell, Cole, Ljungberg (Keown),
Gilberto, Vieira, Pires (Edu),
Henry, Bergkamp

Liverpool
Dudek, Hyypia, Carragher,
Gerrard, Riise, Hamann,
Kewell, Biscan, Diouf (Murphy),
Owen, Heskey (Baros)

Attendance: **38,119**

Six days previously, Arsenal were being touted in the media as possibly the greatest club side to have ever graced the English game. That was the kind of hype Arsène Wenger and his team were being subjected to at the business end of the 2003/04 campaign. The 'double', claimed the experts, was in the bag. The Holy Grail of the 'treble' was more than a distinct possibility.

But by the time Liverpool were to visit Highbury, on Good Friday, Arsenal only had the Premiership to play for. First an inspired Manchester United, who rode their luck on more than one occasion before Paul Scholes' solitary strike, ran out victors in a pulsating FA Cup semi-final at Villa Park. Three days later Chelsea had dealt the Gunners a devastating blow to break their 17-match hoodoo against their north London rivals, winning 2–1 at Highbury in the second leg of the Champions League quarter-final. The dark clouds of failure were making their way to N5.

Arsène Wenger's battered side had lost their air of invincibility and Liverpool were in confident mood, more so when big Finland defender Sami Hyypia glanced a header past Jens Lehmann five minutes in. Hyypia, Michael Owen and Harry Kewell all had opportunities to extend that lead – at least two should have been converted as Arsenal rocked – before Thierry Henry placed the ball under Kop keeper Jerzy Dudek for a 31st minute equaliser.

But again it was Liverpool who took the initiative, and it was England striker Owen who was to do the damage, edging past Sol Campbell and slotting home in typically cool fashion shortly before the interval. What happened during half-time in the home dressing room we'll never fully know. Some players have admitted they were mentally drained. Maybe fear and self-doubt was enveloping the team. But surely such a brilliant season of football would not go unrewarded?

Arsenal redoubled their efforts to turn this game on its head – and Henry was the catalyst. Four minutes after the restart he combined superbly with Freddie Ljungberg, who found Robert Pires, and he did the rest with an accomplished finish. A minute later, the crowd roaring the home side on, Henry picked the ball up just inside his half, raced direct towards the North Bank, danced around two challenges with exquisite balance, before stroking the ball past Dudek for a goal of stunning quality.

But it wasn't over yet; Owen and Kewell both tested Lehmann, giving the home support some heart-stopping moments, before Henry sealed victory with his hat-trick goal after a lucky rebound off Liverpool's Polish keeper.

Relief and defiance – from players and fans – greeted the final whistle. This really was a game for that now famous Arsenal word, 'Togetherness'.

Good Friday? It was a great, great Friday… this was Arsenal's title.

The defining moment of the game: Henry dances through to make it 2–2.

2004

16 April

Arsenal 5 Pires, Henry (4, 1 pen)
Leeds United 0

Arsenal
Lehmann, Lauren, Campbell, Toure, Clichy, Wiltord, Gilberto (Edu), Vieira, Pires (Parlour), Bergkamp (Reyes), Henry

Leeds United
Robinson, Matteo, Caldwell, Kelly, Radebe (Barmby), Harte, Duberry, Pennant, Milner, Smith, Viduka (Johnson)

Attendance: **38,094**

Arsenal all but sealed their 13th league title against the side who had extinguished their Premiership hopes a year before. It was sweet, sweet revenge after that devasting 3–2 home defeat a year previously – the Gunners' last league loss – with a certain Gallic goal-getter unplayable at times in a blistering display.

Thierry Henry, the best striker in the world according to his manager Arsène Wenger after this extravagant showing, notched his 150th goal for the Club – an incredible effort in only his 251st Arsenal game – as he struck four times to push Leeds a step closer to Championship football.

The Gunners had already plundered eight goals against the Whites in two meetings earlier in the season – a pair of 4–1 victories at Elland Road, one in the league, the other in the FA Cup – and again, they had no answer to a scintillating Arsenal side.

It was another Frenchman who was to set the tone for this Friday evening clash, Robert Pires curling a beauty in from the edge of the box after latching on to Dennis Bergkamp's pinpoint through-ball in the sixth minute.

Alan Smith, in the heartbreaking position of seeing his boyhood heroes on the verge of an undignified exit from top-flight football, showed desire to wriggle free of Sol Campbell twice, while Mark Viduka saw his opportunist effort saved by Jens Lehmann, but goals were always more likely to come at the other end. And come they did…

Henry, eyeing a creaking defence with a glint in his eye, took control, springing the offside trap to slide the ball past England keeper Paul Robinson 27 minutes in. Bergkamp then had a hand in the third, collecting Sylvain Wiltord's pass, only for Michael Duberry to stop the ball with his arm. Henry converted the penalty with a cheeky chip into the centre of the goal leaving Robinson on his backside.

The scoreline may have been a little harsh on Leeds but in this mood Henry gave the impression he would have destroyed virtually any side he faced. Henry completed his hat-trick four minutes after the interval with another

Henry stumbles but still manages to make it five.

devastating break, shifting defence into attack in an instant. Gilberto, winning over the Arsenal faithful with a run of dominating performances alongside Patrick Vieira in midfield, made a burst from the edge of his own box. With Leeds retreating, he threaded an inch-perfect ball through to Henry who made the finish look easy.

With a ten-point lead at the top of the table assured, Henry still wanted more and saved his best until last. Another powerful surge saw him clear on goal, and even though he was clipped from behind he still managed to retain his composure to side-foot the ball into the net.

There were no more goals but Henry's sublime handiwork on the night begged the question: is there anyone better in world football?

2005

11 May

Arsenal 7 van Persie, Pires (2), Vieira, Edu (pen), Bergkamp, Flamini
Everton 0

Arsenal
Lehmann, Lauren, Senderos,
Campbell, Cole, Pires (Fabregas),
Edu, Vieira (Flamini), Reyes,
Bergkamp, van Persie (Henry)

Everton
Wright, Hibbert, Weir,
Yobo, Pistone, Watson,
Arteta (Ferguson), Carsley,
Kilbane, McFadden,
Beattie (Bent)

Attendance: **38,073**

Arsenal tore Everton apart in one of the best displays of attacking football seen at Highbury for many years. It was the Gunners' biggest ever win during Arsène Wenger's nine-year tenure, the biggest home win since February 1992, the first time Arsenal had hit seven since 1993 and the last time Arsenal would ever wear their old red and white shirts at Highbury.

It was a most fitting way to temporarily sign off in those famous old jerseys, the final season at the old ground seeing Arsenal don redcurrant jerseys, the colours the Club sported in the first season at N5 in 1913. Brazilian Edu said goodbye after five years with a goal as he departed for Valencia and La Liga, but the name on everyone's lips on a heady night of fantasy football was Dennis Bergkamp, the mercurial Dutchman whose contract was to end in the summer. Would this be his final ever appearance at his home of the last ten years?

The fans demanded he stay another year and he showed his intentions with a virtuoso performance as the Toffees came unstuck in spectacular fashion. Result aside, Arsenal's performance, particularly in the final third of the pitch, reached heights rarely seen before. The pick of the goals came eight minutes from the half-time interval, Bergkamp showing he is blessed with a touch few could ever match, when he instantly deadened Robin van Persie's driven ball into the path of skipper Patrick Vieira, who dinked the most delightful of chipped finishes over former Gunner Richard Wright in the Everton goal.

That had made it 3–0 after rookie Dutch striker van Persie had raced on to an inch-perfect through ball from – yes, you've guessed it – Bergkamp, to give Arsenal an eighth-minute advantage. A further four minutes had elapsed when Bergkamp proved architect again, drilling another super ball into the danger zone, José Antonio Reyes cutting the ball back and Robert Pires heading the ball over the line after Wright parried his initial effort.

It was difficult to imagine any English side who could have lived with Arsenal's attacking – or have replicated it – as Reyes and van Persie both nearly struck again before the break.

Thierry Henry had not played a part in the opening 45, watching from the bench as he nursed a groin injury.

The hugely talented Dutch youngster Robin van Persie races away after opening the goal-fest.

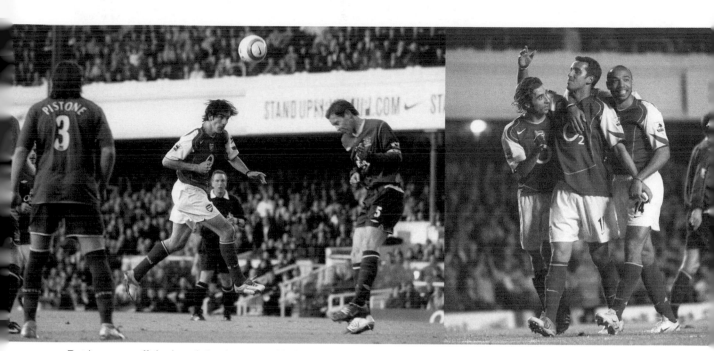

But he came off the bench for the second half and made an instant impact, Pires slotting home after Henry's pass fell into his path via Lee Carsley. Edu, in his Highbury farewell, was given the responsibility of slotting home the penalty after Carsley again tried to intercept another Henry touch, this time with his hand, as Arsenal made it five with 20 minutes remaining.

The hosts' lighting movement and one-touch football continued to bamboozle a thoroughly dispirited Everton, who had arrived at Highbury full of the joys of spring after an unexpected season of consistency had seen them pip arch-rivals Liverpool to fourth place in the Premiership and earn them a stab at the next season's lucrative Champions League.

Fittingly Bergkamp finally got the goal he so deserved – and the heartiest cheer of the evening – when he charged down a clearance and then showed a cool head to roll the ball down and drive it low into the net for the sixth of the evening.

Far from slowing up, Arsenal looked for more and a seventh duly arrived in the 85th minute when sub Mathieu Flamini slotted home Reyes' knock down for his first goal for the Club after another lightning quick move.

Above left: Robert Pires reacts brilliantly to head in the Gunners' second.

Above: Edu celebrates his goal on his final Highbury appearance in an Arsenal shirt.

Below: Fans' favourite Dennis Bergkamp drills in the sixth – and gets the biggest cheer of the night.

2005

21 May

Manchester United 0
Arsenal 0

**Arsenal won
5–4 on penalties
(after extra time)**

Manchester United
Carroll, Brown, Ferdinand,
Silvestre, O'Shea (Fortune),
Fletcher (Giggs), Keane, Scholes,
Ronaldo, van Nistelrooy,
Rooney

Arsenal
Lehmann, Cole, Toure,
Senderos, Lauren, Fabregas
(van Persie), Vieira, Gilberto,
Pires (Edu), Bergkamp (Ljungberg),
Reyes

Attendance: 71,876

Arsenal won the old trophy for a record tenth time with a thrilling penalty shootout victory over Manchester United in Cardiff's last scheduled FA Cup Final. United may have dominated large swathes of play during 120 minutes of frenetic action, but the Gunners took the trophy back to north London with a mix of luck, resilience, fantastic defending and some cool heads.

The Welsh capital proved a home away from home for Arsène Wenger's side at the beginning of the new Millennium, hosting them in no less than four FA Cup Finals out of five. Ironically, Arsenal's most insipid attacking display of the four produced victory over their closest foes of the past decade. It was quite a reverse from that first final in 2001, a game that Arsenal would somehow contrive to lose to Liverpool despite, according to Wenger, producing their most impressive display of the four.

But, as Manchester United themselves will know after beating Bayern Munich in the 1999 Champions League Final with two late goals after conceding possession and space during the majority of the 90 minutes played, the best team is the one with the trophy at the end of game.

Jens Lehmann produced his finest goalkeeping performance in an Arsenal jersey, repelling several goalbound efforts and settling the nerves of youngsters Kolo Toure and Philippe Senderos. Wenger had opted for the fledgling centre-back partnership, omitting Sol Campbell from the starting line-up, and was fully vindicated with an assured display by the pair. But the biggest blow was dealt the previous Monday when talismanic striker Thierry Henry was ruled out with an achilles injury, meaning Dennis Bergkamp was forced to forage for scraps on his own up front.

It was a cagey start to the proceedings by both sides, but United exploded to life with England star Wayne Rooney determined to pick up his first ever trophy. Lehmann had other ideas though, saving well twice and then tipping Rooney's audacious effort away to safety.

United huffed and they puffed but could not blow the Arsenal house down, Lehmann brilliantly denying Paul Scholes and Ruud van Nistelrooy. Robert Pires offered some attacking intent, but it was a heroic rearguard action – Ashley Cole and Lauren both improving as the game wore on following some early scares from Ronaldo and Rooney – which would be the basis for victory.

Captain Patrick Vieira slips the ball past old foe Roy Keane in his final match for his beloved Arsenal.

Left: Jens Lehmann dives to his right to deny Paul Scholes in the penalty shootout, while Vieira (above) hits the winner, his final act after nine years with the Gunners.

With extra time looming van Nistelrooy's header looked to have sealed a United win only for Freddie Ljungberg to stretch and deflect the ball against the underside of the bar. Arsenal were showing an indomitable spirit and stubbornness more closely associated with George Graham's side of a decade and a half before.

The Gunners improved in extra time and for most of the second period were the better side, but the final whistle sounded – just seconds after José Antonio Reyes saw red after receiving a second yellow – and for the first time ever the oldest cup competition in the world would be decided by penalties.

Van Nistelrooy and Lauren traded spot-kicks before Lehmann, Arsenal's man of the match, earned his deserved moment of glory when he pushed out Scholes' fiercely struck effort. The irony was not lost on Arsenal fans; it must have been the first time they had cheered a German saving an Englishman's penalty.

If Arsenal scored all their remaining penalties the cup was theirs. Ljungberg put Arsenal in front and then Ronaldo, van Persie, Rooney, Cole and Keane all tucked their spot kicks away. It was all left for Patrick Vieira, a truly great skipper in the mould of Joe Mercer, Frank McLintock and Tony Adams, who was given the task of converting the winning penalty.

The stadium hushed as, with his usual languid, assured manner, the Frenchman calmly stepped up and fired past Roy Carroll.

The victorious team (left) begin the party and (right) young guns Philippe Senderos, Manuel Almunia, José Antonio Reyes and Cesc Fabregas with the trophy.

Index